P9-DFA-603

Jim Coleman
A Hoofprint
On My Heart

Jim Coleman

A Hoofprint On My Heart

McClelland and Stewart Limited
Toronto/Montreal

Reprinted 1971

0-7710-1994-7

The Canadian Publishers
McClelland and Stewart Limited
25 Hollinger Road, Toronto 374

PRINTED IN CANADA

To D.C.C.

ACKNOWLEDGEMENTS

The writing of this book was instigated by the National Association of Canadian Race Tracks. The officers of that estimable organization cajoled me and prodded me and, now that the book is finished, I am grateful for their encouragement and support.

There were many individuals whose conversational assistance contributed importantly to the completion of this manuscript. Prominent among these were: H. L. Davies, Harry Rudd, William J. Bell, E. Massie White, Robert J. Ramsay and the late Dennis Layzell.

However, it is to the vanished horsemen and the horses themselves that I owe my greatest debt. As I sit here now, cracking my knuckles and cackling in happy recollection, I whisper to them: "Thanks – for the memories."

JAMES A. COLEMAN
Toronto, Canada.
Monday, August 2, 1971.

CONTENTS

1 The Morning Glory 1
2 The Children's Hour 13
3 One Little Sip Won't Hurt You 24
4 Hudson's Bay Rules 34
5 A Little Bit of Help 48
6 There's a Bit of Larceny in Everyone 61
7 The Plainsman 73
8 The School of Pharmacology 89
9 The Open City 104
10 You Could Do Anything You Were Big Enough To Do 120
11 Gentlemen of the Press 135
12 The City Was Swinging 149
14 How To Win A Fortune 165
15 The Good Doctor and the Good Ex-Jockey 178
16 Well, It Was a Good Idea at the Time 193
17 You Remember Only the Good Days 210
18 The Other Side of the Fence 226
19 A Headstone for the Good Ones 241
20 The Second Time Around 251

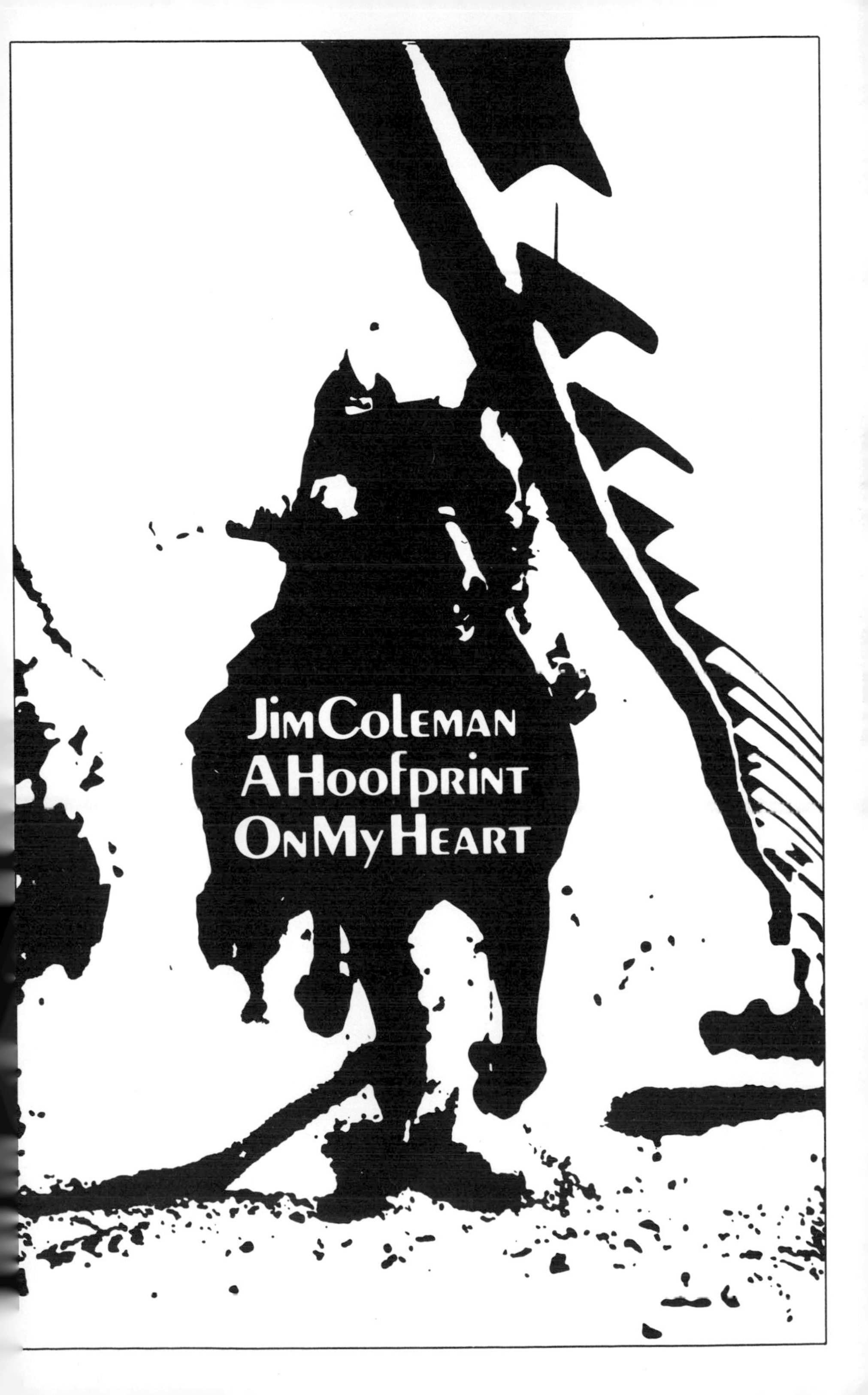
Jim Coleman
A Hoofprint
On My Heart

1

The Morning Glory

I am an evil old man lying here, remembering.

The fingers of the night breeze are twisting the curtain ends lazily and I am thinking: "They could bury me in the infield at Woodbine, close to the rail where I'd hear the thud of the hooves. They could scatter my ashes on the homestretch at Fort Erie. Better still, bury me somewhere on the backstretch, where I could hear the lies."

But no one is left to grant this dying wish. My widow and my children simply wouldn't understand. My widow is crazy enough to make frequent trips to Deacon Allen's grave, where she pours gin on the perennials so that the old man won't be thirsty, but she'd cringe from burying her own husband among the horse manure. The only person who'd really understand is my father and he has been gone for fifteen years.

I die, like this, almost every night. Some people day-dream but I night-dream, particularly when the breeze is blowing into my room from the southwest. It's a good way to go, really; just like drowning, your whole life passes in review before you in wide-screen vistavision.

My nightly death is serene because the shadows of niggling regret are dissipated by the memory of warm laughter, the pleasures shared, the hilarious search for the end of the rainbow. And always in this night-dream there is the compelling and reassuring figure of my father, a wise, gentle, loving man who could see stardust on his sleeve.

Compassionately, he would have accepted my wry conclusion that I was only a Morning Glory, shattering stop-watches in the dawn workouts but running like an inconsistent selling plater in the late afternoon. Better than almost anyone, he realized that human beings, like horses, often display unsuspected frailties. I am the classic Morning Glory; there were the early rich years, rich in promise, then the years of feverish productivity, and finally the long easy slide into comfortable mediocrity. This he could understand, because he and I bet on many a Morning Glory which wilted in the heat of the afternoon sun.

As I lie here dying each night, I remember most the gift of his unquestioning love. Smiling in my night-dream, I accept the fact that the odds against me waking to another dawn are always even-money. If I could have my choice of just one more dawn, it would be beyond the gift of God, for I would wish to return to a long-ago morning in Saratoga.

It was the gentle touch of my father's hand on my cheek which awakened me.

Words were unnecessary. I could hear Daoust, the chef, preparing breakfast in the galley; the aroma of coffee drifted down the corridor. As my father walked away on slippered feet, I threw back the bedclothes and, eagerly, I raised the broad white windowshade.

The Mount Royal was parked on the private-car siding. A gandy-dancer who was raking up invisible specks of paper stared at the Mount Royal, his interest aroused probably by the fact that the shining maroon Canadian Pacific car contrasted abruptly with the row of olive-green private Pullmans on the same siding.

My father was sitting in his accustomed seat at the head of the table, reading the bulldog edition of the *New York Herald Tribune,* when I had dressed and I dropped into the chair at his left. I didn't interrupt him because I could see that he was reading the racing column – Joe Palmer's column or, possibly, Murray Tynan's. The more important world news was ignored on this one day: we had come to Saratoga to go racing.

We breakfasted quickly; I gulped my first cup of coffee

while my father was finishing his second cup of tea. George Grant, the car steward who spent many years with my father, silently moved a plate of dry toast within range of my father's groping hand.

The August sun was felt rather than seen through the branches of the huge elms as we descended from the Mount Royal to be greeted by Mundy, who was standing on the Saratoga depot platform. Ken Mundy had chauffeured down from Montreal the previous evening at the wheel of the outmoded sixteen-cylinder car which my father refused to discard. My father had his little peculiarities—he liked a car with a running-board and a high roof, so that he could walk into the back seat without jack-knifing to duck the door sill. And Mundy was the ideal man to be associated with my father for twenty-two years; he was a genuine sports nut, devoted seasonally to the Montreal Canadiens hockey team, the Montreal Alouettes football team, the Montreal Royals baseball team and, always, devoted to the horses.

Mundy didn't see anything peculiar in carrying a silver shaker of chilled martinis in the sixteen-cylinder barge when my father went racing. Precisely after the official result of the fifth race had been posted each afternoon, Mundy produced the shaker of martinis from a small picnic basket. My father thereupon sipped martinis while the frailer members of the party took tea or lemonade.

It was the hour of the morning when for most human beings in Saratoga life has halted momentarily. We drove through empty streets, past the vast, old-fashioned hotels with their towering white colonnades and their broad, empty verandahs. For once, the high-backed rocking chairs were motionless; their regular occupants still were abed, snoring off the excesses of middle-aged affluence.

Even the last weary gambler had disappeared from the streets. The crap-game had shut down to permit the dice to cool off. Only the gin-rummy players, the most compulsive of all gamblers, were still awake in a few smoky rooms in the big hotels. That particular August, there was one rummy game in a room at the Grand Union which, with alternating pairs of players, ran non-stop for twenty-eight consecutive days. It may or it may not have been a world record.

The gin-mlls were closed, the shades drawn on their dusty windows. A few neon signs remained alight, their ghastly glow paled by the morning sun. Despite the fact that not a soul was in sight, the one traffic light on the main street was operating and, when we stopped for the red, I could hear the neon gas whispering in the tubes of a sign over the door of a corner bar and grill. The gas was going zzzzzzzzzz, ping! zzzzzzzzzz, ping!

As I lie here, dying, I realize that I have been granted the gift of total recall. For instance, I can still hear that neon sign, advertising a temporarily dry watering-hole. I can still feel the comfortable warmth of the car's deep leather seat. I can still smell the smoke of my father's DeReszke cigarette. All this comes back to me because I was happy. You can reach out and actually touch the past when you're recalling a moment of genuine happiness; you can feel the fabric of fancy becoming reality.

Saratoga is two separate worlds. There is the honky tonk downtown, a cynical tourist trap, geared for one month of cold-blooded pillage each summer. As a native said to me in the paddock, later that day: "In August we live off the people who comes to the races – for the other eleven months, we live off each other."

This brazen whore is one Saratoga and the other Saratoga is the race track, a sylvan Victorian anachronism in the twentieth century. It took us only a few minutes to drive out of one world into the other.

Always, I have been fascinated by the manner in which parking lot attendants and gatemen react to the arrival of a large chauffeur-driven car. The gateman didn't even bother to read the note which my father proffered, written by the secretary of The Jockey Club. The man had opened his wicket gate before we descended from the car. He swept us through and trotted behind us for a few paces, pointing out the quickest route to the grandstand, where we could watch the morning workouts. His hand was ready when my father tipped him for his solicitude.

Yes, and there was the tout, being rousted by the Pinkerton. How the tout got into the race track so early in the morning is still a mystery to me. Possibly, he had slept overnight in some tolerant horseman's tackroom. Anyhow, the Pinkerton and his victim passed us, heading for the outside gate as we were walking towards the grandstand. The Pinkerton didn't actually have a hand on the tout; he was walking ominously about two feet behind the shabby turf advisor.

As they reached the gate, the Pinkerton remained inside. The tout straightened his dusty jacket defiantly and, as he retreated, he shouted over his shoulder: "I never asked anyone to make a bet for me in my life. I have LOTS of money. I ain't a tout – I'm a gentleman from South Carolina. If anyone ever offered to make a bet for me, I'd kick his ––––––– teeth out."

The Pinkerton just stood there, with his arms folded. He expectorated judiciously. "On your way, bum," the Pinkerton said, without any apparent rancour.

My father was a gentleman. I don't mean that he was tenth-generation landed gentry with a title which went back to William the Conqueror. He was one of those instinctive gentlemen who never lost his cool in moments of embarrassing crisis. I watched him closely now, and well defined laugh-lines around the corners of his mouth crinkled briefly but he said nothing.

Lying here, I remember that it was much the same one day at Blue Bonnets when I was sitting with my stepmother and him, in their front box, right on the finish line. Actually, it was described officially as the Vice-Regal Box, but the track management always put it at the disposal of my parents. And, I was sitting there when I heard a voice hailing me boisterously from the ground on the esplanade, in front of the boxes. The voice was bawling jarringly: "Hey Coleman! How did you con your way into the Royal Box?"

Blushing, I peered over the balustrade and I realized that these unseemly remarks were being uttered by an old friend, Patsy, who was unshaven, as well as dressed in what might be described as the dregs of fashion.

"Hello, Patsy," I said weakly, pretending that my parents were two complete strangers. "Where have you been?"

"I've been in the can," Patsy howled cheerfully. "They said that I burned down my own barn for the insurance money. You know I wouldn't do a stupid ––––––– thing like that."

I stammered some inane commiserations for this obvious miscarriage of justice and I buried my head in my program, until, fortunately, Patsy went away.

I looked at my father who, face expressionless, was asking Mundy to purchase him a five-dollar straight ticket on the next race. My stepmother, who, as usual, was shuffling the seven different sets of selections which she clipped daily from all the racing papers, said brightly: "My goodness, dear. You have some of the strangest-looking friends."

So it was, this morning at Saratoga. The tout made no visible impression on my father, beyond that brief flicker at the corners of his mouth. I followed him up into the deserted grandstand and we sat down in a couple of seats in the third or fourth row, close enough to watch the horses.

I was just sitting there, sucking in the quiet beauty of the scene, when the whole thing crystalized.

The first beams of that August sun were creeping over the tops of the giant elms as a chestnut colt, his hoofs pounding rhythmically, swung into the stretch.

His coat glistened as the long slanting rays splashed him and threw his racing shadow against the white rails that fenced the track. Each hoof kicked up a tiny puff of dust as it bit into the soil. The air was cool and full of the sweet smells of early morning and as the colt pounded down the stretch his hot breath condensed in little wisps of steam.

The simple splendour of the moment took my breath away. I felt tears starting in my eyes. Stupidly, I didn't risk looking at my father, but I could feel his gaze. And after I had composed myself and turned in his direction, I saw that expression on his face. It was the same expression that he'd worn when I was only an eight-year-old boy, returning with him in the car from my mother's funeral.

The strangeness of the discovery confused me, but the message was clear. This remarkable oldster and his son found the key to communication on a sunny morning on a quiet race track in Saratoga. Our affection always had been very strong but it had been inexpressible in words. There were too many puritanical repressions in our background to permit easy conversation on filial relations. Here, we still were wordless but, suddenly, the lines of communication had been opened – never to be closed again until we buried him beside the river in the little town of Arnprior.

Now I became aware that this trip to Saratoga wasn't merely his whim. This was the pay-off.

A few days later, quite unexpectedly, he was to telephone

me, telling me that he was making me a gift of my first race horse. Just like that! A thoroughbred two-year-old, by Brooms out of Rise, registered owner: "James A. Coleman."

It would be stupid to say that he had been training me for this moment. But he had steered me into the sporting world since I was a small boy – he hadn't shoved me, but he had opened all the doors for me. I was the product of his own over-indulgence; he was giving me the opportunity to do all the things which he might have wished to do when he was younger, but those opportunities had been denied him. For all his hard-earned success in the business world, he was a romanticist and a dreamer; he could envision me standing, with my own horse, in the winner's circle at Woodbine. This was one more dream; earlier, he had envisioned me playing cricket for Oxford at Lord's after being awarded a Rhodes Scholarship. I had goofed quite badly on that dual project. My university career had been distinguished only by my zealous preoccupation with The Daily Racing Form, stud poker and spirituous libations. There was one rather dubious distinction in my dismissal from the halls of Learning: Sir Arthur Currie, the principal of my university, seldom bothered to deal directly with individual students. However, in my case, Sir Arthur had summoned me to his presence, to tell me to get-the-hell-out-of-there before I undermined the entire structure of higher learning in Canada. Sir Arthur didn't exactly escort me to the train, himself. He merely telephoned my father to inform him that I was en route.

Long, long before that academic disaster, my father had encouraged my wild enthusiasm for sports. He took me to my first hockey game when the Winnipeg Falcons, those magnificent Icelanders, came home after winning the world championship. After that, we seldom missed a hockey game when he was home from his travels.

He worked miracles for a small boy. When I was still in short pants, I was sent alone – albeit in the reluctant care of the sleeping-car conductor – from Winnipeg to Regina to see the Vancouver Maroons defeat the Regina Caps for the right to meet Toronto St. Pats in the Stanley Cup Final. And when I was incarcerated in a maximum-security boarding school in Victoria he arranged for my temporary release, to see the Victoria Cougars win the Stanley Cup from the mighty Montreal Canadiens.

He arranged for me to see the very best in every field of

athletics. He took me with him on his business trips in his private railway car. By a remarkable coincidence, our visits to the United States usually meshed with the schedules of the Big League baseball clubs. On one glorious trip, we sat together to see Babe Ruth and Lou Gehrig swatting home runs for the New York Yankees; Ty Cobb invading his spiritual home, Detroit, as an outfielder for the Philadelphia Athletics; Walter Johnson hurling aspirin tablets for the Washington Senators; and, for an encore, we saw Jack Dempsey ruthlessly kayo Jack Sharkey while Sharkey was turning his head towards the referee to whine that Dempsey had been punching him on the testicles, in gross disregard of the Marquess of Queensberry's rules of Pugilism.

And, always, there were the race tracks. There wasn't a race track from Florida to Vancouver Island that we didn't visit. God, how I loved those afternoons that we spent together, in sun or in rain. You may be under the misapprehension that my father was a compulsive gambler. He wasn't. He was a quiet, professorial-appearing railway president. His wagering was confined to a five-dollar straight ticket, plus a six-dollar combination ticket on the horse he fancied. Simply, he loved racing and he loved the horses – or "harses" as he called them. "Harses" was one of the two words which clung to him all his life, as a reminder of his Ottawa Valley Irish background. His other birthright word was "hal-ow" with which, invariably, he answered the telephone. I can hear it now: "hal-ow" as if he was answering the phone in the next room.

You'll gather from all this that I had a deep affection for my father. Well, since I'm making my nightly deathbed confessions, I can tell you a little about it. Even today, I become increasingly grateful for every minute he gave me. He left me no money, but he left me a legacy of love and understanding. He, better than anyone, knew my occasional soul-shattering torments. He never raised his voice to me; he was always there when needed, always loyal, never angry or reproachful. He stuck with me through my countless stupidities. He realized that, frequently, when I drank insanely, I was simply attempting to blot from my mind the embarrassment which many of my witless ecapades must have caused him. When, my friends, a father endures such disappointments from a son and still stands beside him proudly, the word to describe this relationship is "love."

It's just too damn bad that he didn't last long enough to see me after I quit drinking. The abrupt but overdue flip-flop would have rewarded him for his patience. I wish that he could have stayed around to see me, who had been a taker all my life, painfully and slowly learning just a little bit about giving. It was strange that I should have to *learn* about giving because, from the day I was born, he had been there, providing a daily example of giving. How blind can you be?

A wise father recognizes a son's limitations as well as his faults. He had resigned himself to the fact that I appeared to have found my happy niche as a sports writer. After all, he had guided me along that path by exposing me to the world of sports. Someone told me that he read every word I wrote. When he was out of the country, he left instructions that my columns were to be air-mailed to him daily. He knew that I wasn't going to set the world on fire. He knew, too, that better than anything else – better even than the aroma of the juniper berry – I loved the smells and the colours of the race track at dawn. That's why he had made up his mind that he was going to give me a race horse of my own.

So, not knowing what was going through his mind, but glowing with a sense of discovery, I followed him out of the track at Saratoga that wonderful morning. I was walking slightly behind him and I was thinking what an odd-looking little man he was. Always, he wore his hat squarely on his head, with two identical deep clefts in both sides of the hat. Although I've stood for hours examining the passers-by in London, Paris, Rome, Tokyo, Stockholm, I've never found another man who wore his hat exactly the same way. As he raised his cane to salute the Saratoga gateman, I found myself smiling affectionately. He was a very dignified little man.

Mundy drove us back to the Mount Royal and my stepmother was up, fussing with her racing papers. Mundy had picked up copies of *Collyer's Eye* and *The Green Sheet,* two publications which my stepmother valued almost as highly as her missal. By the time that we were ready to sit down for lunch, Sammy Smith had arrived with the selections which had been provided by his personal clocker. Sammy Smith was Victor

Emmanuel's trainer. He was always helpful to Canadian friends of his patron because Sammy had ridden jumpers for Harry Giddings at Woodbine, and he remembered Toronto with considerable affection. Sammy's clocker was a good handicapper. He picked four winners on that afternoon's program.

With my stepmother prattling over her selections and my father beaming at her, it was an exceptionally happy lunch. For once, I used some common sense. I decided before we left the Mount Royal that I'd practise an afternoon of self-denial: I'd stay out of the Club House bar. Looking back, I'm glad that I made that whimsical decision. It turned out to be a glorious afternoon.

We sat in Victor Emmanuel's box, directly behind Mrs. Dodge Sloan, who owned the Brookmeade Stable. My stepmother has a charmingly artless manner of involving herself with almost everyone in the world. She steps into a taxicab and, within forty-five seconds, she has the taxi driver telling her all about his wife and children. She dines in a foreign restaurant and, before the soup has cooled, the maitre d'hotel is displaying his family snapshots. My stepmother is in her eighties now, and perfect strangers still find themselves, mysteriously, in deep conversation with her.

Mrs. Sloan hadn't met my stepmother until that afternoon, but without any preliminaries my stepmother was telling her that she owned a colt sired by Brooms, the horse which won the Hopeful Stakes in Mrs. Sloan's colours at this same Saratoga track. Mrs. Sloan became so engrossed in my stepmother's remarkable discourse that she turned her back on the steeplechase, in which one of her horses was running. My stepmother was exceptionally pretty and, with her animated conversation, she could distract a traffic cop at rush hour.

"My God!" Mrs. Sloan said suddenly. "You made me miss the whole race and I don't even know where my horse finished." Mrs. Sloan had been overmatched conversationally.

I was remembering how many other afternoons the three of us had spent sitting together at race tracks, just like this, when I had been a schoolboy. The same old magic was in the air, my stepmother chattering away to herself and to my father who just nodded silently, occasionally patting her hand. My stepmother had a bewildering habit of betting on two or three horses in the same race. Usually, she cashed at least one of her tickets but, at the day's end, when she counted her money, she never could understand why she hadn't won money. Biting the tip of a pencil in perplexity, she would re-check her figures and then, triumphantly, she would announce that one of the cashiers at the track must have short-changed her. My father would placate her by telling her that he would write a letter of complaint to the track management. "Oh, don't do that," she would say absent-mindedly. "The poor man probably has a very large family."

That afternoon at Saratoga, I caught time between my outstretched fingers and forced it to halt in mid-flight. I can even remember the names of the horses on which we made our modest bets and our happy laughter when they won. Most of all I remember the warmth of our own company, the ease with which we slipped back into the pattern we had established in my childhood at little Whittier Park and Polo Park, in Winnipeg, the quiet exchange of mutual congratulations over our own winners – quiet, because we didn't wish to distress further the people who were sitting in the boxes on either side of us; people who mournfully were discarding bushels of uncashable tickets. I held time between my fingers until the last race of the afternoon had been run and then, with a shrug, I turned it loose.

That evening, after dinner at the Gideon Putnam, we sat on the lawn chairs outside until it became quite dark. We talked easily of the old times and the old horses: Jingo, Son O Unc, Olds Eight, Colonel Boyle and Duchess of York. In the darkness, I could hear my father clicking open his little pocket watch and I knew that it was time to leave.

We drove back to the Mount Royal, still parked on the private-car siding in the Saratoga Springs station. I went on board briefly to pick up my suitcase because I was leaving them. Mundy was driving me to Albany to catch the midnight train for Toronto. They were returning to their Montreal home.

While I was collecting my suitcase, and my stepmother was fussing over me, straightening my tie and looking in her purse for the new St. Christopher's medal which she had obtained for me at St. Peter's in Rome, my father had seated himself in his favourite chair and he was scanning the front page of the airmail edition of the *London Times*.

We weren't much for saying goodbyes, so I just walked over

to his chair and leaned over far enough for my lips to brush the top of his thinning grey hair and said: "Thanks, Dad, for a wonderful day."

He smiled and he stood up and he followed me through the door of the private car. He stood alone on the observation platform of the Mount Royal waving to me, as Mundy drove me away. I could see his slight figure, still framed in light, as we turned into Saratoga's main street.

As we drove down the road to Albany, the old car's big tires singing on the empty highway, I sat in the front seat beside Mundy, gnawed by the growing realization that again I had failed myself. I had been so close – but I'd missed. The opportunity had been there for me to tell him exactly how grateful I felt for his years of unselfish devotion to his family. Before I left him that night, I should have put my arms around his shoulders and said: "Thanks, Dad, for ALL the wonderful days." There I was, with every turn of the wheels taking me further from Saratoga and never again in his lifetime was I to have another such appropriate moment to tell him what was in my heart.

As I lie here, now, I remember . . . I remember . . . I remember.

2

The Children's Hour

It's going to take me a couple of hours of night-dreaming before I get around to the horse-racing portion of this deathbed confession. My thoughts are likely to take a few violent detours, too, because I can't make a cohesive, all-encompassing confession about horse racing unless I make some references to Deacon Jack Allen the eccentric boxing promoter, or the Good Kid, or the Battling Colcloughs, or Stanley Zedd, the proprietor of the world's oldest permanent floating crap game. They weren't associated primarily with horse racing but they were woven into the rich colourful fabric of the sport.

I must tell you something of my own background, too, because you may be wondering how anyone can get hooked on horse racing at the age of ten or so and then go through an entire lifetime without shaking the habit. It's easy, really. All you require is the spirit of perseverance.

My childhood probably wasn't quite normal, when judged by the rather prim standards of its era. After my mother died, my father got rid of our old house on Donald Street and we moved into a seven room suite on the fifth floor of the Royal Alexandra Hotel in Winnipeg. In the interval before my father remarried, my younger brother and I were supervised by our two maternal aunts, both of whom shall have their reward in heaven for courageous devotion above and far beyond the call of duty.

The Royal Alexandra wasn't designed to be a children's

playground. However, it acquired quite a reputation for extra-curricular athletic events in the period of our residence. Among the permanent guests were seven or eight other lively children of approximately our own ages.

In the apocrypha of the Canadian Pacific Railway, there is a hardy legend that, when the company was seeking a valid excuse for the dismissal of an assistant-manager in their hotel system, they would send him to the Royal Alexandra. It was assumed that after he had been exposed to six months of dealing with the children who lived in the Royal Alexandra he would seek surcease in dope or strong drink. Either of these reprehensible habits provided good grounds for dismissal.

We weren't malicious children; nevertheless we were quite energetic. We played hockey on the marble floor of the basement lobby, using real hockey sticks and a tennis ball. The hockey sticks thumping on the marble floor and the outraged cries of the youthful players who were tripped or body-checked combined to produce a din which one doesn't associate commonly with a dignified and expensive hostelry. Whenever the unfortunate incumbent assistant-manager arrived hurriedly on the scene to ask us to desist from our manly enterprises, it was noticeable that, invariably, he was ashen-cheeked and suffering from the early symptoms of palsy.

Far from sulking when our hockey game was terminated abruptly, we would repair cheerfully to the Crystal Ballroom where we would amuse ourselves by drop-kicking an English rugby ball over the magnificent glass chandeliers. One young assistant-manager, who came upon this scene unexpectedly, fainted dead away. His career in the hotel business was doomed from that moment – obviously, he never would be sturdy enough to withstand the maledictions heaped upon him by an indignant traveller who upon arriving at the hotel after a wearying trip must be informed that the hotel's accommodations already are over-booked.

My bosom companion in the halcyon days of the Royal Alexandra was a young gentleman, named T. Jeffares Porte, Jr., who was only a year older than I. T. Jeffares Porte, Jr., dabbled in chemistry with extremely gratifying results.

T. Jeffares Porte, Jr., anticipated the H-Bomb by more

than thirty years. He concocted a mixture of chemicals which, when exposed to water, would "explode," tossing a geyser of water high in the air. T. Jeffares, Jr., would build a couple of these water-bombs and we would tape them beneath the seats of the toilets in the public washroom on the basement level of the hotel.

We used to hang around the door of the washroom until we saw an unsuspecting victim enter one of the cubicles in which we had planted our bombs.

Crossing our legs in excitement, we would wait eagerly until the victim flushed the toilet – whooosh! the bomb would precipitate a geyser of cold water and the curses of the victim enriched our childish vocabulary. By the time that the soaked gentleman emerged from the cubicle, we were far from the scene of the crime; cadging chocolate éclairs from Phillippe, the hotel pastry-cook who wore a pair of wooden sabots as he manufactured his delicious confections.

Actually, of all the children in the Royal Alexandra, only two could be classed as potentially dangerous. They were brothers, slightly older than ourselves, and even at this late date, delicacy dissuades me from mentioning them by name.

These two adolescent brigands conducted a course in petty larceny for the younger children in the hotel. They showed us how to jimmy the coin-boxes and extract money from the pay-telephones which were housed in a neat row of booths along the south wall of the main lobby. The booths were in a location of such eminent seclusion that even Jack The Ripper could have practised unlicensed surgery there without attracting a crowd. Fortunately, most of us were appalled by the mere suggestion of theft and we expunged their lessons from our minds, quickly. Although I have suffered from acute financial anaemia on many occasions, I haven't found it necessary, as yet, to tap a telephone coin-box to obtain working capital.

The brothers departed from our lives before any genuine damage was wrought on our twisted little souls. Their residence in the Royal Alexandra was brief, if spectacular.

One day, about noon, two large representatives of the Winnipeg Constabulary strode into the hotel and, after a rumbling consultation at the front desk, an assistant manager led the peace officers to the suite of rooms occupied by the good doctor and his family.

Unknown to the rest of us, the two brothers had a .22 calibre rifle and ammunition in their room. In moments of boredom, they would amuse themselves by opening their own bedroom window and firing shots into the rooms of the Alberta Hotel, about fifty yards down Main Street. A .22 rifle had no real striking-power at that range, but a few of the stuffier residents of the Alberta Hotel objected to having their afternoon naps disturbed by snipers. To no one's real sorrow, the doctor and his unusual brood vacated the Royal Alexandra soon thereafter.

Actually, I am convinced that it was our adventures in the Royal Alexandra which instilled in me a curiosity concerning those human beings who were considered to be slightly unconventional. There were some highly unusual residents of the hostelry and, unknown to our father, my brother and I struck up a warm friendship with Mr. Harry Sokol.

Mr. Sokol has been ignored unjustly by historians who have written about Canadian commerce. Mr. Sokol built the first Canada-U.S. pipeline, many years before natural gas was tapped from the underbelly of Alberta and Saskatchewan.

Mr. Sokol built a pipeline which had its source in a cattle barn on the Canadian side of the border, down near Emerson, Manitoba. The pipeline travelled underground for several thousands of feet to its southern terminus in another cattle barn on the U.S. side of the border.

Mr. Sokol poured thousands of gallons of good Canadian whiskey into the Canadian end of his pipeline. The Volstead Act was being enforced in the United States at the time and Mr. Sokol's whiskey, which bubbled endlessly into the U.S. barn, assuaged the thirst of thousands of grateful Americans who, otherwise, might have been blinded by drinking illegally-distilled domestic bathtub gin.

In my childish but probably accurate estimate, Mr. Sokol was a great humanitarian. He was a non-drinker and a non-smoker and a bachelor, but he had many relatives, astonishingly attractive young ladies whom he introduced to me as his "nieces."

My faith in Mr. Sokol's innate humanitarianism was vindicated many years later, in 1950, when Winnipeg was inundated by the Flood. The repeal of Prohibition in the United States had made Mr. Sokol's pipeline redundant but, far from resenting the United States government's destruction of his business venture, he had gone to make his permanent home in California. When he heard that Winnipeg was beleaguered by the cresting waters of the Assiniboine and Red Rivers, he chartered a four-engine airplane; loaded it to the roof with rubber boots, pumps and lengths of hose and he flew back to Canada to succour his former fellow-citizens. Mr. Sokol was one of nature's gentlemen – he did harm to no man, and to many men he supplied comfort, liquid and practical.

About the time that the rifle-toting brothers removed themselves from our jolly little group, Aunt Ella Grant, who was acutely sensitive to some muttering among the more staid adult residents of the Royal Alexandra, suggested that she should take my brother and me on a long, stimulating holiday at Qualicum Beach, on Vancouver Island. My father agreed with surprising alacrity. I imagine that in his quasi-landlord capacity (well, he was the senior western official of the railway company which owned the hotel) he was beginning to receive a few poison-pen letters from moustachioed old gentlemen who objected to being struck over the toes with hockey sticks when they walked through the basement lobby.

Although you may have gathered the impression that my father was primarily responsible for my lifelong addiction to horse racing, it was actually Aunt Ella Grant who first exposed me to the siren. She shall forever be hallowed as my benefactor, even if I am quite sure that when she shepherded us westward from Winnipeg that summer she didn't have the vaguest suspicion that she was introducing me to my first and most enduring passion.

It should be explained that my own mother's family, The Grants, were considered even by their closest friends to be mildly off-beat. The Grants didn't pay much attention to clocks in an era when smalltown Canadians were regimented into a nine-to-five working day with scant consideration given to frivolity. The Grants simply ignored what was considered to be normalcy. As my father used to say, with wry admiration: "The Grants think that the day is just beginning, about the time that everyone else is ready to go to bed."

It was this unconventionality which always caused my

brother and me to look forward to our visits to Grandmother Grant's home in Edmonton. My grandmother was a merry but paradoxically stately lady who had been christened, imposingly, Hectorina Rowan. Grandmother loved to play bridge and, while we were still in short pants, my brother and I were indoctrinated with the rudimentary skills of the finesse, the demand-bid and the simple club-ruff. If a stranger had dropped in and observed us concentrating with knitted brows on the cards at the ages of six and nine, respectively, the stranger might have suspected that he had stumbled upon a gambling session of the American theatrical troupe of lilliputians known as Singer's Midgets.

Sometime after midnight, it was usual for our grandmother to put down the cards firmly and announce: "We all need some fresh air – I think that we should go out for a little ride in the car."

Cackling happily, we would get the car out of the garage and, although ninety-nine per cent of Edmonton's population was sleeping soundly, we would drive for an hour or so through the deserted streets. My grandmother invariably was stimulated by these post-midnight rides. Before we went to bed, she would insist that we have "a little snack," consisting of coffee, toasted scones and curds. Refreshed by the night air and surfeited by the little snack, nevertheless we slept the deep untroubled sleep of innocent babes.

Aunt Ella was the reluctant iconoclast of the family. Whereas Uncle Rowan Grant cheerfully ran away from home one summer to groom race horses for Billy Field of Calgary, Aunt Ella seldom spoke of being the first lady bank-teller in Vancouver. Really, her family's lack of inhibitions outraged her Presbyterian conscience. But deep down inside, Aunt Ella was a gambler. A dead give-away was the manner in which her eyes would light up like pinball machines when the horse on which she had ventured a two-dollar wager was light-footing through the homestretch. She, too, loved horse racing, though until she had seated herself in the multitudinous anonymity of the crowded grandstand she acted as if she was being lured into a bordello.

So Aunt Ella was the culprit who took me to the races for the first time. The trip from Winnipeg to the Pacific Coast began innocently. Ella had suggested that a close friend, Mrs. Hugh Baird, should accompany us with her three children. My father, who was equal to all emergencies, announced calmly that there was a spare Canadian Pacific private car which would be put at our disposal, since it was being hauled to Vancouver, dead-head, to pick up an Oriental princeling who was coming from the Orient aboard The Empress of Australia. My father was no fool – he had no intention of permitting five children to run wild in the corridors of the regular passenger train. He had great confidence in Ella Grant and, Mrs. Baird was one of his very favorite ladies but, essentially, his sympathies were with those passengers who paid cash to travel via Canadian Pacific.

The private car was the "Penticton," an ancient wooden travelling caravanserai which once had belonged to James J. Hill, the American transportation tycoon. The permanent steward aboard the Penticton was Archie Gray, who hated the car with a glowing intensity and who referred to it, publicly and scathingly, as "The Penitentiary."

Archie Gray's hatred for the Penticton stemmed from the fact that the old private car was accident-prone. If there was a derailment at even the most remote section of the Canadian Pacific's 23,000 miles of trackage, the Penticton was certain to be involved in that catastrophe. The Penticton had survived four or five snowslides and rockslides in the passes of the Rockies and the Selkirks and, on each of those occasions, Archie Gray had been battered by flying crockery and uprooted furniture. After each accident, he prayed fervently that the Penticton would be junked. He cursed the genii of the car-repair department who twisted and wrestled the Penticton back into shape, gave it a fresh coat of paint and restored it to regular service.

For all his pessimism, Archie was a delightful man who, in his youth, had performed in English music halls. He loved children and from the time we left Winnipeg he had an enraptured audience as he entertained us between meals with his repertoire of sleight-of-hand, card tricks and music-hall drolleries. All the while, he punctuated his performance with dire prophecies of the ultimate fate of the Penticton. He was almost correct – while we were travelling across the prairies, we received word that the main line had been blocked by a tremendous rockslide in the Kicking Horse Pass. It was necessary to detour our train to Vancouver by way of the Crow's Nest Pass and the Kettle Valley, an expediency which added four or five hours to our trip.

Was it the hand of fate which triggered that rockslide? We arrived in Vancouver too late to catch the morning-boat for Nanaimo, en route to our final destination at Qualicum Beach.

With an afternoon to waste, Aunt Ella Grant decided to take all of us to the horse races at Brighouse Park. I don't know what mad whim inspired her to take five small children to a race track – but the die had been cast.

There must have been an easy way of travelling from the Hotel Vancouver to Brighouse Park, but Aunt Ella chose the long, hard way. She was becoming crafty after three days aboard the Penticton – she thought that the Vancouver scenery would occupy our attention, giving her time to compose herself for any unforseen emergencies.

Exuding false enthusiasm from every pore, she walked us, bitching and whining, to an interurban tram terminal. There we boarded the electric railcar which ran from downtown Vancouver to Lulu Island in the delta of the Fraser River. Brighouse Park, which really was picnicking-distance from the metropolitan centre, had been built in the Lulu Island farming district where real estate was cheap and the loam was rich.

Aunt Ella acted as a tour conductor while the interurban car lumbered across the False Creek bridge, grunted past the back gardens of the Shaughnessy Heights residential district, and thundered down into the suburb of Eburne before crossing the river to Lulu Island. Aunt Ella, who had lived previously in this evergreen jungle, described the sights in a chauvinistic manner which would have done credit to a shill from the Chamber of Commerce. She managed even to wax rhapsodic over the Eburne sawmill, which was belching sparks, smoke and an evil stench. When we passed a salmon cannery, she caught herself before she launched into a graphic description of the manner in which the piscatorial dainties were eviscerated prior to being enrobed in tin. As a matter of fact, she wrestled to close the window of the car when the odours from the cannery threatened to provoke a mass attack of mal de mer in her enchanted audience.

The afternoon's first two races had been run before the interurban car reached Brighouse Park. Aunt Ella and Mrs. Baird tidied our clothing on the station platform and then they led us across the dusty parking lot to the admission booth.

Thereupon, Aunt Ella was confronted with the first of the unforseen emergencies for which she had been gathering strength. Children weren't welcome on Canadian race tracks in those days. The ticket seller quailed in an agony of uncertainty as he watched Mrs. Baird and Aunt Ella bearing down on him like two galleons trailed by five little pinnaces. Protected by the wire grille in his booth, he protested the invasion.

Aunt Ella was magnificent. She was quite a large lady and when she extended her bosom and expelled her breath through the nostrils of her patrician nose she could be genuinely imposing. Indignantly she told the poor overmatched man that she had brought these five little children all the way from Winnipeg for the sole and express purpose of taking them to the races at Brighouse Park. She had, she emphasized, no intention of breaking their little hearts by permitting a race track flunky to deny them the privileges of the course.

The man retreated from his box nervously. He held a whispered consultation with two gatemen, who had been listening to Aunt Ella's declamation with considerable interest. Finally, the ticket-seller returned to his booth to announce that he was prepared to compromise. He would admit us to the track on the condition that we promised to sit – and remain – in the very top row of the grandstand where we wouldn't bother the adult patrons.

Aunt Ella paid for the tickets and she swept us through the gates, with a regal and condescending nod to the cowed attendants.

I wasn't dazzled instantly by the unfamiliar surroundings. The grandstand at Brighouse Park wasn't an architectural masterpiece which rivalled the Taj Mahal or the Palace of the Doges in Venice. My first impression was that the place was dusty and the wooden seats were hard.

A race went to the post just as we were settling into our seats, and the event made no immediate impact on me. There was a lot of cheering as the horses turned into the homestretch. I wasn't smart enough to stand on my seat and consequently all

I saw was a swirl of dust through a forest of bobbing heads. When the horses cantered back to the unsaddling barrier, I regarded them without any undue curiosity. Horses weren't new to me; I had my own pony back on Smith's farm at Birds Hill, Manitoba, and there were many other horses with whom I had a talking acquaintance. Furthermore, bread, milk and other household necessities were still delivered by horse-drawn vehicles in Winnipeg in those days. A horse was just a horse.

Then, attempting to stir my interest, Aunt Ella showed me a program and she pointed to the next race. She asked me to select a name which appealed to me. Solely to humour the lady, I solemnly pondered the program and announced that the name I liked was "Mineral Jim."

Aunt Ella bustled out of her seat and informed me that she was going to buy a place ticket on Mineral Jim. She explained carefully that, if Mineral Jim finished either first or second, we would win money. I was still unimpressed but, I found myself looking forward to the next race with mild interest.

Aunt Ella had returned with a ticket clenched in her hand before the horses paraded to the post. I saw Mineral Jim. My gaze was glued on him throughout the very long post-parade. They paraded for fifteen minutes or more in that era, to squeeze every possible two-dollar bet out of the crowd.

Brighouse Park hadn't yet been desecrated by such modern inventions as the starting gate and the public address system. The assistant starters simply wrestled the horses into a semblance of a straight line behind a tape which was stretched across the track, head-high on the horses. The official starter, who occupied a tall, flimsy stand inside the infield fence, was usually noted for his patience and his profanity. Sometimes, it required ten or fifteen minutes of wrestling to heave the horses into a ragged line.

In this particular race on this particular afternoon the horses didn't dally at the post. The starter – a gentleman who rejoiced in the name of Quarter-Horse Neary – released the tape and the crowd yipped in unison, "They're off!"

My eyes never had left Mineral Jim from the moment he appeared on the track. I could see that he was off to a good start and he was close to the pace-setter in the early stages of the race. Suddenly, Aunt Ella climbed up onto the seat and she pulled me up beside her. The horses were turning into the homestretch and Aunt Ella began to yell encouragement to our horse. Swept up in the enthusiasm, I began to yell too. Mrs. Baird and the Baird children first looked at me in astonishment and then *they* began to yell.

Down the stretch Mineral Jim ran, his jockey booting and scuffling. Three horses rushed for the finish-wire together and Mineral Jim was one of them.

"We won," Aunt Ella shouted triumphantly. "We won!" I echoed, jumping up and down in glee. "We won," shouted the Baird family. We were still shouting as the jockeys eased their horses and the crowd in the seats below us turned around to stare at the noisy celebrants.

We hadn't won. The placing judges hung up the numbers of the first four finishers and Mineral Jim had finished third. We had lost, but Mineral Jim had given us a hell of a good run for our money.

I was still jumping up and down in excitement and I threw my arms around Aunt Ella. She looked at me in alarm as the enormity of what she had done to me began to dawn on her. She tried to calm me. I wasn't about to be calmed, I was deliriously excited.

I was hooked – I was hooked for a lifetime.

3

One Little Sip Won't Hurt You

You question the accuracy of my memory? You quibble over the precise detail in which I describe long-ago incidents?

For the purposes of this night-dream, I have been granted the gift of total recall. Consider the fact that I am lying here, remembering the enduring love affair of my life. Any man is capable of recalling his one satisfactory love affair in the most intimate detail: the sound of her voice, the colour of her eyes, the curve of her lips, her walk, her every gesture. Lie back and test your own memory. You see her as she was, *then.* If you saw her today you wouldn't recognize her. Memory is the only true, faultless mirror.

So I can tell you with absolute certainty that this is how it happened. I can remember, for instance, that Stub Barnes had a mustard stain exactly two inches below the breast pocket of his shirt on the afternoon that he sent Shasta Sheik to the post, higher than a Georgia Pine. I can remember the color of the barn roofs at Whittier Park; I can remember where High-Ball Kelly hid his hypodermic needle; I can remember every cuss-word in Jim Donovan's extensive vocabulary; I can remember the look on Cowboy Parker's dead face when they found him murdered at Old Woodbine; I can remember exactly how the tobacco juice caked at the corners of Doc Ronald's mouth; I can remember, with every inflection, the voices of "Whittlin' " Knifong, Cougar Smith, Sleepy Armstrong and Big Jim Fair. I can remember the wording of the inscription in the gold watch which had been given to The Blow-Back Kid by his admirers when he swam clear across the Yukon River, right after the ice breakup. Right now, I can see and hear those things.

Thus, I can tell you that the first race horse which I appraised at close range was Merry Marquis, owned by Captain Stanley Harrison, the poet laureate of the turf. The confrontation occurred in Edmonton, the summer following our circuitous trip to Qualicum Beach. My younger brother and I were visiting our Grant relatives in Edmonton and, again, our revered Aunt Ella was the instrument of our ruin. On the Sunday before the opening of the Edmonton race meeting, she took us to the barns at the Edmonton exhibition grounds to inspect the livestock. Undoubtedly Aunt Ella was intent upon extracting feed-box information from some carelessly loquacious horsemen.

Captain Harrison made a practice of nailing portable nameplates on his horses' stall doors. I remember Merry Marquis because he was a stallion and accordingly he occupied the position of honour, in the stall adjoining the tackroom in which the grooms slept. Merry Marquis eyed us in grim malevolence, but he was considerably gentler than most stallions and he accepted sugar from us while Aunt Ella quizzed the grooms. It was notable that, after feeding the sugar to Merry Marquis, my cautious younger brother wryly counted his own fingers.

In fairness to my brother, it should be explained at this point that he never shared my consuming affection for the racing world. His natural antipathy was probably accentuated by my habit, developed a few years later, of rousing him from bed at 6 a.m. to attend the morning workouts at Whittier Park and Polo Park in Winnipeg. He was a wily child and at an early age he contrived to contract hay fever and pinkeye, which in all probability were self-induced. The gleam of triumph was discernible in his eyes when our family physician announced that he should stay away from race tracks.

When he had graduated from law school and volunteered to join the Canadian Army in the frenzied autumn of 1939, he was still a bit bitter about the unjust coercions of his childhood. In the early weeks of World War II, the Canadian Army was treating volunteers with charming deference. As my brother offered himself to his country's cause, the recruiting officer said with impeccable good manners of the Royal Military College: "In what branch of the service do you wish to serve?"

"I'll serve anywhere," my brother replied bluntly, "as long as you don't assign me to the bloody cavalry!" They gave him the infantry. Six years later, he came home with a D.S.O. and a Military Cross and a couple of impressive holes in his pelt. So much for his childish caution. When he became a Colonel, he still looked so young that Jimmy Krakeel, the bartender at the Carleton, in London, asked him to grow a moustache so that the hotel wouldn't lose its licence for selling double Scotches to minors.

From Merry Marquis's stall door, my path led directly to the grandstand of every race track in Canada. During his few years of renewed bachelorhood, my father decided to take me with him in his railway car when he made his frequent business trips during the school summer holidays. Possibly he reasoned that the residents of the Royal Alexandra Hotel would feel more secure when they learned that I had been separated from the inspiring company of T. Jeffares Porte, Jr. In any event, we visited a great many cities where, by a remarkable coincidence, race meetings were in progress. My father was much too busy to go racing every day but when his own business appointments detained him he sent me to the track, chaperoned by his private secretary.

By another remarkable coincidence, my father always selected private secretaries whose arteries gushed sporting blood. There were no computers in thosc days, but my father must have submitted prospective secretaries to an exhaustive quiz on hockey, baseball and horse racing before they joined his family. Looking back on it, I realize that everyone in his business-family circle was a sports buff. It was, therefore, no great sacrifice for a secretary to take his boss's small boy for a pleasant afternoon of horse racing.

One of these secretaries, who generously contributed a great deal of off-duty time to providing me with warm companionship, was a highly unusual man named Andrew C. Manson. When he got me safely on the way into university, he left the railway service and, later, became the president of an insurance company. Andy Manson was multi-talented; he composed music which was published successfully; he played piano in a dance band; he had been a good baseball pitcher and he had an encyclopaedic knowledge of sports trivia. Furthermore, he was one of the few men in the world who could read both my father's handwriting and my father's mind.

Andy Manson knew that, when we were on the road, my father would cease dictating letters to him precisely at 1:45 p.m., so that we would have time to reach the track for the first race at 2:30. Andy gravely would hand the day's racing entries to my father, who would mark one horse in each race. No questions were necessary – he knew that my father expected him to bet two dollars to win on each horse. My father would dismiss the pair of us with the slightly envious words: "Have a good time."

One of these summer trips took us to Victoria, B.C., where for the first time the prospects of the great riches which could be amassed by wagering on horses stirred the larceny in my soul. Years of painful research have taught me that you lose much oftener than you win. My father used to refer to losing wagers as "character builders." Since that afternoon in Victoria, my unsuccessful racing investments have built me enough character for ultimate sainthood.

Andy Manson and I climbed into a taxi in front of the Empress Hotel and we were driven to The Willows, a half-mile track which was the centrepiece of the somnolent little city's exhibition grounds. We arrived just as the horses were parading to the post for the first race and Andy dutifully wagered two dollars on my father's marked selection. It was a horse named Truelane.

In the argot of the equine industry, Truelane won the first race by as far as a strong-armed farm boy can throw a big rosy red apple. While we watched in awe, a track functionary chalked the winning price on the infield odds-board – $207.45 for a two dollar ticket! Naturally, there weren't too many people in the two-dollar straight cashier's line after that upheaval and Andy became quite embarrassed by the curious stares of rueful onlookers who watched him collecting the money. He counted the money carefully several times and almost forgot to bet on my father's selection in the second race. Fortunately, he remembered in time. My father's horse, Quinam, won the second race and paid $23.40.

If Victoria still occupies a soft corner of my heart, the affection probably was born that afternoon. In any event, a few years later, when my father offered to remove me from a boarding school in Lennoxville, Quebec, to another boarding school in Victoria, I greeted the suggestion with moderate enthusiasm.

The truth of the matter was that I hated the confinement of boarding school. I missed my quaint friends in the Royal Alexandra Hotel. I missed the warmth of my own family. My father had remarried before I was sent away to school for the first time and, although I loved my stepmother in my childish fashion, I felt that she was somehow responsible for my banishment. It was an unfair assumption on my part although I am reasonably confident that my stepmother must have become emotionally exhausted, waiting for the next complaint from hotel guests who took a singularly narrow-minded view of my habit of riding my mini-bicycle through the hotel corridors at reckless speeds. Never did I actually collide with anyone, but I must have scared the hell out of a few stately dowagers. Anyhow, if my incarceration in boarding schools was to be my fate, I had an infinite preference for incarceration in Victoria, which was equipped with two race tracks.

Appropriately, I was sent from Winnipeg to Victoria for enrollment in University School, under plainclothes escort. My warder was another of my father's private secretaries, Clarence B. Horne, who knew all my basic peculiarities. Forty-eight hours after leaving Winnipeg, another little boy and his father boarded the train at Kamloops. There is a peculiar instinct for recognition which exists between small boys who are headed for the same boarding school. Possibly, I sensed his reluctant acceptance of impending doom. Although no words passed between us – in fact, we weren't introduced informally until the second day of school – my instinct was accurate. He was Nicholas E. Morant, later to become a famous Canadian photographer of snorting locomotives, mountain peaks and assorted native flora and fauna. (Some of my schoolmates came to a rather sticky end in later years, but Nick Morant was our only graduate who survived the ordeal of being mauled by a grizzly bear in Banff National Park. The she-bear must have been camera-shy because she damn nearly killed poor old Nick.)

We arrived in Victoria on the overnight boat from Vancouver. It wasn't necessary to report to the school until seven o'clock that evening. In view of the fact that it was my final day of freedom, Clarence Horne generously permitted me to select the full program of activities. Promptly, I opted for an afternoon of racing at The Willows and an early dinner at the Empress Hotel.

The afternoon of watching the horses in the bright September sunlight temporarily lifted the clouds of depression from my ten-year-old shoulders. I don't recall that we picked any winners. Simply, I wished that the afternoon never would end. Sniffing slightly with regret, I permitted Mr. Horne to take me by taxi to the Empress for my last hearty meal. When he was a very old man, living in retirement in Vancouver, I ran into him and he could still remember exactly what I ate that night in the main dining room of the Empress: jellied consomme, a Lancashire hot pot and seven chocolate éclairs. My display of calorie-inhalation imbedded itself in his mind. I was no fool – already I had considerable experience with boarding school food and I was intent upon keeping some flesh on my bones until the Thanksgiving holidays. Nevertheless, I was groaning slightly in the taxi as we drove up to the school on Mount Tolmie where the twinkling lights in the dormitory windows gave me no welcome, only a profound sense of desertion.

Actually, Victoria was an ideal place to go to school when you compared its physical attributes with Winnipeg's. In Winnipeg, the climate was disparaged nationally as "ten months of winter and two months of poor skating." Victoria seldom experienced a snowfall. It was a residential city of 50,000 populated by many retired persons of moderate and considerable wealth, including some notably eccentric British expatriates.

They say that if you dumped an Englishman on a tropical island he'd found two enterprises: a tea plantation and a race track. Although Montreal and Toronto may claim priority in Canada, it is recorded that race meetings were conducted in Victoria as early as 1860. Those antediluvian race meetings took place on Beacon Hill, a rocky parkland overlooking the Straits of Georgia. Undoubtedly, those were the first horse races ever to be staged in Western Canada.

By the time that I was lodged in University School, Beacon Hill Park had become a trysting place for audacious young lovers and any traces of a race course long since had disappeared. However, there was racing at The Willows and some emigrant heirs to the Coventry estates in England had built a one-mile course at Colwood, ten or fifteen miles from downtown Victoria. I visited The Willows every Saturday morning because I had been enrolled in a weekly riding class which was conducted by the formidable Major Proby, ex-RCMP, who stabled his sterling steeds in the covered arena of the exhibition grounds. In his rare moments of carelessness, the good Major permitted us to gallop our steeds around the half-mile race track. Little did my classmates realize that when we were galloping our stylishly stout plodders I was Jockey Snapper Garrison, in mufti. Major Proby did not pemit us to carry whips, a restriction which deprived me of the opportunity to show my classmates how The Snapper could gun a horse through the final furlong. Major Proby also forced us to ride with a long stirrup, heels-down, a type of seat which would have been deplored in the flat-racing set.

The racing season at The Willows didn't coincide with our school year, but a few horsemen always wintered their stock in the exhibition grounds. Because the University School curriculum didn't include a course in four letter words, we were warned to avoid the stabling area at The Willows, a region which was inhabited by profane and irreverent horsemen. It required some ingenious contriving for me to miss at least one streetcar back to school each Saturday morning as, undetected by the authorities, I made a brief but satisfactory survey of the race-horse barns. Well, the medical report which was supplied to the school with my application for enrollment, stressed that among my other gruesome deficiencies I had weak kidneys.

For some reason, George Addison deserted Calgary to winter his horses at The Willows in one of my early school years. The star of the Addison barn was Col. Boyle. I was familiar with Col. Boyle because he won the feature race at The Willows on the same afternoon when my father bet on Truelane and Quinam. Col. Boyle was a chunky, dark bay horse who excelled on the bull-rings of Western Canada. As a matter of actual fact, he ran so close to the inner rails that when he came back to the barn after a race the whitewash from the fence streaked the left side of his glossy coat. On my illegal visits to The Willows barns, I never failed to pet Col. Boyle, who was generally tractable, though he had one spectacular eccentricity.

Col. Boyle was a farm boy at heart and he hated to wear shoes. When it came time to shoe him in the spring to prepare for the summer's racing, it was necessary to import a farrier from Calgary to tackle this exhausting assignment. The farrier was Jimmy Smith, who later shod the immortal New Zealand horse Phar Lap for his one North American race, a smashing victory in the $100,000 Agua Caliente Handicap.

Even under the familiar hands of Jimmy Smith, Col. Boyle acted like a maniac. He screamed and fought, lashing out furiously with his feet. It was necessary to rope and hog-tie him, a task which exhausted three or four men and which elicited some extremely colourful language from Mr. Addison and his perspiring assistants. Even when he was hog-tied and lying in the dust, Col. Boyle would snort and glare murderously at Jimmy Smith. Strangely enough, once the ordeal was over, Col. Boyle permitted Smith to pet him as if he was a collie dog.

Racing at Colwood extended into September and, usually, I could escape to the track on the first two Saturday afternoons of the school year. My indulgent parents had left instructions that I could sign their names to dining-room checks at the Empress Hotel, and the bill would be sent to them at the end of each month. News of my carte blanche spread quickly through University School, and when we were freed each Saturday morning many older boys who ignored me during the week suddenly offered to accompany me to lunch. When my absent father had fed them well, these older boys would go off to a movie and, secretly, I would go off to Colwood.

There were friendly agents on the staff of the Empress Hotel who aided and abetted my racing adventures. Mr. Hudson, who managed the newsstand, had at least a telephonic connection with some unseen bookmaker and, additionally, he permitted me to peruse the past-performance charts in the *Green Sheet*. Tony, who operated the shoeshine stand in the hotel basement, was a discreet source of information which he had collected from jockeys and trainers who chatted together over his bent silent head while he was applying a high gloss to their expensive brogans. Tony wasn't an expansive conversationalist, but he imparted highly classified information to me because he admired my father, who in some mysterious manner had assisted him in the distant past.

The Japanese bellboys in the Empress were also my confederates. With a few notable exceptions, the bellboys were gamblers. When I smoked out a tip on a "live one" at Colwood, I would seek one of my bellboy friends who would take my two dollars and bet it on the horse. Thus, at an age when I should have still been gnawing rusks, I was making the occasional cautious but informed wager on thoroughbreds.

Getting to Colwood in those days was half the fun. For fifty cents, Barney Olson would drive you from the hotel to the track in one of his open sightseeing buses. They were old-fashioned buses with double-decked running-boards. The passengers sat four abreast in wide seats. While the bus was rocketing around the curvy road, Barney would send his assistant, an enormously fat taxi-driver named Winnipeg Chilton, to collect the fares. Puffing and sweating, Winnipeg would crawl along the upper running board on the outside of the bus, clinging desperately to the doors. In retrospect, I suspect Barney Olson of slightly sadistic tendencies because he would roar with delight whenever Chilton was almost dislodged by the overhanging branches of evergreen trees as we surged along the narrow island highway.

The Good Lord alone knows how Lord Coventry was induced to sink his money into the construction of Colwood Park. It was a one-mile track, situated in a valley in some of the most rugged terrain on the coast of Vancouver Island. The backstretch ran downhill and the homestretch was an uphill gradient. On a quiet day, you could actually hear the laboured wheezing of the horses as they toiled uphill to the finish-line. There was a towering mound of rock in the infield, obscuring your view of a hundred yards of the backstretch when you were watching a race from the grandstand. Some very strange shuffling in the positions of the horses took place in the few seconds while they were hidden behind that small mountain.

There were other unusual sights at Colwood. A farmer raised turkeys in the track's infield and the birds were permitted to run loose all year. Frequently, the turkeys became excited by the crowd's cheering and they ran wildly onto the track, creating traffic hazards for the startled jockeys. There is a completely apocryphal story that a jockey once won a race at Colwood with a tom turkey perched on his shoulder and his horse was disqualified for carrying more than the statutory five pounds of overweight.

There is nothing apocryphal about the story of the elderly lady who stood alone in the infield at Colwood, wildly shaking her tartan ankle-length skirt. While shaking her skirt, the lady would be singing a highland war-chant in a loud if slightly cracked Scottish contralto.

This was no ordinary Victoria eccentric. This was Mrs. Jessie Mackenzie, a former stage beauty from Scotland, who trained her own horses. When one of her horses was running in a race, Mrs. Mackenzie encouraged them by singing to them and waving them on with flourishes of her Mackenzie tartan skirt.

Colwood was also the home ground of Asah Smith, the Baron Munchhausen of cougar hunters. Asah Smith's stable jockey was Red Pollard, later to achieve some international renown as Seabiscuit's regular rider.

On a Saturday afternoon, Red rode one of Asah's horses to a driving finish at Colwood. Pollard was certain that he had won the race, and when he came back to dismount in front of the judges' stand, he glanced at the result-board. To his astonishment, his horse had been placed second.

A man of violent impulses, Red reached down beside the scales on the finish-line. He picked up a handful of gravel and, with unerring accuracy, he hurled the gravel at the windowed front of the judges' stand, causing Presiding Judge Samuel Rothert to duck to avoid the cascading shards of glass.

On any other one-mile race track in North America, a jockey who was so demonstratively discourteous to the presiding officials would have been suspended for the remainder of the season – or, possibly, ruled off for life.

The next morning, Jockey Red Pollard was summoned to the prisoner's bar to receive the solemn sentence from Judge Samuel Rothert.

Jockey Red Pollard was fined $25.

You will gather that racing at Colwood Park could be quite interesting.

4

Hudson's Bay Rules

The salubrious climate of the Pacific coastal slope has a peculiar effect on many human beings. It is notable that the great majority of off-beat characters in the United States gravitate ultimately to California, where they discover their spiritual home. Much the same situation prevails in British Columbia, which is Canada's paradise for active eccentrics.

In my Victoria school days, the territory still abounded in genteel oddballs. Lower British Columbia – or, more particularly, Vancouver Island – still had the lingering atmosphere of a Crown Colony. The Union Jack waved proudly from atop the Parliament Buildings and the Empress Hotel in Victoria. Victoria's population still had a small, hard core of well-heeled British expatriates who descended on this benighted land equipped only with impeccable pedigrees, impeccable public school educations and little or no training for the hurly-burly of North American commercial practices.

Cushioned by their income from family estates in England, they settled down in the great tradition of the British Empire, as if they were living in Hong Kong or Singapore. They sauntered about in their shaggy tweeds and good thick-soled English Brogans. They were delightfully anachronistic.A contemporary cartoon in the *New Yorker* magazine epitomized Victoria's type of colonizer. The cartoon shows two moustachioed Englishmen quaffing cool drinks in some outpost of the Empire. And one Englishman is recalling dreamily to the other: "I can see the old girl now – striding about in her flat heels and smelling of saddle soap."

British colonizers always invaded new territory equipped with two toys – cricket and horse racing – to amuse themselves and to charm the hostile natives. Undoubtedly, the British influence was strong in British Columbia. Only a scion of the noble house of Coventry could have been reckless enough to build a one-mile track at Colwood, in the timbered jungles of Vancouver Island. The project was doomed from the start, due to comparative inaccessibility and lack of patrons, but it staggered through fifteen years of operation from 1924 until 1939.

Such profligacy is incredible, reviewed in the light of the Canadian economy of the 1970's, but the cities of Vancouver and Victoria had a total of five race tracks operating in the period between 1925 and 1939. Vancouver had Brighouse Park, Lansdowne Park and Hastings Park. Tiny Victoria had Colwood Park and The Willows.

Five race tracks to serve a combined two-city population which in the late twenties was less than 350,000!

Such a climate was propitious for the ripening of individualists. British Columbia harboured some highly individualistic horsemen, highly individualistic thoroughbreds and several unusual racing officials. The standard of jurisprudence on B.C. tracks was uneven.

Occupying a position of unquestioned integrity was Judge Robert F. Leighton, a courtly Englishman. Like many other English émigrés, Mr. Leighton had come into reduced financial circumstances after his arrival in Vancouver, and for a time he had stomached his pride and had maintained his family by tending bar in the old Bodega Hotel on Cordova Street. Judge Leighton was a no-nonsense Presiding Steward who governed with innate dignity. However, he was also a compassionate gentleman, fully aware that many of the horsemen who race in his jurisdiction were no better than God had intended them to be.

In my time on Canadian tracks, there have been three truly outstanding Presiding Stewards. Judge Leighton was one of these. Another was Judge Francis Nelson, a Toronto sports editor, who presided for many years on the major Eastern

Canada tracks, in addition to conducting the winter meetings at Agua Caliente and Santa Anita. The third was Judge George Washington Schilling, who came from the San Francisco bay area to be the supreme arbiter of racing on the Canadian prairies.

However, there were some other B.C. stewards who permitted racing to be conducted under what horsemen described sardonically as "Hudson's Bay Rules." That descriptive phrase suggests that, in a crisis, horsemen and horses could fall back on their most primitive instincts.

There were judges such as Sam Rothert, who gave Jockey Red Pollard a twenty-five dollar fine for hurling stones at him. And there was Judge Tom Wellman, whose casual advice to the jockeys before a race was: "take your best holt – but keep your hands on your own horse." I always had a particular reverence for Judge Wellman because he told me in a reminiscent mood that he had saved the life of my Grandfather Grant. In their barnstorming days in the Crow's Nest Pass region, Judge Wellman had been driving their buckboard and my Grandfather had been sitting whittling with his legs dangling over the tailgate. The good Judge carelessly drove over a large rock and my grandfather was dislodged, the knife slashing a main artery in his arm as he clattered to the rocky ground. Judge Wellman ripped off his own shirt, applied a tourniquet to my expiring grandfather, lashed the horses into activity and sped to the nearest hospital. I don't recall that my grandfather left anything to Judge Wellman in his will. Possibly, my grandfather reasoned that the Judge's teamstering wasn't above reproach.

Tom Wellman's offhand dispensation of frontier justice appalled serious-minded devotees of horse racing. Nevertheless his rulings often had the wisdom of Solomon.

There was the case of an Indian lady, Mrs. Crawford, who lost her favorite horse, Boot Top, in a claiming race at Colwood. In front of the judges' stand, when the groom from the new owner's stable presented the claim-slip and attempted to put his halter on Boot Top, Mrs. Crawford, who was large and extremely emotional, caused a terrible scene. Tears pouring down her dark cheeks, Mrs. Crawford sat right down on the race track and she refused to budge. Her lamentations rent the afternoon air and, while the curious crowd peered over the inner rails at this fascinating spectacle, Judge Wellman instructed four of his sturdiest henchmen to coax Mrs. Crawford into absenting herself. She was led away, wailing. She howled and sobbed in the manner of a widow at an old-fashioned Italian funeral.

Judge Wellman then summoned the unfortunate gentleman who had claimed Boot Top. The judge ordered the man to enter Boot Top in another race, two days later, for exactly the same claiming-price.

The following morning, The Judge called a meeting of all horsemen who entered their steeds in the race with Boot Top.

"Listen to me carefully," the Judge said solemnly, when the horsemen had assembled. "Mrs. Crawford is going to claim Boot Top out of this race, tomorrow afternoon. If any of you other burglars put in a claim for Boot Top, I'll run you so far down the road that it'll take you a year-and-a-half to find your way back."

Boot Top returned to Mrs. Crawford's barn the following afternoon, via the claiming route, and peace and tranquility once again reigned at sylvan Colwood.

At other times, Judge Wellman displayed a lofty disregard of the impartially inflexible duties of his judicial office.

One afternoon, he summoned Massie White, a clerk on the racing staff, to the stand and he said to him: "Here's a hundred dollars. Bet it for me on the Number Seven horse in this race."

"Good God, Judge, you can't do that," blurted White. "You're the presiding steward."

"Why the hell can't I?" thundered Wellman. "This horse is going to win and those idiots in the crowd are letting him go at ten-to-one. Now, get out of here and bet my money!"

British Columbia race tracks promulgated their own rules to suit their peculiar convenience. For instance, in an era when the presence of women on the backstretch was considered to be as incongruous and as improbable as a Salvation Army lass soliciting alms in a loggers' brothel, Mrs. Jessie Mackenzie had a licence to train her own horses on the tracks in Vancouver and Victoria.

Quite apart from her habit of waving her tartan skirts in the infield while her horses were running, Mrs. Jessie Mackenzie was no ordinary lady. She had been beautiful in her youth and, always, she retained some of her airy theatrical mannerisms and a gift of declamatory speech. Although she went a bit to seed in her declining years, she retained her regal bearing and no rash horseman ever dared to take liberties with the old girl.

The most loyal and patient of Mrs. Mackenzie's racing patrons was the redoubtable General "One-Arm" Sutton, who settled in Victoria to dissipate his loot which he had carried home from China. This soldier of fortune had carved quite a gaudy career as a bellicose advisor to Chinese warlords.

General Sutton's first confrontation with Mrs. Mackenzie was a meeting of the giants. The General was in the mood to assemble a racing stable and he was directed to Mrs. Mackenzie who, temporarily, was suffering from the shorts. Consequently, Mrs. Mackenzie was ready to sell her gallant little horse, Jim Rogan, on two conditions: the price must be right and she must continue to train Jim Rogan.

At the sight of General Sutton, who gleamed with fresh wealth, Mrs. Mackenzie went into her sales pitch. Summoning all her resources of richly colorful eloquence, the lady extolled Jim Rogan's conformation, his long pedigree and his stupendous racing abilities. As Mrs. Mackenzie expanded on her theme, she extended Jim Rogan's pedigree all the way back to the Darley Arabian and, as a racer, she compared him favourably with Man O War and John P. Grier.

General Sutton, who had played poker with some rather wily Chinese brigands, listened patiently until Mrs. Mackenzie developed a slitch hitch in her verbal gait.

"My dear lady," he said, tapping her on one shoulder, "let's get down to business. How much for your story – and how much for your horse?"

General Sutton was a generous patron and Mrs. Mackenzie's racing fortunes flourished for a few years. Then, regretably, the General went broke during the Depression. Mrs. Mackenzie finally moved into a shack on the backstretch at Brighouse, but always she maintained a home for gallant old Jim Rogan. The horse proved to be quite as durable as his mistress and, at the incredible age of thirty-eight, he was paraded before the crowd one afternoon at Hastings Park in Vancouver. He lived until he was thirty-nine; in terms of human existence he was 117 years old.

Mrs. Mackenzie was unique on the distaff side of the B.C. racing family, but a determinedly insular breed of horseman flourished in the evergreen forest on the Pacific Slopes. That moist but temperate region exercised a peculiarly strong grip on visitors who strayed from other, harsher climates. The B.C. racing colony included several U.S. emigrés who, after one exploratory visit, stayed for the remainder of their lives.

British Columbia's racing fraternity was a closely-knit group. Seldom did they venture from their home grounds. A few shipped their horses south to the Juarez and Tia Juana tracks in Mexico for winter racing but they always came home for the B.C. season. The number of B.C. horsemen who shipped their stables to the Canadian prairies wasn't high. And if a B.C. horseman shipped all the way to Ontario for autumn racing he usually desired a holiday from a domineering wife.

Notable among these emigrees – but certainly not typical of them – was Charles C. "Gyp" Emmert. His nickname had no larcenous connotations. He was one of the breed of horsemen who travelled constantly from track to track with a few old selling-platers, living in the barns and accumulating little more than bare living expenses. Those itinerant horsemen were known as Gypsies.

Gyp Emmert came out of a small town in Missouri, where he had worked for ten cents a day cleaning out the local poolroom. Out of his pay he saved five cents a day, so that he could take out his girl friend on Sundays. The girl friend, who became "Ma" Emmert, was worth every nickel of Gyp's self-deprivation. Ma Emmert was a lady of tremendous character, a foster mother to countless young jockeys and stableboys, a Florence Nightingale in manure-stained shoes.

Even after the Emmerts settled on Vancouver Island, Gyp was one horseman who declined to become involved in the prevalent preoccupation with isolation. He persisted in his gypsy way, shipping to the prairies, shipping to Mexico, and eventually he made one of his shrewd purchases which had a profound effect on British Columbia's breeding industry. While racing at Tia Juana in the late winter of 1927, Emmert found himself making a daily habit of wandering past a stall occupied by the five-year-old horse named Simony. Whittlin' John Strite owned Simony but, the horse originally had belonged to the Seagram Stable, of Waterloo, Ontario. Emmert horse-traded with Whittlin' John for several days and, eventually, he bought Simony for $1,000 down, plus $500 on-the-cuff.

Billy Bell, later to become a steward on B.C. tracks, rode Simony in his first race in Emmert's colours. The horse won for a claiming-price of $1,500; he won for $1,800; he won for $4,500; and on February 4, 1928, he won a handicap at Tia Juana. However, his racing career was of secondary importance; Emmert took Simony home to British Columbia where the black horse became a foundation-sire who dominated two generations of thoroughbred stock on the Pacific Coast.

Simony proved to be an exceptionally tractable stallion. There was a local legend that when Gyp Emmert took his stallion to breed him to a neighboring mare, he would climb on the horse's back and ride him down the paved Island Highway.

The actual fact wasn't quite as colourful as the legend. However, Gyp always loaded Simony into a tiny one-horse trailer which he hauled behind his car. And as soon as he was out of Ma Emmert's sight Gyp would drive to a nearby estaminet, the Colwood House.

Emmert would repair to the bar room for a few cool, refreshing lagers. Meanwhile the old horse, his head hanging over the back of the trailer, would doze contentedly in the morning sunlight. Passing children would pet and feed apples to Simony, innocently unaware that he was a thoroughbred stallion. Sensing that his master, enjoying himself in the malty atmosphere of the Colwood House, expected him to behave as a gentleman, Simony never onced gnawed a childish human finger and, when Emmert emerged and drove him to his male animal destiny, Simony sired some of the best horses ever to be seen in Western Canada.

The proprietor of the Colwood House was Mrs. Asah Smith. There is an important distinction in the above statement: Mrs. Asah Smith owned the hotel, Mrs. Asah Smith had the money, Mrs. Asah Smith ruled the roost – Mr. Asah Smith wryly played second fiddle in the Colwood House Symphony.

"Acie" Smith was Idaho's gift to British Columbia. A bandy-legged ex-jockey, he had a humorously crumpled face which gave him a resemblance to a happy bulldog. His wife, who out-weighed him by a few pounds, ruled him with a whim of iron. One day, Gyp Emmert strolled into the Colwood House just after Mrs. Smith had expressed herself rather vehemently to her spouse.

"I seen Acie standing outside," said Mr. Emmert, as he called for a beer. "He was lookin' like a bulldog that had been whipped with a wet hose."

In the circumstances, it is understandable that Asah Smith devoted a good deal of time to campaigning his modest stable on distant tracks. Mrs. Smith refused to wander more than a few feet from her cash register in the hotel. She didn't give a damn where Asah went, as long as he didn't spend any money.

Whenever Acie had a horse which was worth more than five dollars, he would ship off to Winnipeg, and on one epic safari he took two of his steeds, Goldstream and Bear Tamer, all the way to Toronto. He had a very successful meeting in Toronto, and when he returned home in October he triumphantly dumped a wad of bank notes into Mrs. Smith's eager hands.

"You aren't holding out on me, are you?" asked Mrs. Smith shrewdly.

Asah recoiled as if he had been bitten by a puff-adder. The enormity of his wife's suggestion cut him to the heart. Manfully, he shouldered his wounded pride; he merely gave her a look of forgiving benediction.

Two weeks later, one of those open-window envelopes arrived at the Colwood House. Mrs. Smith steamed open the envelope. It was a bill for four hundred dollars from the Canadian Pacific Railway. Through some fatal oversight, Acie had neglected to pay the railway for shipping his two horses from Toronto.

Asah didn't attempt to explain the oversight to his enraged lady. Wisely choosing the path of discretion, he spent the next two nights sleeping in the barn with his horses.

The walls of that particular barn were lined with cougar pelts. It would be obvious that any man who could talk the formidable Mrs. Smith into marriage must be an exceptionally talented conversationalist. Asah, by his own boast, was the veritable monarch of cougar-hunters. According to Asah, the nearby city of Victoria would have been overrun by cougars if he personally hadn't repelled the annual invasion of mountain lions.

Acie's stories of his prowess with a rifle were constantly at the tip of his lips, waiting to be released when some ready listener opened a bottle. His colourful descriptions of his one-man war against the predator cats were heard on race tracks from coast to coast and, indeed, many enchanted horsemen still remember him as "Cougar" Smith.

When he had a suitably receptive audience, Asah would modestly give some of the credit for his cougar-hunting success to his gallant old broodmare, Bee's Wing. If there is such a thing as a Thoroughbred Hall of Fame in Canada, Bee's Wing deserves admission.

Asah used to tell a story of how two cougars invaded his barn one winter night. Bee's Wing used her teeth to open her stall door. Then the old mare trapped the two cougars in one corner of the barn, turned her back to them, and kicked them to death. When Asah went to the barn in the morning, he found the two dead cougars. Bee's Wing had gone back into her stall and she had used her teeth to re-lock the door.

When I was a teenager, I sat in Asah's tackroom at Polo Park in Winnipeg. Taking one of his regular holidays from Mrs. Smith's imperious surveillance, he had shipped a colt named Prince Goldstream to race in the inaugural running of the Manitoba Derby.

"Yup, that old Bee's Wing was half-human," Asah said, while my eyeballs bulged from their sockets. "And she hated cougars. She could smell a cougar a mile away and when she smelled one she'd go crazier than a peach orchard boar.

"There was a little lake near my place at Goldstream. When the lake froze over in mid-winter the cougars would come down from the hills to try to get water. When I saw a cougar out on the ice, I'd turn loose Bee's Wing.

"The old mare would chase the cougar, round and round on the ice. Finally the cougar would get so tired that he'd have to set down on his haunches. The cougar would be sweating, and as soon as he sat down he'd freeze to the ice in a sitting position. He wouldn't be able to move.

"I'd walk up to him, pull out my hunting knife, and I'd slit him from the base of the chin right down to his rump.

"Then, I'd give the cougar a good kick in the ass. He'd jump right out of his skin and run away, leaving me with an unmarked pelt."

In addition to being the scourge of the cougar population, Bee's Wing was a productive broodmare. Asah bred her to Simony several times and, one of her colts was Goldstream, a stakes-winning horse who inherited some of his mother's rugged individualism. Goldstream was lying in his paddock one day and a yappy little terrier persisted in circling him, barking incessantly. Goldstream ignored the racket for some time, but finally the horse arose with slow dignity. With one quick snap, Goldstream seized the terrier by the nape of the neck, walked across the paddock, and dropped the frightened dog into a water trough.

My earliest excursions to Colwood and The Willows were confined to my weekly Saturday escapes from boarding school supervision. The drug had entered my bloodstream. I became the school's resident authority on thoroughbred bloodlines, a circumstance which was deplored by the headmaster, a gentleman whose only vicarious association with the turf was the riding-crop which hung on his office wall and with which he chastised aspiring juvenile delinquents. His corrective measures were an exercise in futility – I was already beyond redemption.

From a spectator's viewpoint, the three essential ingredients of horse racing are: the horses themselves, the owner-trainers, and the jockeys. Initially, it was the horses which fascinated me in my years of innocence. Slowly I became aware of the existence of the men who trained and owned the horses and, even more slowly, the robust personalities of a few jockeys impinged on my growing consciousness.

The two British Columbia jockeys whom I remember most vividly from my boarding school days were Acie Smith's trigger-tempered rider, Red Pollard, and the exceptionally durable John "Scotty" Craigmyle. Both gentlemen were highly talented.

Pollard's mercurial disposition had earned him the nickname, "The Red-Headed Skull Basher" and the redoubtable Asah Smith handled him with kid gloves. There were no breathalizer tests on race tracks in those days and it was rumoured that Pollard, weakened by his daily strenuous efforts to control his weight, occasionally required a restorative shot of whiskey in the jockeys' quarters to tune him to the proper riding pitch. It was obvious, even to a small schoolboy peering over the fence beside the weighing-in scales, that there were certain jockeys who, upon dismounting and strolling past the fence on their way back to their quarters, appeared to be expelling the vapours of some drink which was more robust than milk. Mr. Pollard's language, when he lost a close finish, left a profound impression upon my own private vocabulary. It was during my observations of those daily unsaddling ceremonies that I had my first exposure to the Great English Adjective.

In terms of personality Jockey Craigmayle was almost the direct antithesis of Jockey Pollard. He was a solemn little Scotsman with a pronounced stutter.

Johnny Craigmyle was born in Scotland, where his father was a successful barber. Intrigued by the tales of vast wealth to be acquired in the British overseas dominions, Craigmyle *père* sold his tonsorial parlour on his native heath, moved his entire family by ship to Montreal, and bought another barbershop in the French-Canadian metropolis. It wasn't long before Craigmyle *père* realized that he had made an unwise purchase: his new shop was situated in a completely French section of Montreal and he was unable to speak the language of his prospective patrons. Reselling his shop at a substantial loss, Craigmyle moved his family to Vancouver, where at least the natives spoke a less incomprehensible language.

Possibly it was his father's business misadventure which caused Scotty Craigmyle to grow up with an inclination to taciturnity. Possibly it was his stammer which caused him to be slightly introverted. In any event, Craigmyle, even in his earliest days on the track, was regarded among the cognoscenti as a cold-nerved "money-rider," a jockey who would beat the hair off a horse to earn a fifty-dollar gratuity from a winning owner.

Years later, I was to see Craigmyle win the Canadian Derby at Winnipeg with one of his "money rides." Ten to Ace, a colt which had won the Queen's Plate in Toronto with ridiculous ease, had been shipped to Winnipeg for the race. Ten to Ace appeared to outclass his Winnipeg rivals and, accordingly, the track management ruled that there would be no public betting on the Canadian Derby. Six other horses entered the Derby, but their owners had no serious designs on first-moneys; they were running second, third and fourth prizes.

As was expected, Ten to Ace sprinted into a lengthy lead.

Craigmyle, riding a horse named Maginot Line, was restraining his mount carefully, intent on making a run through the stretch to grab second-money.

As they galloped along, Craigmyle noticed something which escaped the attention of his less vigilant rivals. Ten to Ace was losing his smooth action; the chestnut colt from Toronto was faltering. Although Ten to Ace still was leading by twenty-five lengths, Craigmyle suddenly began to whip Maginot Line furiously. He pulled away from the pack and he set out after Ten to Ace. Too late, the other jockeys realized what was happening; they too went to their whips, but Craigmyle had the jump on them.

Craigmyle, lashing and slashing, hit Maginot Line every step of the way through the final six furlongs as he literally stole the Canadian Derby. Ten to Ace, which subsequently was discovered to be a very sick horse, finished dead-last.

Maginot Line earned a very long rest from his victory in the Canadian Derby. He had been whipped and booted so enthusiastically by Craigmyle that he couldn't eat his feed that night. In fact, a few days later, Maginot Line was shipped home to British Columbia to recuperate. The Canadian Derby had taken such a toll from the horse that Maginot Line didn't race again for fourteen months.

When I first saw Scotty Craigmyle in action at Colwood, the richly gusty spirit of horse racing hadn't been diluted by the introduction of the saliva-test or those electronic snoopers, the film-patrol cameras. A jockey still rode with two distinct objectives – to win or to lose – and he had small choice in the matter. He obeyed implicitly the orders of the man who owned or trained the horses which he rode.

Horse race purses were small. The horseman who wished to keep his budget balanced, augmented his income with judicious winning wagers. In the circumstances, few trainers desired to see their horses winning until they were betting on them. Any jockey who consistently disobeyed a trainer's laconic instructions to "give this horse an easy one" soon found himself out of regular employment. This was fairly common practice on smaller race tracks throughout North America. It wasn't regarded as felonious – it was a matter of simple economic necessity. A horseman, like anyone else, must earn enough money to feed himself and his family, not to mention his ravenous horses.

Scotty Craigmyle grew up in this restrictive atmosphere, where a sensible jockey who wished to prosper in his profession listened carefully to the instructions of the men who commissioned his services.

Thus, one of Scotty's most memorable feats of horsemanship was performed in a losing cause. Mr. Thomas R. Stone had shipped his stable of horses from Calgary to campaign on the British Columbia tracks. Mr. Stone not only raced his horses on Western Canada tracks, but he operated the Calgary Club in his home town. A great deal of gambling took place at the Calgary Club, and the gambling included wagering on horse races. Every person of any financial importance in Calgary was aware that Mr. Stone's club engaged in bookmaking. It was not at all unusual in those days for bookmakers to own stables of race horses. Bookmakers usually were heavy bettors themselves and the track owners were enchanted by the spectacle of bookmakers grinding their own money in the pari-mutuel machines. When Mr. Stone appeared on a Canadian track, the management was extremely happy to encourage his presence.

Shortly after opening his invasion of British Columbia, Mr. Stone entered his horse, Peach Stone, in a race. Astutely, he secured the services of Scotty Craigmyle as Peach Stone's jockey. Peach Stone was as fit as a fiddle, Scotty was riding in top form, and Mr. Stone was confident of victory.

Shortly before he left for the track on the afternoon of the race, Mr. Stone placed a long-distance telephone call to the man who was tending his store back in Calgary. A few minutes later, Mr. Stone, ashen faced, put down the telephone receiver. The news from his little store was shocking. Mr. Stone's bookmaking establishment was "loaded" with bets on Peach Stone. Furthermore, Mr. Stone's storekeeper couldn't move any of the money; every other bookmaker was loaded with action on Peach Stone. Even the bookmakers in Winnipeg were up to their eyeballs in bets on Peach Stone.

Mr. Stone's course of action was quite plain. Peach Stone must lose – or Mr. Stone's bookmaking operation would sustain grievous losses.

Tom Stone sped to the track and, just before the race, he had an earnest little chat with Jockey Craigmyle. He explained the situation to Jockey Craigmyle tersely. As he boosted Jockey Craigmyle into the saddle, Mr. Stone said quietly and coldly, "Get this horse beaten, somehow! I will be very upset with you if Peach Stone happens to win!"

Scotty Craigmyle was young, but he was astute. During the long parade to the post, he assessed the most efficacious and honourable methods of losing the race. He hit upon a solution – he would bolt into an early lead and drive Peach Stone so rigorously in the first half-mile that the horse would become exhausted. Peach Stone was slightly touched in the wind and, habitually, he choked up if he was asked to expend his top speed in the early part of the race. The tactics appeared to be perfect; Peach Stone, gasping for breath, would be overtaken in the late stages of the race.

When the starter sprang the latch, Craigmyle gunned Peach Stone away from the gate. He hammered a tatto on Peach Stone's hide. Sure enough, after they had gone a half-mile at this furious pace, the horse began to wheeze like an asthmatic accordion.

Scotty looked back over his shoulder and, to his horror, he saw that his closest pursuer was twelve lengths behind.

But he saw something else which caused his heart to freeze – no one was trying to overtake him! The enormity of the situation struck him full force. He was being "shooed in;" the other jockeys in the race had bet on Peach Stone. The books in Calgary and Winnipeg were loaded with Peach Stone bets for the very simple reason that the jockeys had advised their numerous clients that Craigmyle's mount wouldn't lose this particular race.

His steel-trap mind clicking rapidly, Craigmyle considered his dilemma. He was turning into the homestretch with a ten-length lead. He envisioned Mr. Thomas Stone waiting for him at the finish-line. Mr. Stone would lose thousands and thousands of dollars if Peach Stone won and Mr. Stone would be very, very angry.

Peach Stone still was winging along three hundred yards from the finish-line when Scotty Craigmyle solved his desperate problem.

Smoothly, he slipped his two feet from his stirrup irons – and he fell off!

5

A Little Bit of Help

The end of each school year was always followed by the careless rapture of the long hot prairie summer.

It was in this annual hiatus between my periods of confinement-in-exile that my budding interest in thoroughbred horses – and in the men who raced them – was given the opportunity and the climate to burst into full flower. It was fate, I am certain, that prescribed that my return from school coincided exactly with the opening of Winnipeg's first race meeting of the season.

Winters in Winnipeg were cruelly cold; it was the type of cold which you could feel right down in your lungs. Summers in Winnipeg were as mercifully hot and rewarding as the winters were pitiless. Winnipeg was reborn each summer. There was the sun, tall in the sky which stretched from horizon to horizon like a benevolent blue canopy. There were the incredibly long twilights when you could read a book on the front stoop at nine o'clock at night.

Horse racing is a sensual recreation. Even today, due to the happy circumstances of my early indoctrination, I still associate horse racing with the warmth and langour of the prairie summer. For me, horse racing still is a summer sport, just as baseball and cricket are summer sports. When the day came for the track operators to extend their season into the bleaker, colder months and they built glass-enclosed, heated grandstands,

I was overwhelmed by a sense of loss. They had destroyed one of my most pleasant illusions.

Glass-enclosed grandstands were one million light-years in the future when my father and my stepmother began to take me to River Park in Winnipeg, my younger brother tagging along, grunting moodily. River Park certainly wasn't Royal Ascot. It was bare and dusty, but to me it was glamorous and exciting.

Within a year or two, R. James Speers moved his racing operations out of River Park and he built two new tracks, Whittier Park and Polo Park. In my childish perspective, they were magnificent; Whittier with its white buildings and cottage-barns, roofed in green, and Polo Park with similar gleaming white buildings, roofed in maroon. It was on those two tracks that I learned about life and harmless larceny.

In this respect, Mr. Speers, who was to become one of my mentors, early gave me some valuable cautionary advice when he told me: "There's a little larceny in every man – but you notice it more around a race track."

Racing at Whittier and Polo was very much a family sport. Children who accompanied their parents and who were well behaved were indulged by the management. Each track had a neat little club house where the ladies of the St. Agnes Guild served tea each afternoon. The St. Agnes Guild was a formidable charitable organization and by providing the ladies with a means of raising funds for their good works Mr. Speers effectively charmed a powerful element in the community which, under less fortuitous circumstances, might have been inclined to inveigh publicly against horse racing as an abomination of the devil. I can still see the dear ladies, who occasionally included my devoutly Roman Catholic stepmother, serving restorative provender to the club members. They went about their duties happily, clad in blue smocks with gold collars and cuffs. It was the closest my stepmother came to wearing the official colours of the Loyal Orange Lodge.

To his dying day, Mr. Speers opposed the sale of liquor on race tracks. Nevertheless, he realized that a gentleman who had blown a wager on a beaten favourite required frequent injections of plasma. On the main floor of the club house there was a room to which the male club members retired at regular intervals. Many of the gentlemen emerged from that room refreshed, rosy-cheeked and uncommonly merry.

If I were granted a return into the past for another day of my life, I believe that I would choose to relive an afternoon at Whittier Park. There we would be again on the grass lawns in front of the white club house. From where I sat on a garden bench, secure between my father and my stepmother, I could see those two regal old ladies, Mrs. G. V. Hastings and Mrs. Patrick Shea, sitting in their adjacent black limousines beside the club house fence. We'd sit there, watching the horses run again – Duchess of York, Cappy Ricks, Son O Unc, McGonigle, Formic and little Joey – and when the last race had been run, we'd get into the waiting taxi for the leisurely ride home. And my stepmother, digging into her purse, would be fretting about the winning ticket which she was sure that she had dropped somewhere and my father would be smiling quietly.

When we entered the lobby of the Royal Alexandra, we'd stop first at the news stand where the entries for the next day's races were piled neatly on the counter; just little sheets of paper with the names of the horses and the jockeys. We'd go to our suite on the fifth floor and my father would order dinner from room service. And after dinner, as we sat by our west-facing windows, watching the sun slipping over the horizon, we'd lock hands on the chesterfield and we'd talk happily about our selections for tomorrow's program. We were very close then. Very close and very happy.

It didn't take me long to find my way to the barns at Whittier Park and Polo Park. My father inadvertently opened the gates to the stable area by telling me that Duchess of York, which was one of the family favourites, had been bred by Charlie Yeandle, a locomotive engineer on the CPR line between Calgary and Edmonton. My father was the type of old-fashioned railway official who knew every locomotive engineer between Fort William and Vancouver. Choosing an appropriate moment, I implored my father to take me to the barns to meet Mr. Yeandle and his race horse. Mr. Yeandle was a bit nonplussed when his company's vice-president and a small boy drove up to his barn, but he rallied gamely. My father had told me previously that Mr. Yeandle "raised Duchess of York with kid gloves." To my surprise, Mr. Yeandle was wearing no gloves, let alone kid gloves at our first meeting. His strong capable hands were calloused, a result of years of grasping the Johnson-bar and tugging on the huge brake lever of his passenger locomotive.

This tenuous acquaintanceship with the affable locomotive engineer was my "open sesame" to the stable areas of Canadian tracks. Stable-gate security was rather slipshod in those days, and after that first introduction I would walk up boldly to the gate and tell the gateman: "I'm going to see Charlie Yeandle." The gateman never questioned me. I was small and he probably thought that I was an aspiring jockey. After a few tentative ventures into the barns, I merely waved to the gateman as I sped past him. One morning, I brought the gateman a box of my father's De Reszke cigarettes and thereafter I received the red-carpet treatment.

The racing public, sitting daily in the grandstand or the club house, sees the finished product. The real drama and colour of the race track can be seen only on the backstretch, in the early mornings. Men who spend their lives around horses are unique. They have no taste for the world of commerce. They are, in the words of the 1970's, dropouts. They exist like a tribe of happy, untroubled aboriginees. They are tribal in that they protect one another against the encroachments of the outside world. As in any other social group, they have their misfits, but generally speaking they are warmly friendly and garrulous. Although they have their occasional petty feuds, they have a greater spirit of camaraderie than you can find in any other profession.

As soon as I discerned the subtle but important distinction between "the races" and "the morning workouts," I sought and received parental permission to visit the stable area while the sun was rising. Each night before I went to bed I asked the hotel telephone operator to give me a wake-up call at 5 or 6 a.m. When the phone rang in the morning, my brother would pull the covers over his head and feign deep slumber. Disgusted by the fact that he did not share my enthusiasm for the horses, I would ride to the track in state in a taxi which I charged to my father's account. Considering the meals which I charged to my father's account at the Empress Hotel in Victoria and the taxis which I charged to his account in Winnipeg, it is small wonder that my father didn't retire from business until he was seventy. I imagine, though, he accepted my matinal race track excursions as eminently preferable to my games with my extroverted playmates in the hotel.

Once I was through the stable gate, on the specious excuse of "going to see Mr. Yeandle," my Presbyterian conscience impelled me to pay a morning courtesy call at Duchess of York's stall. I would give her a couple of lumps of sugar which I had filched from a room-service tray on my way out of the hotel and then I would make a complete tour of the entire stable area. I must have been a quiet and inoffensive intruder because no one took exception to my presence. At least, no one ever shouted, "Get the hell out of here, sonny."

I believe that I must have puzzled some of the horsemen because I was dressed in what you might call "hotel attire" and obviously I had no right to be nosing around stall doors. The ginnies and swipes who worked around the barns in that era wore the same rough clothes for weeks on end and bathtubs weren't standard equipment on the backstretch. I am equally certain that my presence in the stable area was reported to Mr. Speers, but possibly he was amused by my unmitigated gall. In any event, no one bothered me and before many days passed some of the horsemen actually fell into the habit of greeting me by name.

There were no rules prohibiting the use of stimulants in those days and many of the most respected horsemen had no compunction about giving their horses "a little bit of help." Stimulation was deplored publicly by the S.P.C.A., and it wasn't condoned officially by racing stewards, but it was one of the sturdy realities of racing life in North America. As soon as the horsemen, through oblique questioning, had established the fact that I wasn't a midget undercover investigator for the S.P.C.A., they didn't bother to hide their little gadgets when I wandered along their shedrows.

Even in those days, when inhibiting rules were minimal and elastic, the vast majority of horses usually ran without medicinal assistance. There were, though, many horses of dubious quality who lacked both celerity and courage.

Speed and bravery for these underprivileged and underpowered steers could be provided, in many cases, by a judicious injection of stimulating drugs. The changes which were wrought in the personality and performance of these steeds when they were injected with a stimulant were quite startling. They would develop temporary delusions of grandeur. They became as brave as Jack Armstrong the All-American Boy and they wore the winged hooves of Mercury. There is no evidence, physiologically, that a stimulant actually increased the speed of a horse. It was a matter of the mind – psychologically, the stimulated horse was equipped to approach his task with carefree abandon.

And although every respectable trainer had an amply equipped medicine chest, drugs weren't used indiscriminately. The stable areas of North American tracks were quiet monasteries when compared with the Yorkvilles and Haight-Ashburys of the 1970's.

Not every trainer had the skill or the knowledge to administer drugs effectively. There was a highly professional group of trainers, the revered inner circle of the equine industry, who were the acknowledged maestros in the fine art of stimulation. Some of these gentlemen were so greatly skilled in the use of the hypodermic needle that their technique would have been envied by America's pre-eminent neurosurgeons, Dr. Wilder Penfield and Dr. Harvey Cushing.

My morning peregrinations on the backstretch led me inevitably to the racing establishment of the Barnes Brothers. The Barnes boys were gypsying horsemen who spent their winters in Mexico and their summers on the tracks of Western Canada. They were known affectionately among their confrères as "The James Brothers," a facetious reference to the American family of minor banditti whose activities had been glorified by the *Police Gazette* and other periodicals of dubious distinction. I had been aware of the existence of the Barnes brothers since my first visit to River Park, because they had assisted in Mr. Speers' pioneering efforts by bringing their two sterling runners, Olds Eight and Utelus, to Winnipeg. The name Olds Eight stuck in my mind because we owned an eight-cylinder Oldsmobile, a mechanical monster which devoured gasoline at an alarming rate.

Now the opportunity was offered for a personal relationship with the two itinerant American horsemen. The principal racing patron of the Barnes brothers at the moment was W. A. Dutton, a railway construction tycoon. Big Bill Dutton, a tall, powerful man with a magnificent grey soup-strainer moustache, was currently a resident of the Royal Alexandra Hotel. I admired him intensely and I followed him around the race track in the manner of an eager puppy. Mr. Dutton was one of those high-rollers who bet with both hands. The heavy contractors of Western Canada conducted most of their business from the McArthur Building, at the corner of Portage and Main in Winnipeg, and Mr. Dutton's office was headquarters for their regular noonday sessions of pitch, a mysterious card game in which large sums of money changed hands rapidly.

When I was in my early teens, I would sit in that office daily at noon, watching the contractors silently playing their hands before we went to the races. Dan McLeod, a constantly agitated little man who was Mr. Dutton's confidential clerk-accountant, barred the door to the inner office and intercepted all phone calls which might have interrupted the brow-knitted card sessions. I doubt that the President of the United States could have put through a call to that inner office, even if he were offering the boys a guaranteed cost-plus contract to build another Panama Canal. When the cards were put away and accounts had been settled for the day, the contractors would summon their personal bookmaker, who operated a haberdashery around the corner, next to the Province Theatre. After pondering the entries at the Chicago and New York tracks, Mr. Dutton would bet $1,000 straight, $1,000 place and $1,000 show on a couple of horses, as casually as if money were going out of fashion.

Without a doubt, Mr. Dutton bankrolled the racing adventures of the Barnes brothers handsomely, and when he gave them the nod, my acceptance at their barn was immediate although it may have been tainted by coercion. The senior partner of the establishment was Stub Barnes, a short stout man who wore a deceptive look of bland innocence. He was accompanied to the track daily by his wife, Babe, a laconic, cigarette-smoking lady whose lined face testified to their years of gypsying from coast to coast across North America. Unlike many of the backstretch set, Stub and Babe lived downtown while they were racing at Winnipeg, in the Leland Hotel, an establishment which was never rated by the Michelin guide or Duncan Hines.

Stub was the senior partner, but the recognized genius of the ménage was his younger brother, Dooge. Among the members of his own profession, Dooge Barnes was regarded as the peer of Dr. Joseph L. Lister and the Mayo Brothers.

Somewhat larger than Stub and even more contented in appearance than his brother, Dooge Barnes was amazingly skilled in the use of stimulating drugs for tardy horses. Although he was self-schooled, his knowledge of pharmacology was reputed to be encyclopaedic. Watching him work with a loaded syringe was an experience akin to watching Dégas completing one of his impressionist paintings. Admirers said that Dooge Barnes "could send a horse so high that the horse would climb up into the branch of a tree and recite Lincoln's Gettysburg Address."

If the Nobel selectors, in their annual search for worthy scientists, had bothered to investigate the little-known activities on the backstretch of North American race racks, I feel reasonably confident that Dooge Barnes would ultimately have been awarded the Nobel Prize for Chemistry.

An unselfish man, Dooge Barnes was always ready to share his skill, even if he didn't share the secret of his private prescriptions. He would give one of his own horses a stimulating injection and then he might be summoned by a trainer who was running a horse in the very same race. Generously, Dooge would unpack his little pharmaceutical kit; he would assess the problem carefully; appraising the horse's weight and girth; and, he would insert the needle in the vital zone. Dooge's generous assistance, so freely offered to rivals, was frequently deplored by his older brother – particularly when the beneficiary of Dooge's ministrations was running in the same race, against one of their own horses. "One of these days," Stub predicted dourly "that brother of mine is going to needle us right into the Old Folks' Home."

My dogged daily trailing of Mr. Dutton and my tenuous friendship with the Barnes brothers led to me owning my first race horse, about the same time that I owned my first long pants.

From the time that I was two years old, I always had owned a horse – a horse of some type. My father bought me a pony in Calgary and, when we moved to a house on Donald Street in Winnipeg, the pony went along. The pony was kept in a garage behind the house. Often I used to ride the pony through the streets of Winnipeg and across Osborne Street Bridge to visit our friends, the Bairds, who lived on River Avenue. Now, when I cross Osborne Street Bridge on my visits to Winnipeg, I marvel at the recollection of my childish temerity and stupidity. I can only assume that the traffic on the bridge was considerably less intense in the days of my carefree equestrian excursions.

When we moved from Donald Street to the Royal Alexandra Hotel, my father resisted any suggestions that the pony could be stabled in the Crystal Ballroom. The pony was shipped to Nelson Smith's farm at Birds Hill, where I could still ride him – and I did ride him until he was eighteen.

Long before I stopped riding him, the poor old pony had been relegated to second-class citizenship in my rapidly changing world. My pony wasn't the first childhood pet to be abandoned heartlessly by a boy who goes after bigger game. This is human nature: I was to learn in later life that otherwise sensible men occasionally discarded an old wife in favour of a younger, flashier model. In my case I didn't abandon my pony entirely: I was dazzled by the visions of racing thoroughbreds. The old pony, who had grown fat through long months of inactivity, couldn't run a quarter-mile without gasping and wheezing in the manner of a beached whale.

Now that I was thoroughly horse-struck, I dreamed of one day owning a race horse of my own. This was my private dream, and I am quite positive that I never expressed my longings aloud.

Mr. Dutton was a patient man but, in all probability, he had become a bit tired of having me underfoot, particularly when he was attempting to skunk his business competitors in his regular noonday game of Pitch. One day, when I went down to his office in the morning before we went to lunch in Child's Restaurant downstairs, Mr. Dutton told Dan McLeod to shut his office door as soon as I had been ushered into his presence.

From his jacket pocket, Mr. Dutton produced a racing badge. It was on Owner-Trainer badge, issued by the management of Whittier Park. On the space reserved for the name of the bearer, I could see that a clerk in the Racing Secretary's office had written MY name: "Jim Coleman."

I almost swooned with excitement. I didn't trust myself to speak, beacuse I feared that Mr. Dutton was playing a little joke on me.

While I stammered questions, Mr. Dutton explained to me that he had a chat with Stub Barnes earlier that morning. They owned, in partnership, a chestnut gelding named A. Lester. The horse was my particular favorite around the barn – he was a sprinter who held the five furlong record at Salt Lake City. Mr. Dutton said that he and Stub Barnes had decided to make me a gift of a quarter-interest in A. Lester. Furthermore, they had registered the horse in my name at the Racing Secretary's office, a circumstance which entitled me to wear the owner's badge which he had presented to me. Furthermore, the badge entitled me to all the rights and privileges of the race course.

Babbling my thanks, I sped out of the McArthur Building as if Dooge Barnes had squirted heroin into my bloodstream. I rushed all the way to my father's office to tell him the good news.

My father's reception sobered me as if I had been plunged into an ice-cold showerbath. In a matter of seconds, my mood of wild ecstasy was shattered – it became stark tragedy.

For the first time in my life, but certainly not for the last time, I crashed head-on into the inflexible code of my father's business and personal life. Seating me in a large chair on the other side of his desk, my father carefully explained the facts of life to me. He told me that, as vice-president of the railroad with jurisdiction from Fort William to Victoria, it was his prerogative to award all contracts for construction of new branch lines. He pointed out that Mr. Dutton was one of Canada's major railroad construction contractors. I heard him but I was shaking my head in crushed bewilderment. My father went on, speaking carefully and gently. He explained that if I accepted Mr. Dutton's gift of a race horse Mr. Dutton's competitors in the construction business would shout "foul" the next time Mr. Dutton was awarded a contract by my father's company.

There was no alternative, my father said: much as he regretted breaking my miserable little heart, I must decline Mr. Dutton's gift, with thanks.

I am quite certain that my father never suspected Mr.

Dutton of any ulterior motivation. I know that my father was genuinely grateful for the hours of companionship which Mr. Dutton whimsically devoted to me. Years later, when my adolescent drinking became a matter of family concern, my father, aware of Mr. Dutton's considerable influence on me, asked him to lend a corrective hand. With gratitude and humility, I can remember the big, old man taking me into his office, closing the door and twisting his moustache ends in an agony of embarrassment as he lectured me on the evils of the Demon Rum. I loved that rough-hewn old man.

In less than an hour, then, I had been lifted to the dizziest heights, only to crash into the deepest pit of disappointment. It was like betting twenty dollars on a fifty-to-one winner, only to have the stewards disqualify the horse after the numbers had been posted on the odds-board. It was one of those ghastly experiences which my father used to describe as "character builders."

I surrendered A. Lester's registration papers, of course. My father said that he would return them to Mr. Dutton, personally. My grief was assuaged almost completely by the fact that the Racing Secretary told Mr. Dutton that as far as his department was concerned I would be permitted to keep my new Owner-Trainer badge. In all probability, Mr. Dutton, whose stable of fashionably bred horses attracted many bettors to the Winnipeg tracks, had a chat with Mr. Speers and informed him of my tragedy. In any event, throughout the remainder of my years in Winnipeg, the track management never failed to mail me an Owner-Trainer badge for every meeting, although my only horse was the pony on Mr. Nelson Smith's farm at Birds Hill.

You can imagine how my childish ego was inflated by that Owner-Trainer badge. I wore it on my jacket lapel, displayed as prominently as a locomotive headlight. On rainy days, I left my topcoat unbuttoned, to be sure that no one missed my badge. When I passed through the paddock gate, I pointed at my badge, wordlessly. Gatemen merely nodded and waved me through, as if I was Alfred Gwynne Vanderbilt or C. V. Whitney. The badge earned me a certain celebrity among the dear old ladies in the Club House. Aware that I had access to the barns, they questioned me concerning the chances of certain horses. I learned quickly to gladden all of them with the stock answer: "the trainer says that he has a good chance."

My friendship with the Barnes brothers ripened instantaneously after the A. Lester incident had been settled. Stub and Dooge had been understandably reluctant parties to the deal. They had no overwhelming desire to give a portion of one of their best horses to an importunate moppet, but since W. A. Dutton kept them well supplied with greenbacked goodies they didn't protest too vehemently. When they realized that I wasn't going to pose any threat to their financial future, they became considerably more cordial and I believe that they actually felt a litle bit sorry for me.

Dooge no longer looked over his shoulder nervously when I was mousing along the shedrow while he was examining the contents of his medicine chest. He didn't even shoo me away if I followed him when he went into a stall to give a laggardly horse a nerve treatment. He'd merely say to me: "Don't block the light. You've got to be careful where you put this stuff. If you put it in the wrong spot, this horse is liable to turn meaner than cat piss."

Naturally, I became privy to some truly remarkable information around the barns. Making my way cautiously, I began to persuade my father to make the occasional small wager for me. We had a deal – any moneys which I won would be banked for me until I was twenty-one. Coaxing my father only occasionally, when I really "knew something," he made bets for me on an astonishingly high percentage of winners. My father began to regard me with some unusual parental curiosity. He asked me where I was getting my information. I told him blandly that I sat with the clockers during the morning workouts and listened to them talking among themselves. This was literally true, but it wasn't the entire truth. My information was genuine feed-box information.

One afternoon, my father almost had a fit when I asked him to bet $10 straight, $10 place and $10 show on one of Mr. Dutton's horses which rejoiced in the name of Shasta Sheik. Mr. Dutton also owned a horse named Shasta Rabbi. Obviously, he was an early One World advocate who never envisioned the Middle East turmoils of the later decades of this century.

My father eventually agreed to bet the money, but only afer he assured me that he hoped fervently that I would blow my bet – it would be a lesson, he said, which would teach me the utter folly of wagering on horses.

I knew what I was doing, or at least I was fairly confident that I knew what I was doing. Earlier that afternoon, I had been down in the stable area and I had leaned against Shasta Sheik's stall door. I noticed that the horse was wearing a muzzle, which was unusual. I noticed, too, that Shasta Sheik had a particularly roguish look in his eyes. I had seen that same look in the eyes of some other horses. I realized instantly that Dooge Barnes, that dean of the faculty of Equine Psychology, had paid a quiet visit to Shasta Sheik's stall.

Choosing a moment when no one else was around, I walked over to Stub Barnes and I asked politely: "Mr. Barnes. Is Shasta Sheik going to win this afternoon?"

"Sonny," said Stub Barnes in a low confident voice, "he'll win – or he'll blow up with a roar that they'll hear all the way to Portage La Prairie."

Stub Barnes never lied . . . much. Shasta Sheik didn't blow up!

Shasta Sheik ran head-and-head with a mare named Miss Ida Brown for one mile and one-quarter and he beat her, right on the wire. In so doing, he established a Polo Park track record which survived for fifteen years.

6

There's a Bit of Larceny in Everyone

Those early mornings on the backstretch provided an education which couldn't have been acquired for £10,000 in the capitals of the Old World, in the Sorbonne or the London School of Economics, or even in the Casbah. After all, it is a lucky student whose studies are directed by a faculty composed of such celebrated authorities as Stub Barnes, Dr. Levi Ronald, Sir Lester R. Knifong, Sleepy Armstrong and Bullshit Brown.

As for acquiring a vocabulary? My vocabulary was enriched beyond the wildest dreams of a lexicographer by my close observation of James Donovan, the official starter on the tracks of the Canadian prairies. Mr. Donovan had a command of the language which seldom has been equalled on this continent. The toughest drill sergeant in the U.S. Marine Corps, if he heard Mr. Donovan in action, would have been suffused with such envy that he would have destroyed himself by munching his own hand grenades.

It is a matter of record that Jim Donovan, who had been foaled in Colorado during The Great Blizzard of '77, had visited Canada in his youth and he had vowed stoutly that he'd never return. Donovan's antipathy to the Canadian West stemmed from the fact that he had been playing nursemaid to a thoroughbred horse which was being shipped from Winnipeg to the Pacific Coast in a freight car. The season was early winter and they were travelling on a very slow freight train. Mr. Donovan's other companions were a half-starved exercise boy and an oversized, perpetually hungry bulldog. Before embarking on his journey, Mr. Donovan had expended his last funds on a handsome roast of beef which had been cooked for him by a friendly chef in a flea-bag hotel. With only this roast to sustain him, Mr. Donovan sighed resignedly as the train creaked and groaned out of the Winnipeg freight yards.

At nightfall, Mr. Donovan pitched some hay to the horse, carved off a couple of slices of beef for himself and his fellow-human, and tossed a few scraps to the bulldog. It was cold outside on the prairies and, for that matter, it was very cold inside the boxcar. The snow was whistling through the gap beneath the door of their wheeled ark. Pulling his overcoat around him, Donovan settled down to sleep, covering himself with straw.

In the morning Mr. Donovan shook himself free of his straw shroud and decided to have a little snack of cold roast beef. Search as he might, he could not find the roast. Then he looked at the bulldog – the dog was snoring contentedly, his stomach distended by his nocturnal gluttony.

In the ensuing sixty hours, as the train laboured towards the Pacific Coast, Donovan developed a hatred of bulldogs, a slightly paranoiac fixation which pursued him for years. Possibly it was incidents such as this which provided Mr. Donovan with an irritable disposition in moments of stress and, concurrently, a magnificent command of outraged profanity.

My Owner-Trainer badge gave me the right to stand in the infield within earshot of Mr. Donovan when he was starting a race from the old six-and-one-half furlong chute at Whittier Park. There were no mechanical starting-gates at that time.

Certainly, prior to the invention of electrically operated gates, the starts of races on North American tracks bore little resemblance to the Household Cavalry parading for the Queen's Birthday, but an astonishingly small percentage of horses were left at the post in the course of an entire season.

There were other occupational hazards for a starter. Many horses are just naturally spooky or addle-pated. And when an injudicious trainer had over-administered a stimulant to a horse, those delays at the starting-post often had cataclysmic results. In such crises Mr. Donovan's language was shocking. His rich invective was echoed feelingly by his assistants, who were struggling with the wild-eyed horses. One of the assistants, Mr.

Wampus Fuller, was quite as profane as Mr. Donovan and he offered colourful contrapuntal embellishments to Mr. Donovan's vengeful threnody.

By the standards of boarding school boys my own vocabulary was not inadequate but I learned new words and new phrases almost daily when I lurked in the vicinity of the starting-post. I would squirm there, crossing my legs to avoid wetting my pants in vicarious delight as Mr. Donovan and his assistants vented their frustrations on the clean afternoon air.

Mr. Donovan worked under the gaze of two critics every afternoon at Whittier Park. One was a gaunt lady dressed in black who carried an umbrella even on the fairest afternoons. She was an inspector for the S.P.C.A. and she stationed herself in stern proximity, to assure the world's do-gooders that Mr. Donovan and his assistants didn't abuse any of our four-footed friends. To be truthful, Mr. Donovan and his crew didn't abuse the horses nearly as much as the horses abused human patience.

Despite his rococo vocabulary, Mr. Donovan was essentially a gentleman.

Whenever he had despatched a field with more than a normal flow of profanity he would turn to the lady, doff his hat, and say courteously: "Begging your pardon, ma'am." As far as I can recall, she never answered him directly. She merely sniffed loudly. She was pretty creepy.

Mr. Donovan's other critic was a large crow, which perched in the branch of a tree directly above the six-and-one-half furlong chute. This bird was called "the Clocker Crow" because he perched there every morning watching the post-dawn workouts.

After the workouts were finished the crow would fly away, only to return in time for the afternoon's racing.

When Mr. Donovan would begin to curse, the crow would caw loudly and derisively. The more angry Mr. Donovan became, the more loudly the crow would heckle him. Mr. Donovan frequently threw his hat and small boulders at the bird, but his aim was lamentable. I am quite sure that Mr. Donovan's detestation of that crow almost equalled his detestation of the bulldog which had blighted his earlier visit to Canada.

Surprisingly enough, you didn't hear an inordinate share of

bad language around the stable area, apart from the witless obscenities of the younger hot-walkers and grooms who hoped to establish some claim to manhood through the excessive employment of four-lettered words. The respected trainers such as Sleepy Armstrong, Lester Knifong, and the Barnes brothers swore only in moments of extreme provocation. Possibly the brooding presence of the saturnine Mrs. Babe Barnes imposed a genteel restraint. On reflection, I withdraw this observation: Mrs. Barnes looked like a lady who in her time had heard almost everything.

When I first was introduced to Sir Lester R. Knifong, he had arrived in Winnipeg from Austin, Texas, with a small stable of useful selling-platers, the most consistently honest of which was Sixpence. Knifong was one of America's best-known gypsy trainers and because of his devotion to carving stray chunks of wood with an old pocket knife he was known more familiarly as Whittlin' Knifey. His knighthood was bestowed upon him gratuitously by racing stewards who he charmed with his drawling courtesy.

Knifey, like most of the other gypsy trainers, wore a well-travelled cattleman's hat, not one of those white ten-gallon monstrosities which became the vogue with ersatz westerners in the fifties and sixties, but a genuine stockman's hat, tan, sweat-stained, with a moderately low crown and a brim just wide enough to shade the eyes from the slanting rays of the sun. Sleepy Armstrong, another Texan, wore one of those hats too, as did the Barnes brothers. Horsemen weren't much for dressing up around the prairie tracks. I don't remember Knifey wearing a jacket or tie at a track with the exception of those occasions when he invaded Woodbine in Toronto. For a few years he wore a sweater which had been knitted for him by his wife, a labour of love which filled him with distress rather than gratitude. "My wife used to be a great cook," Knifey lamented. "Then she got around to building me this sweater – now she can't cook worth a lick."

For all his droopy-eyed lugubriousness, Knifey was actually sharper than a serpent's tooth. He existed and even prospered in the racing business for many years without making any important capital investments in livestock. His modus operandi was an occasional visit to the office of R. James Speers, who in addition to operating the prairie tracks bred large numbers of useful thoroughbreds. Drawling and whittling until the office floor was knee-deep in shavings, Knifong would persuade Speers to give him a couple of horses on-the-cuff.

This type of financial transaction was primeval in its simplicity. Knifey put up no cash – simply, he agreed to pay Speers later from purses which, hopefully, would be won by the horses. Speers, who had immense faith in Knifong's probity and skill, must have given him over the years a couple of dozen horses on-the-cuff. Even when he was an old man, Knifong lost none of his shrewdness. I can remember him, in his declining years, taking two Speers cuff-horses named Frilly and Hoops My Dear to Bay Meadows.

Knifey waited until his larder was almost empty and then he entered his two horses on the same day's program. Cautiously, he bet five dollars on Frilly, which won and paid $124 for every two-dollar ticket. Cashing his tickets, he bet his entire bundle on Hoops My Dear which also won, paying thirty dollars. The purses for the two races totalled $1,400, which meant that Knifong picked up $6,000 from his afternoon's activities. Before he went to bed that night, he telegraphed $5,000 to Winnipeg to be applied to his floating debt.

Knifey's personal hang-up was transportation. He spent a considerable portion of his life travelling in box cars with his horses. Earl Sande, who became the most famous American rider of his generation, told me that when he was running away from his Idaho home, intent upon becoming a jockey, he began his journey to fame and fortune by scrambling through the door of a boxcar on a freight train. When he settled down on the straw, Sande shyly introduced himself to his fellow-travellers: seven horses, Lester R. Knifong, Mrs. Knifong and their baby daughter. "He treated me like one of his family," Sande recalled, "but the horses always got fed before the family."

In pioneering days, the wagon-trains made many tedious and exhausting journeys across North America but during World War II Knifey set some type of record for transcontinental dilly-dallying. He was in California training Jim Speers' colt, Gower Mon, for the Queen's Plate, which was scheduled to be run at Toronto in May. Early in April, Knifong loaded the colt into a boxcar and, as usual, he climbed into the boxcar too. Wartime transportation of freight was a tricky business, and instead of heading in the direction of Toronto the train travelled slowly to New Orleans. After a couple of days in New Orleans the boxcar headed north, and Knifey felt reasonably confident that he was bound for Toronto.

Several days later, Knifey looked out of the boxcar and he realized that he was pulling into Chicago. The next leg of his epic journey was even more improbable – instead of heading east from Chicago, Knifey's boxcar was attached to a freight train heading west. Ignoring his protests, the railway took him all the way to Portland, Oregon.

When Gower Mon and Knifong eventually arrived in Toronto, they had been in the boxcar for sixteen days. Knifong's drawled description of his misadventures required almost as much time as the actual journey.

In the autumn of the same year, Knifong decided to send Hoops My Dear from Winnipeg to race at the Thorncliffe track in Toronto. Wishing to have no repetition of his earlier journey, he loaded Hoops My Dear into a boxcar, alone. Then he got into his automobile and began to drive to Toronto via the paved highways of the northern United States.

Knifey made one grave error. Gasoline was rationed in the United States during World War II and Knifong didn't have any U.S. gasoline ration-coupons.

With his gas gauge registering empty, he pulled into a garage in a small Michigan town.

"It looks as if I'm in trouble," Knifey said to the garage owner.

"You're in trouble if you don't have any gas coupons," the garage owner agreed, unfeelingly.

Sir Lester, a man of infinite ingenuity, said confidently: "Well, don't sell my car. I'll be right back." Whereupon he walked slowly through the streets of the little Michigan town until he saw a church. On the same plot of land with the church was a small, well-kept white house. Obviously, the house was the residence of the parish priest.

Knifey knocked on the door and when the parish priest appeared the man of God was exposed to the persuasive charms of one of racing's most revered raconteurs. "Reverend Father," said Knifey, twisting his hat in his hands, "I'm just a poor old horseman who has run into difficulties. I have a nice mare, Hoops My Dear, waiting for me up at the Thorncliffe track in Toronto, Canada. I have her all tuned up like a Stradivarius and she'll win, first crack out of the box. But I can't get to Toronto to start her in a race unless I have some ration coupons to buy gasoline for my car. Now, Reverend Father, I'm quite sure that you must know some of your parishioners who would be willing to help a poor old horseman in distress. Particularly when they have my personal assurance that Hoops My Dear will tow-rope her field. I hate to think of her pining in her stall, wondering what's become of me."

The priest listened, solemn-faced. He went into the house, leaving Knifey on the doorstep. In a few minutes, the priest returned and he said, still solemn-faced: "Your story has touched my heart. Obviously, you are a kind man who loves animals. It would be inhuman to detain you further from a reunion with your horse. Here are coupons to buy fifteen gallons of fuel to complete your journey."

Four days later, Hoops My Dear made her first start at Thorncliffe and, as Sir Lester Knifong had predicted, she won first crack out of the box. The winning-price was approximately fifteen-to-one.

As Knifey contemplated the profits of his coup, he lifted his eyes heavenward gratefully and he murmured: "I sure hope that nice priest in Michigan knows the telephone number of a good reliable bookmaker."

Dr. Levi Ronald and Sir Lester Knifong were kindred souls although Knifey was a Texan and Doc was a strayling from Fergus, Ontario. Doc originally had been a trotting-horse man but the thoroughbreds routed the standardbreds from the major cities of Western Canada, and rather than suffer from what was known in the horse industry as "the miss-meal cramps" Doc gravitated to the runners.

As with Sir Lester Knifong, Dr. Levi Ronald did not acquire his doctorate through traditional channels. In my youth, I addressed him respectfully as Doctor Ronald, assuming that he was a physician, surgeon, dentist or licensed veterinarian. In my mind I placed him in the latter category because Doc, whose chin habitually was caked with dried tobacco juice, didn't appear to be sufficiently antiseptic for the human-healing professions.

My later investigations revealed that Dr. Ronald's degree had been conferred on him not by the Royal College of Physicians and Surgeons nor the Synod of the Anglican Church but by the grateful horsemen of Western Canada.

In the days of alcoholic prohibition, Levi Ronald was the official bootlegger on western tracks. It was his practice to carry his supply of bottled goods in a black medical satchel and he would retail his merchandise at twenty-five cents a shot.

In the early mornings on the backstretch, many horsemen who had been foxed with the grape overnight would lying about in varying stages of distress. Their throats would be parched, their brows fevered, their stomachs knotted in pain.

Then Levi Ronald, carrying his medical bag, would appear at the end of the shedrow. Gladly the stricken horsemen would arise from their beds of misery and they would chorus happily: "Here comes the doctor!" Indeed, as Levi Ronald poured out his medicinal spirits, he was as welcome as Dr. Albert Schweitzer in a cholera-ridden African village. He carried the title "Doc" to his grave as a token of his early-morning patients' eternal gratitude.

His humanitarian practice long since forgotten, Dr. Ronald was buried in Toronto in 1964. There were only eight people clustered in the tiny chapel for his funeral service. Four of us were racetrackers with long memories.

Knifey and Doc Ronald shared a lack of faith in stimulating drugs and electric persuaders, which were then widely regarded as the two most efficacious agents for improving the speed of a horse. Some jockeys could be importuned to carry a small battery concealed in the palm of their hand while riding in a race. When this small battery, which was known as a "joint," was applied to the perspiring flank or neck of a horse, the effects often were electrifying. The horse spurted forward as if he had been attacked by a swarm of angry bees. Frequently, too, a trainer would take one of those batteries into a stall to "wake up" a dull horse prior to a race. Some horses merely swished their tails when, in the vernacular, they were "hit with a joint." Other, more flighty horses were quite likely to climb right up the walls of their stalls.

Levi Ronald's humanitarian ministrations to hung-over

horsemen earned him the eternal gratitude of his manure-stained confrères. In a mildly irreverent profession, he was regarded as a likely candidate for deification.

One morning at Whittier Park I eavesdropped on an emergency meeting of well-wishers outside the good Doctor's tackroom. A noble beast, which Ronald had campaigned with success for several seasons, had lost its competitive urge. Organically, there appeared to be nothing amiss with the horse. His ankles were sound; his suspensory ligaments had lost none of their elasticity; his appetite was undiminished. The horse's ills were spiritual rather than physical.

News of Levi Ronald's dilemma spread quickly through the stable area. His distress and concern was shared by every horseman whose morning thirst had been allayed in moments of crisis by the soothing medications which Doc carried in his black bag.

"Don't know what's happened to this horse," Doc was saying to the circle of self-appointed consultants. "He's as sound as a bell of brass, but all of a sudden he can't run fast enough to beat a fat man."

The assembled trainers examined the horse speculatively. They opened his mouth and peered in. They felt his ankles, then ran their hands over his shoulders. A ginny took one end of the shank and he jogged the horse up and down the open space between two barns. The trainers stroked their jaws thoughtfully and they scratched their scalps as they agreed that, without a shadow of doubt, the horse was sounder than the American dollar.

"There's nothing wrong with him – he just needs to be waked up!" said my helpful friend, Dooge Barnes. "I've got some heroin over in my tackroom. Just spit a little heroin on his tongue, and he'll light up like a Greek church."

There was a murmur of approval from most of the horsemen; a murmur which was checked by one voice of dissent. The dissenter was a brash invader from the United States, recently arrived and well-equipped.

"Naw, don't waste any heroin on him; he may not be a hop horse," quoth this oracle. "This old horse is just sluggish. If you want to wake him up, hit him with a joint. I'll go and get my joint from my tack box."

Doc Ronald had been strangely silent during this intriguing

conversation. He was gnawing a cigar as, thoughtfully, he appeared to be considering the respective merits of the offers of heroin and a battery. Slowly, he walked over to his horse, looked the steed in the eye, patted the animal on the neck, and turned to face his circle of consultants.

"Thank you, my friends," Doc said wryly. "But, I ain't a druggist and I ain't an electrician. So, I guess that I'll just have to get me a rifle and shoot this poor old son-of-a-bitch."

Doctor Ronald, despite his professed disdain for drugs, batteries and similar types of illegal persuaders, was far from being a Pollyanna. He was an inveterate schemer who, in the opinion of his countless admirers, was "sharper than jail house coffee." He would go to incredible lengths of skullduggery to win a horse race when the price was right and when his wealthy clients, most of whom were gambling owners of hotels, had agreed to wager in his behalf.

Doc didn't believe in taking unnecessary risks: when he was betting, he was betting with other persons' money. And when the bets were down, Doc seldom missed the target.

For evidence of Levi Ronald's depths of genial perfidy, it is necessary only to examine the published record of the inaugural running of the Manitoba Derby at Polo Park in 1930. The race was won by a horse named Jack Whittier and the owner-trainer of the winning horse is listed as "L. Ronald."

I remember the race with some clarity although it wasn't until some years later that a much older Doc Ronald, sitting in my office at the Woodbine track in Toronto, cackled happily as he confessed that he had resorted to the most devious tactics to win the race.

Doc bought Jack Whittier from breeder Jim Speers for $500, on-the-cuff. He didn't race the horse extensively as a three-year-old, but he did some experimenting. Long before dawn, when other trainers still were abed, Ronald had the colt out on the track, being exercised by a jockey named Dwight Hurlburt. The Doc didn't tell Hurlburt what plans he had in mind for Jack Whittier, and his reticence in this matter necessitated some future chicanery. In any event, Ronald and Hurlburt were the only two persons who knew how fast Jack Whittier could run, and since Doc was holding the watch in those pre-dawn workouts he didn't bother to give the full facts to Hurlburt. If the colt worked five furlongs in 1.05, Doc would tell the jockey blandly: "He went pretty good – he just shaded 1.07."

A week before the running of the Derby, Doc Ronald learned that Asah Smith was shipping Prince Goldstream from Vancouver for the race. To his horror, Doc also discovered that Asah had refused to ship to Winnipeg unless the Racing Secretary guaranteed that he would have the riding-services of Jockey Hurlburt. Doc was stuck – he hadn't told Hurlburt that he planned to run Jack Whittier in the Derby.

Doc solved the problem skilfully. He consulted with one of his hotel-owner clients and they took Jockey Hurlburt on the town for the next three nights. They wined him and they dined him. Jockey Hurlburt, who was enchanted by their lavish entertainment, waxed fat. In fact, Jockey Hurlburt, who always had difficulty in keeping down to riding-weight, suddenly gained twelve pounds. He was supposed to weigh 117 pounds to ride Prince Goldstream in the Derby – four days before the race, Hurlburt weighed 129 pounds and he was gaining steadily.

When Asah Smith arrived at Polo Park three days before the race Doc Ronald met him at the stable gate. "Too bad about your jockey," Doc said brightly, by way of greeting. "I saw him last night and he must have a tumour – he's so heavy that he couldn't ride an elephant."

Fuming, Asah scurried around Winnipeg until he located Hurlburt. He took one look at the sadly bloated jockey and he fired him on the spot. Still fuming, Asah went back to the track and engaged the services of his old friend, Red Pollard, to ride Prince Goldstream in the Derby.

As soon as he saw Asah striding wrathfully into the Racing Secretary's office, Doc Ronald, who had been lounging on a bench outside the building, was galvanized into action. He raced to Jockey Hurlburt's rooming house where the distraught rider tearfully was contemplating himself in a mirror. "Don't worry about losing the ride on Prince Goldstream," Ronald said consolingly. "I'm going to give you the mount on Jack Whittier – he'll win by as far as you can throw a rock."

Jockey Hurlburt wasn't seen around Polo Park the day before the running of the Derby. He wasn't seen for the very simple reason that Doc Ronald had him locked in the steam-box in the Swedish Baths at the Royal Alexandra Hotel. The bath house attendants were under instructions to steam Hurlburt until he was shrunk down to skin and bone.

When Doc Ronald boosted Dwight Hurlburt into the saddle for the Derby, the jockey, complete with saddle, weighed only 118 pounds. The rest of him was lying on the floor of the steam-cabinet in the Swedish Baths.

Jack Whittier won the Derby by one-half length. Prince Goldstream finished second. Asah Smith's rage was monumental – he stormed out of the track, vowing never again to return to Winnipeg where the racing establishment was infested with rogues and scoundrels.

There was one curious aftermath of the race. Jack Whittier paid only $8.20 for a two-dollar ticket, a shockingly low price, in view of the fact that he never had won a race in his life prior to that afternoon. Someone, obviously, "knew something." Three or four weeks later, a certain Winnipeg hotel-owner issued a contract for a large addition to his beer parlour.

7

The Plainsman

The bulky figure in the background, the man who was to play an important role in my destiny, a man who I was to revere until his dying day and beyond, was Robert James Speers.

Speers was the architect, builder and benevolent dictator of a prairie racing empire which extended from Winnipeg to Calgary. Like many other latter-day imperialists, he learned a costly lesson when he invaded the United States and built a one-mile track at Butte, Montana. He retreated thirteen months later in financial disorder. He was the proprietor of Whittier Park and Polo Park in Winnipeg and Chinook Park in Calgary. Additionally, he operated the annual one-week racing meetings for the Civic Exhibition associations in Calgary, Edmonton, Saskatoon and Regina.

In order to provide thoroughbreds to race on his tracks, he established his own breeding farm in Manitoba. He raced some of the stock in his own colours but the majority of the horses were auctioned or disposed of, on-the-cuff, to carefully selected trainers whose trustworthiness had withstood the trials of years. Jim Speers was benevolent and he was far-sighted; he knew that the men who owed him money for livestock also owed him an obligation to race on his tracks. They were unlikely to ship their steeds to other tracks, where the purses were larger.

The skilful management of his diversified racing enterprises eventually enabled Jim Speers to become Canada's leading breeder of thoroughbred horses. He dethroned Colonel R. S.

McLaughlin, the cheery old Ontario sportsman who was the Chairman of General Motors of Canada.

"Speers is a marvel," Colonel Sam McLaughlin said with wry amusement. "I've spent millions of dollars on my horse breeding activities. Speers operates his farm on a $50,000 bank overdraft."

Essentially, Col. McLaughlin's estimate of the situation was correct. Although Jim Speers died a wealthy man in 1955, his business fortunes were subject to frequent violent fluctuations. He was a man of such overpowering charm and his shrewd gambling instincts were admired so highly in the business community that the occasional problem of raising a fresh bankroll was, for him, never insoluble.

I had my first sight of Jim Speers when my father took me to the opening of the racing season at River Park in Winnipeg, before the construction of Whittier Park and Polo Park. There was an official ceremony before the first race: a band paraded to the flag pole in the infield and Mr. Speers, a portly man with a pronounced limp, stumped along behind them and raised the Red Ensign on the pole while the band played God Save The King. My father told me that Mr. Speers' game leg was a legacy from a train wreck on the Spokane International, a U.S. subsidiary of the Canadian Pacific Railway.

Unknown to me, my morning adventures in the stable area were permitted only because they were condoned by Mr. Speers. It was he who had authorized the Racing Secretary's office to provide Mr. Dutton with an Owner-Trainer badge with my name inscribed on it. Like all benevolent dictators, Mr. Speers discretely maintained a highly efficient intelligence system. There wasn't a mouse which built a new nest in the barn area without Mr. Spears being apprised of the intrusion. He knew how many bottles Doc Ronald carried in his medical bag when the healer made his morning rounds; he knew which trainers were using needles and he knew which trainers were equipped with dry-cell batteries. In those circumstances it would have been incongruous for him to be unaware of the fact that a skinny, bespectacled boy, wearing a boarding-school blazer, was haunting the shedrows.

I kept out of his sight as much as possible, and he never spoke to me, but several times I felt him gazing at me curiously in the afternoons when I was persuading the Japanese bellboys from the Royal Alexandra Hotel to make my modest wagers in the pari-mutuel machines. Years later, he told me: "Oh, I knew that you were prowling around the barns. I let you stay because I knew that like myself you'd grow up to love horse racing."

Jim Speers had owned his first race horse at the age of nine, when his blacksmith father operated the forge on the present site of Toronto International Airport. He went to Winnipeg at the age of eighteen and five years later started out on a bicycle to seek his fortune at Old Battleford, six hundred miles northwest. Before he had gone many miles, he traded the bicycle and some cash for a horse and buckboard and rode the remaining distance in greater comfort.

He opened a feed and grain business and borrowed enough money from a Winnipeg manufacturer to build six small grain elevators in the vicinity of Wilkie, Saskatchewan, to which metropolis he removed himself and his family. Notably unsuccessful in his homesteading enterprises up to this point, he made an incursion into politics as the Conservative candidate in the Tramping Lake provincial election.

As he described his situation at that moment: "I had been frozen out, hailed out, dried out and finally starved out and someone suggested that, since I'd been a failure at everything else, I'd make a good politican."

The morning after the Tramping Lake election, Speers went into his Wilkie feed and grain store and he said to his clerk, Harry Rudd: "Well, how do we stand?"

Rudd, who had been compiling some figures on his desk, arose, took a deep breath and recited precisely: "You've spent five and one-half months of your time; you've spent $10,500 of your own money; you owe for 1,100 gallons of beer for German campaign picnics at Grosswerder and Cactus Lake; the opposition has arrested three of your campaign workers and one of them still is in jail; you're sued for $50,000 libel and you're licked by 239 votes."

"My boy," said Speers, putting one arm around Rudd's shoulders, "with your head for figures, you're assured of a job with me for the rest of your life." Speers was as good as his word, although the future was clouded for both of them at that particular moment. Harry Rudd, who had borrowed twenty pounds from his grandfather to pay his passage from England to Saskatchewan nine years earlier, was employed by Speers until his patron died. And, in 1971, Harry Rudd still was employed in the Racing Secretary's office of the Western Canada Racing Association, successors to the Speers regime.

I have reason to believe that much later, when I was a racing-oriented sports columnist, Mr. Speers had selected me to be his turf biographer. It was a project which never became airborne for the simple reason that Mrs. Speers objected strongly to any public references to her husband's deep and abiding affection for gambling. Writing a story about Jim Speers without mentioning his gambling proclivities would have been tantamount to attempting to cook an omelet without using eggs. Mrs. Speers always deplored her husband's financial plunging; stubbornly, she declined to accept the fact that it was his ability to gamble boldly which established the family fortune. Indeed, it was Speers' reputation as a good gambler which set him apart from lesser men and which caused him to be revered as one of the truly colourful and successful pioneers of Western Canada's business community.

Speers seldom if ever gambled on his own race tracks. He didn't discover the stock market until his declining years. He gambled in the grain market and he gambled in livestock. The poker table was his favorite arena and he was a tough, calculating card player. He accepted his wins and his losses with deceptive equanimity. If you saw Speers emerging from an all-night poker session, his cheerful countenance could be misleading.

He told me once that in their Battleford days he and Mrs. Speers decided to spend Christmas visiting their parents in the vicinity of Malton, Ontario. Mrs. Speers left Battleford about a week before Christmas. He stayed behind, saying that some pressing business required his immediate attention. He arrived in Malton about five days after Mrs. Speers had settled into the family Christmastide gathering.

They enjoyed a delightful holiday with their respective families, visiting the two parental homes and observing all the yuletide amenities.

After the New Year, Mrs. Speers said quietly to her husband: "This has been a wonderful holiday. But, now, I can hardly wait to get back to our own little house in Battleford."

"Well, we'll leave for Battleford tomorrow," said Jim Speers agreeably, "but we won't be going back to the same little house – not immediately, anyhow. I lost the little house in a poker game, the night before I left Battleford."

I suppose that it was quaint misadventures of this type which occasioned Mrs. Speers to impose strictures on those who desired to write about her husband. Nevertheless, the incident is factual. Jim Speers could bluff the eyeballs right out of your head at the poker table but he was a thoroughly frank man.

In 1914, still pursuing the elusive rainbow, Speers moved from Saskatchewan to Calgary with the faithful Harry Rudd in attendance. The oil market had been booming and Speers went into the oil brokerage business – just in time for the big 1914 crash. However, two fortuitous events occured almost simultaneously: he met Charlie Roe, who later was to become general manager of all the Speers racing enterprises, and he received a sub-contract to buy horses for the French government.

The French were scouring the western world for horses to equip their beleaguered military machine. Anyone who has eaten in a French restaurant in wartime will tell you that horses were used for purposes other than hauling cannon or carrying overloaded cavalrymen, but officially he was purchasing horses for the French Army.

It was on one of his scouting trips into the horselands of the neighboring state of Idaho that he was involved in the wreck of a passenger train which cost him the mobility of one leg. He was trapped in the wreckage for many hours, and throughout the remainder of his life he wore a raised heel on the shoe of his leg, the knee of which was locked forever in a rigid upright position.

He spent nine months in hospital at Spokane, Washington and, in the meantime, a lawsuit in his behalf was taken against the Spokane International by R. B. Bennett, who later became Prime Minister of Canada. When Jim Speers was released from hospital in 1917, Bennett had obtained for him $13,000 for medical expenses, plus a cash settlement of $25,000 The lawsuit had its little ironies in that Mr. Bennett also was solicitor for the Canadian Pacific Railway, which owned stock control of the Spokane International. Jim Speers was a man who made friends quickly. Mr. Bennett was Calgary's leading legal eagle and he had become aware of Speers in the brief time which Speers spent in that city.

"It was the first time in my life that I had any really important money of my own," Mr. Speers said later. "Up to that point, I had been able to raise lots of money, but it had to be repaid eventually."

During his convalescence in hospital, he had been pondering the possibility of disposing of his grain and feed business, which he still owned in Wilkie, and of moving to Winnipeg with the intention of going into the horse business on a full-time basis. Even then, he had been considering the possibility of owning a race track.

So, en route from Spokane to Wilkie, he detoured through Winnipeg to re-establish his commercial contacts. The news that he was in town spread rapidly through Winnipeg. The news also spread that Jim Speers was equipped with a bankroll. His friends decided joyfully that his return should be celebrated with a poker party in a suite at the Empire Hotel, a hostelry which was unofficial headquarters for the card-playing set.

On the day when the poker party began, the ubiquitous Harry Rudd, who was shepherding his convalescent patron homeward, was sitting in the lobby of the Empire Hotel. Harry's income and his inclinations did not extend to table-stakes poker, a sport which could result in severe financial debilitation. Rudd was just sitting there, contemplating how many days might pass before Mr. Speers cleaned out his friends or, God forbid, blow the bonanza which resulted from his lawsuit, when a local character named "Seven Dollar" sashayed into the lobby. "Seven Dollar" was a conductor on the passenger trains of the Canadian Pacific Railway, on the run between Winnipeg and Saskatoon.

His nickname stemmed from the fact that, although the regular passenger-fare from Winnipeg to Saskatoon was fourteen dollars, he had an arrangement with his acquaintances whereby he charged them only seven dollars. Naturally, his acquaintances didn't buy their tickets at the regular depot ticket offices in Winnipeg or Saskatoon – they waited until they were aboard the moving train and made their private transactions with "Seven Dollar."

In those carefree days, some passenger-train conductors became quite wealthy as a result of short-circuiting the railways' collection of passenger tolls. According to the legend, after a conductor had collected these fares illegally he would throw all the banknotes high in the air as he stood in the corridor of the coach. Any banknotes which landed on the overhead emergency-cord, on which the conductor exchanged signals with the locomotive engineer, were dutifully turned into the railway's auditing department. He kept the rest.

Seven Dollar had achieved both fame and prosperity and although he was noted for personal frugality he loved to play poker. Paradoxically, he frowned on poker being played on his passenger trains and he would threaten to disembark passengers in mid-journey if he caught them indulging in any card game which was more venomous than solitaire or whist. "You're not going to turn MY train into a gambling hell," he would roar at them indignantly.

In any event, Harry Rudd saw Seven Dollar coming into the Empire Hotel lobby and since he, too, had previous occasion to avail himself of Seven Dollar's cut-rate fares between Winnipeg and Saskatoon he greeted the conductor in a friendly fashion, saying: "They're having a poker game upstairs, to welcome Jim Speers back from hospital in Spokane. Why don't you go up and take a hand?"

"Speers!" ejaculated the saintly railway conductor. "I'm not going to get into any poker game with that son of bitch he'll raise you $1,000 on the turn of a single card, without batting an eye."

The welcome-home poker party lasted for three days and Jim Speers routed the opposition. He went back to Wilkie for three years; then he moved to Winnipeg to operate a horse-sales barn, and two years after that he staged his inaugural thoroughbred horse racing meeting at River Park.

Inducing horsemen to ship their livestock to the landlocked and unproven racing centre of Winnipeg presented a formidable obstacle. It was the warm, colourful personality of Jim Speers which overcame this problem. Once met, Speers never was forgotten.

British Columbia horsemen such as Gyp Emmert and George Addison, who always were willing and ready to travel, shipped their stock to Winnipeg without qualm. Speers scoured the tracks of the American southwest, soliciting horses for the early Winnipeg meetings, and his journeys led him eventually to Juarez and Tia Juana in Mexico. It was in Tia Juana that he had the good fortune to bump into J. B. McGinn, who trained a large string of hard-hitting platers, including McGonigle, who was unquestionably the worst post-horse in the history of the American turf. When McGonigle was wheeling, sun-fishing and kicking behind the starting-tapes, he could buck a jockey so high out of the saddle that the frightened rider often came back to earth with badly sunburnt ears.

J. B. McGinn was a man who had reason to recall an earlier encounter with Speers, and in the circumstances he could have been less than cordial.

Back in 1915, when Speers was buying horses for the French government, McGinn was buying horses for the U.S. Cavalry. The pickings were becoming lean by the time the two men met on a hotel verandah in a dusty little Montana town; the ranges had been swept almost bare of horses as the rival governments' agents bought any animal which was reasonably sound in wind and limb.

"I've got eighteen horses and I know that you've bought nineteen," Speers said to McGinn after they had introduced themselves. "Neither of us has enough to load a boxcar and there isn't another fit animal within thirty miles of this god-forsaken hole.

"I'll tell you what I'll do. I'll toss a coin for the whole outfit. If you win the toss, you get these thirty-seven horses. If you lose the toss, I ship the thirty-seven on the next train that passes through this town."

Speers won the toss and, within twenty-four hours, his load of range-strays was en route to the eastern seaboard. McGinn, empty-handed, went away to scout distant and desolate range-lands.

Now, when they met in Tia Juana, their roles had changed. McGinn owned and trained a string of twenty-eight horses, almost enough to fill an entire afternoon's program of racing. Speers desperately required livestock to assure the success of his meeting.

"I remember that you're quite a gambler," McGinn growled, after he had listened to Speers' sales pitch. "So I'll take a gamble on you and your race meeting. I'll ship my whole outfit to Winnipeg."

Annually, when the winter and spring meeting closed at Tia Juana, a trainload of horses and men made the long journey to Winnipeg. The American invaders were led by such distinguished gentry as McGinn, Sir Lester Knifong, Sleepy Armstrong, Sam Gorbet and those charming rascals, the Barnes Brothers. It is probable that Jim Speers paid the shipping-charges from Tia Juana to Winnipeg. It is equally probable that Speers – who usually was sailing quite close to the wind in his pioneering days – deducted the shipping costs from the purses which the invaders won on his prairie racing circuit.

Despite the restrictions imposed on him by his nervous budget-comptrollers, Jim Speers frequently erupted in seemingly senseless outbursts of profligacy. When his meeting at Butte, Montana, went belly-up in the summer of 1930, he summoned all the horsemen to his office and, unblinkingly, he told them that he would ship them and their horses to any track in North America at his personal expense.

The Butte disaster, including his unnecessary gesture of paying the shipping-charges for more than two hundred and fifty horses to distant points, cost him $250,000 when the world was sliding into a cataclysmic financial depression. In terms of today's money, his whim probably cost him more than $1,000,000.

Speers, however, recognized the value of personal relations in an era when the term "public relations" hadn't crept into the business language. He knew that in the tougher times which lay ahead he could count on those particular horsemen to honor a moral obligation. He was correct – almost without exception, they came back to race on his tracks in the depression years.

For similar reasons, Jim Speers enjoyed a remarkable immunity from the touts who infested the tracks of North America. The day before the opening of his second summer meeting in Winnipeg, a group of the roughest hustlers in the annals of race track larceny arrived from Chicago intent on fleecing the unsophisticated Canadian turf patrons. Charlie Roe, who could smell a tout at a range of five hundred yards, summoned the Winnipeg Police morality squad on opening day. The constabulary rounded up the Chicago hustlers and they were paraded into Speers' office.

"Now, boys," Speers said, "We don't want you around our track, but we're not going to throw you into jail. I'm prepared to pay your train-fares and give you some expense-money to get back to Chicago." They departed, with Charlie Roe waving godspeed from the railway station platform, and throughout the length and breath of the continent they spread the good name of R. J. Speers as "a square-gee who treats you like a gentleman." This does not imply that touts did not operate on Speers' tracks, but the hustlers who were tolerated – The Blow-Back Kid and Doc Burns, to name two of them – were Canadian citizens who were so well known to the track officials that their activities could be kept within bounds.

The touting fraternity's respect for Mr. Speers became legendary. Almost twenty years after the Chicago touts had been shipped out of Winnipeg, I was standing with Mr. Speers waiting for a taxi at the Orchard Park Hotel across the street from the Old Woodbine track in Toronto.

One of the survivors of the Chicago mob, an internationally harassed tout named Michigan Ike, lurched out of the Orchard Park bar and bumped into Mr. Speers. "Hey, Buster," demanded Michigan Ike drunkenly, "gimme a buck for a couple of drinks." Speers, without a word, gave him a dollar-bill.

Michigan Ike reeled away. Then he spun on his heels and did a double-take. He rushed back, full of apologies.

"Migawd, Mr. Speers, I didn't recognize you," the tout blurted. "I would insult you by asking you for a lousy buck – I should have asked YOU for five bucks!"

The consuming desire of Speers' life was a personal victory in the Queen's Plate, North America's oldest thoroughbred fixture which is raced annually at Woodbine. His ambition never was fulfilled although one of his horses, Lord Fairmond, finished second to Last Mark in the 1948 running of the Queen's Plate.

It is a thoroughly normal ambition for the prodigal son to wish to return to the scene of his birth in circumstances of triumph. Speers became a chauvinistic Westerner, mildly resentful of the fact that much of Canada's financial and political power was concentrated in southwestern Ontario. Furthermore, although he never would have admitted it publicly, he fumed with the knowledge that some of the insular directors of the

Ontario Jockey Club regarded his efficiently operated Western Canada racing enterprises as a raffish collection of "leaky roof" tracks.

Possibly his antipathy for the nabobs of Eastern racing was occasioned by a horse named Leihand. In his pioneering Saskatchewan era, Jim Speers usually owned at least one standardbred pacer or trotter. Even then he was a racing devotee. Once, he drove a horse and buckboard all the way from Battleford to Calgary, a return trip of eight hundred miles, to attend a one-day race meeting.

In this period, he leased a good thoroughbred named Leihand and shipped the horse from Battleford to Hamilton, Ontario, with the laudable intention of "killing the country." Pari-mutuel wagering hadn't been introduced to Canada and the betting at the Hamilton Jockey Club was accommodated by official bookmakers, the presiding genius of whom was Tom Shaw of New York. Shaw established the odds on each horse and every other bookmaker obediently copied his prices.

A few days after his arrival in Hamilton, Speers worked Leihand before dawn and the horse ran a hole in the wind. He entered Leihand in a race for the following afternoon.

Since Leihand was known merely to be a visitor from Saskatchewan, a region which was considered suitable only for the breeding of bison and gophers, Tom Shaw listed an opening price of 100-to-1 against the horse's chances. Speers sent a couple of trusted friends into the betting-ring and they wagered cautiously. Meanwhile, Speers was in the paddock, giving instructions to Leihand's jockey.

Just before the horses were due to begin the post-parade, Tom Shaw totalled the money which had been bet on Leihand and he suspected, accurately, that he was being dry-gulched. Shaw rushed to the stewards' stand and he demanded that the stewards remove Leihand from the race.

The stewards despatched a clerk to the paddock with an order that Speers produce Leihand's registration papers for official examination. The registration papers were back in the barn.

Speers sent a friend running to the barn for the papers. Meanwhile Leihand pawed fretfully in the paddock while the other horses in the field paraded to the post.

The starter, who had been alerted by the stewards, didn't waste any time. He sent the field on its way from the starting-tape and the race was over before Speers' friend returned to the paddock with Leihand's identification papers.

Since Leihand was a non-starter, Tom Shaw graciously refunded the money which had been wagered by the Speers entourage. "Too bad, boys," Shaw told them. "But I never forget a face and I'll always remember that Speers fellow, even if he turns up at New Orleans or Latonia."

Jim Speers more than evened the score in later years. However, when he was sending an "eagle bird" to the post on eastern tracks, he was careful to absent himself from the immediate vicinity. Thus, when Rochester II won at Toronto in 1928, Speers was two hundred and fifty miles away, in the Chateau Laurier in Ottawa. Mr. Speers had equipped himself with the telephone-numbers of a few of Tom Shaw's bookmaking heirs in New York and Chicago and, just before Rochester II went to the post, Speers made enough long-distance calls to win $60,000.

Sixty thousand dollars sounds like an extravagant amount to be won by a prairie sod-buster in a single afternoon, but this is the figure which was accepted by the Canadian Government's painstakingly persistent income tax assessors. The Income Tax Department accepted the $60,000 figure when it was accompanied by an affidavit sworn by Judge George Schilling, who had been with Jim Speers in his Ottawa hotel room while the wagers were being made on the long-distance telephone.

Jim Speers was a creature of habit. Each year, when the activities on his own prairie racing circuit had been concluded shortly after Labour Day, he customarily paid a long visit to Toronto, taking in the autumn meetings at Woodbine, Thorncliffe, Long Branch and little Dufferin Park. The Christmas holidays were always spent in the family home in Winnipeg, after which he would be chauffeur-driven all the way to Arcadia, California, for the winter meeting at Santa Anita.

The prospect of winning a bet would jog him out of his normal annual routine. It was under such circumstances that he accompanied Lord Cheylesmore to Baltimore. Francis Ormond Henry Eaton, D.S.O., was – and he still is – a horsey farmer, maintaining a spread near the village of Alix, Alberta. Captain

Eaton was known as "Cap" around the prairie race tracks and he never bothered to tell any of his fellow horsemen that he was the fourth Baron Cheylesmore, educated at Eton and Cambridge, decorated with the Distinguished Service Order while serving with the Grenadier Guards in World War I. His salty colleagues respected him for his horsemanship – they would have been unimpressed if they had learned that he was a member of the House of Lords.

Cap Eaton was no greenhorn and, when he decided to "let one run," victory was almost certain. One autumn, Lord Cheylesmore shipped a couple of horses to Baltimore and Speers went along to see the fun. Cap Eaton dressed with the casually expensive informality of a prosperous western farmer and Speers – despite the fact that he habitually wore custom-tailored navy blue suits – also wore a black modified cattleman's hat as a badge of western citizenship. Undoubtedly, the sharpies around Bowie and Pimlico must have appraised the pair as a couple of well-heeled western suckers.

Cap Eaton selected the Havre De Grace track as the scene of their Maryland coup. On Thursday, September 25, 1930, he entered his good horse, Baltimore, in a claiming race. The name Baltimore aroused no chauvinism in the Maryland bettors, who ignored him because he had been racing in the Canadian "sticks." Baltimore won, and paid $42.20. The next afternoon, Eaton dropped his second horse, Guilder, into a claiming race. Guilder paid $18.00 and Speers collected handsomely as he parlayed Thursday's profits onto Friday's winner.

Later that evening, the two western gentlemen went to an expensive Baltimore seafood restaurant to celebrate. They celebrated with more enthusiasm than wisdom. Before the restaurant closed, both men were on their knees on the kitchen floor staging a race between two large live lobsters. Each was armed with a kitchen pepper-shaker and, they were dumping pepper on their lobsters, to accelerate their progress to the finish-line.

The next morning, physically and emotionally frazzled by the excessive excitement of the previous evening, they surveyed one another in their Baltimore hotel suite and vowed "never to take another drink of whiskey."

Lord Cheylesmore, who in 1971 was still active in the racing business at the age of seventy-eight, never took another drink of hard liquor. Speers, after examining the fine print in their mutual contract, discovered a semantic loophole. He contended to his own satisfaction that the word "whiskey" did not encompass gin or rum and, although he was an exceptionally conservative man in his consumption of alcohol, he relaxed the terms of his vow to avail himself of the odd dollop of non-whiskey spirits.

Where R. James Speers was concerned, I contracted a lifelong case of hero worship. He dominated the Canadian racing scene in his time; next to my father, it was his counsel which guided me through my formative years in the racing world. There were times when I turned to him for assistance when I was too deeply embarrassed to turn to my father.

When I was a $75-per-week newspaper reporter in Toronto, a temporary lapse in my penchant for picking winners caused me to run up a tab of $300 with my bookmaker. I lost it in little dribs and drabs, $20 here, $35 there. The bookmaker was a patient man, but he suggested that I should do something about settling my overdue account.

Mr. Speers had arrived in Toronto for the Thorncliffe autumn meeting and he was en suite at the Royal York Hotel. I waited until we had dinner one evening and then I asked if I could borrow $300 to pay off my bookmaker.

"How did you get in that deep, on your salary?" he asked.

My story had been prepared. Straight-faced I replied: "I lost a $300-bet on Western Prince." It was a Machiavellian stroke. Western Prince was a horse owned by my father. Mr. Speers had bred Western Prince and sold him to my father as a yearling. Mr. Speers would be touched by my loyalty to the produce of his breeding farm.

"Come and have lunch with me at the hotel tomorrow," Mr. Speers said. "I'll get the money when I go to the bank in the morning."

I felt a cold chill of doubt. I knew that Mr. Speers was going out to play poker that evening. I knew that one of his fellow-players was an associate of my personal bookmaker. I knew Mr. Speers well enough to realize that, within a few hours, he would have all the details of my miserable gambling activities.

Nevertheless, I presented myself for lunch the next day. Mr.

Speers peeled six fifty-dollar bills from his bankroll and he sat with the money in his right hand, resting on the table. "Now tell me again," he said, looking at me carefully, "how did you lose this money?"

I looked him squarely in the eyes and I said: "I lost a $300-bet on Western Prince."

"Good boy," laughed Mr. Speers, handing me the $300. "When you're borrowing money, never change your story in the middle of the negotiations."

I accepted the money and the sardonic rebuke gratefully. It cost me some blood and sweat to repay him. I wrote five stories for Mayfair Magazine at the rock bottom price of sixty dollars per story.

I stuck as closely as I could to Jim Speers, listening, studying and learning. For some service I performed for him he gave me a lifetime membership in the Winnipeg Jockey Club. He was aware that my heart still belonged to the backstretch at Whittier Park and Polo Park. Although my newspapering chores had taken me to live in Toronto, I always managed to convince my employers that my presence at the Winnipeg race meetings was a journalistic necessity. Even in the football season, I arranged my travelling schedules so that I would spend at least three or four days in Winnipeg on each trip, listening to Jim Speers raconteuring on the colourful past of The Last Great West.

It was on one of those late autumn trips that Mr. Speers – who was confined to bed in his Kingsway home after a serious heart attack – despatched me to inspect his ten thousand acre Pine River Ranch near Carberry, Manitoba. Duke Campbell, who had retired temporarily from training the Speers racing stable to assume the foremanship of the cattle-and-horse ranch, drove me from Winnipeg and we spent two days travelling to every remote corner of the magnificent spread. Speers had leased two airstrips close to his ranch; they had been Commonwealth Air Training Schools during World War II, and he had planted them in hay. The hay had been harvested a few weeks previously and Campbell and I estimated that the crop exceeded five thousand tons.

All the way back to Winnipeg I was thinking of those five thousand tons of hay lying in Carberry, and I was conscious of the fact that the Coleman family's horses were racing in New Orleans. We were paying seventy-five dollars per ton for hay at the Fair Grounds track in New Orleans.

Back in Winnipeg, I rushed to Mr. Speers' sickroom to deliver my report. Breathlessly I blurted, "Duke and I figure that you have five thousand tons of hay at Carberry. If you could get that hay into New Orleans, you could sell it at seventy-five dollars a ton."

The old man was pretty sick and I imagine that this was one of the occasions when my energetically sophomoric stupidity gave him a pain in the ass. He glared at me and grumped: "Yes! And if I could get Lake Louise into hell, I could sell it at ten dollars per glass!"

He recovered from that heart attack, despite any irritation which my boisterous intrusion might have caused him, and he resumed his same old pace around the continent's race tracks for another nine years. Then he died, quite suddenly and easily.

I was an official of the Ontario Jockey Club when he died and my employers, knowing my affection for Mr. Speers, sent me to Winnipeg to represent them at the funeral. They buried him in Elmwood Cemetery not far from my own mother's little plot, and the final juxtaposition of the mortal remains of two persons whom I had adored stirred my emotions terribly.

While the clergyman was intoning the burial rites, all the aphorisms which I had heard from Jim Speers were racing through my mind. Funny, but one of his lines returned again and again: "Every man who has acquired a bit of money should have a hobby and a worry – and he can have both, if he owns a race horse."

He was so right – so bloody right!

8

The School of Pharmacology

There were some old-fashioned trainers who, when the saliva test and other restrictive measures were first introduced to North American tracks, moaned that they would be forced to retire from the profession. Sulkily, they complained that the anti-stimulation measures "have killed my best horse."

The lamentations were premature and baseless. Human ingenuity copes with privations; the human spirit adapts slowly but surely to a new environment. As far as I can recall, not a single trainer tossed in the sponge along with his hypodermic needle and his pill-boxes.

On the contrary, Bob Ramsey still was saddling winners in 1971, thirty-six years after he achieved the dubious distinction of being the first trainer in Western Canada who was "caught" by a saliva test. The infamous incident occured at Whittier Park in 1935 when Ramsey went once too often to the well with a horse named Just Cost. The horse's saliva, upon being tested in a government laboratory, caused all the lights in the building to blink warningly.

In justice to many of the distinguished mentors of my childhood, it should be pointed out again that there were no rules prohibiting stimulation during the first third of this century. Secondly, drug use wasn't as fashionable as it became in the 1970's; the drug-users were a few horses, not millions of human beings. Thirdly, veterinary medicine never has produced any conclusive evidence that drugs, administered for the purposes of stimulation, actually shortened a horse's life. After he had received "a little bit of help" a horse's behaviour was as eccentric as a drunk's behaviour for ten or twelve hours, but the effects wore off almost as quickly as the effects of alcohol are shaken off by a healthy human being.

The doping of horses wasn't as widespread as the suspicious racing public would have cared to believe. Usually there were five or six trainers around any track whose credentials for skill in the field of stimulation were unquestionable. Other trainers, who feared or merely declined to tamper with drugs, would summon one of the experts in time of financial emergency. As Doc Ronald once said to me: "If you was going to have a brain operation you wouldn't let the postman handle them knives."

Those trainers who were skilled in using drugs to persuade a slow horse to run with astonishing speed were known facetiously among their colleagues as "chemists." They weren't, by any means, merely run-of-the-mill chemists.

Heroin, diluted judiciously in solvents, could be administered intravenously. Some experts preferred to drop a smidgin of powdered heroin on a horse's tongue. This latter practice was known among unlicensed practitioners as "spitting on his tongue" or "giving him a foo-foo powder." Other trainers administered caffeine, and a few relied on pills which were sold to them by gambling-minded druggists who wished to insure their own bets at the track. In terms of today's sporting practices, when professional football players sharpen their pre-game perceptions by munching benzedrine tablets as if they were salted peanuts, the old-fashioned horse trainers weren't criminally motivated.

The effects of some of these so-called drugs were often merely psychological and they bolstered the morale and confidence of the trainers, rather than improving the performance of their horses. Happy Anderson, who was no stranger to equine chemistry, was fond of telling a story about another trainer, whose faith was stronger than reality.

The trainer sent his wife over to the neighboring "chemist's" barn to borrow a heroin-powder, which he wished to give to his horse before a race. On the way back to their own barn. the wife stubbed her toe, stumbled, and spilled the heroin which was in a folded strip of chemist's paper – about the size and shape of a wrapper for a stick of chewing-gum.

The lady opened her compact and carefully poured some of her white face-powder into the paper. Unquestioningly, the trainer gave the contents of the paper to the horse.

The horse won.

"That's great stuff," the trainer said to his wife. "We'll have to borrow some more the next time we want to win a bet."

Bob Ramsey never was a man who was seeking psychological gimmicks. I saw him in 1971, when he had attained the age of seventy-nine, a genial larceny still very apparent in his bright-eyed glance. Cheerfully, he recalled the details of his suspension of 1935 and proudly produced the press clippings which he had preserved. "I've done everything in the book," he said, "but I never went to jail."

Just Cost was nine years old when the saliva test was introduced to Western Canada tracks. Just Cost was bred in Missouri but he was foaled in Allan Ramsey's livery-barn, just a few yards from the present site of Winnipeg's most opulent hotel, the Winnipeg Inn. Bob bought the horse from his brother for eight hundred dollars, as a yearling.

From the time that he was a two-year-old, the horse campaigned with great success for Ramsey, who in partnership with another brother, Bill, raced under the name of the Bar-Ace Stable.

"He was a hop-horse most of his life," Bob said. "I'd light him up with a concoction of my own, belladonna and a grain and one-half of heroin, mixed in a 26-ounce bottle of brandy. It smelled good enough to drink yourself, if you wanted a free trip to the moon."

When they lowered the boom on Bob on September 14, 1935, Just Cost had won five consecutive races in seven days of racing. It wasn't unusual for thoroughbreds to run three or more times in a single week on Western tracks thirty-five or forty years ago, but Just Cost was exceptionally durable. His winning career provided dramatic refutation of any complaints that the habitual use of drugs injures a horse's health.

"He had won five in a row," Ramsey said. "In that particular week, he won on Monday, Wednesday and Thursday and we were going after our sixth consecutive win on Friday. Then Judge Schilling called me into the office on Friday morning and he told me that the horse was scratched and suspended because his saliva test had been positive.

"He won five in a row," the old man continued, "and he led every step of the way in each of those five races. He came out of the starting-gate in the lead and he just tow-roped those critters."

As usual, Ramsey knew exactly what he was doing when he sent out Just Cost to run in that final week of racing, and he had weighed the possible consequences. Late in the previous week, Judge George Schilling had posted a notice advising all horsemen that a saliva test was going to be taken of the winners of all races.

Ramsey had discovered that no facilities for analysing the saliva-samples were available in Winnipeg. The glass tubes containing the saliva-samples were collected at the end of each day's racing program and they were shipped to the Connaught Laboratory in Toronto. Ramsay estimated that the train-trip to Toronto would take thirty-six hours; add another twenty-four or thirty-six hours for completing the analyses of each sample; add onther thirty-six or forty-eight hours for the chemist's report to reach Winnipeg.

The prairie racing season was due to end on September 15. Ramsey reckoned craftily that the season might be over, and he might have taken his horses into winter quarters before the first report on Just Cost's saliva tests reached Winnipeg. In addition to which, he was a sceptic: he wasn't convinced that these new-fangled tests could untangle a judicious mixture of brandy, belladonna and heroin.

He overlooked one important factor: the long-distance telephone. The chief chemist in Toronto, after breaking down Just Cost's saliva sample and detecting the presence of heroin, telephoned the information to Judge Schilling in Winnipeg.

Judge Schilling was incredulous. "Why the hell did you do it, Bob?" he demanded when the unrepentant Ramsey was bought before him for sentence. "We had warnings posted all over the track – you knew that we were taking saliva tests."

"I need the money from those four extra purses," Robert replied frankly. "The meeting ends this week; the winters out here last six months and those snowballs make damn poor eating."

The sentence which Judge Schilling imposed was compassionate, almost ridiculous. He suspended Ramsey for nine months. This meant that Ramsey missed only the last two racing-days of the 1935 season and the first six days of the 1936 season at Calgary. But the case was widely publicized on North American tracks and Ramsey's suspension was regarded hopefully as a deterrent to any other "chemists" who might feel impelled to stimulate their horses by methods which, now, had been nullified by pharmaceutical research.

Ramsey perversely enjoys the questionable celebrity which still clings to him. When I last saw him at Assiniboia Downs in Winnipeg, he was cackling toothlessly over the fact that thirty-six years after the Just Cost incident investigators for the Manitoba Racing Commission still sniff around his barn to ascertain whether he is concealing any contraband.

Bob Ramsey is unique in the modern genre of horse racing; he is an anachronism, a lively relic of the fabled past. With his huge beaked nose, his rasping voice and his humorous, twinkling old eyes, he reminds me of my imaginative personification of two of my favourite childhood fictional "heavies," Long John Silver and Captain Hook.

He has been everything and he has done everything. Born in Grand Point, twelve miles south of Winnipeg, he was helping to support his family when he was ten years old. His father was crippled by rheumatism. Bob, who spoke French as well as English, used to get five or six dollars for driving a load of hay to Winnipeg and pitchforking the hay into a livery-barn loft at the age of ten. He'd take the five or six dollars to a Winnipeg store and buy sufficient groceries to keep his parents and other children for a week.

He was a gun-carrying rum runner in the days of U.S. Prohibition; he ran bootlegging joints in Winnipeg and he operated the official crap game on Winnipeg race tracks. When Samuel Bronfman, the multimillionaire distiller, owned three hotels in Winnipeg, Ramsey drove the two-horse stage which carted the hotels' patrons to and from the city's railroad depots. When the bars closed in 1916 and Sam Bronfman decided to move to Montreal, he offered Ramsey five dollars a day to go to Montreal to speak French for him in his new milieu. Ramsey, who shrewdly suspected that the closing of the legal bars would be followed by an era of profitable bootlegging, decided to remain in Winnipeg, where he was sure he could earn considerably more than five dollars per day.

Since most of his misdeeds have been outlawed by the Statute of Limitations, he has no compunction about talking of them now, quite openly.

"One night in my whiskey-running days I was driving back across the prairies in the middle of the night in my roadster," he recalls. "I'd just finished making my last run of the season – it was snowing and it was as dark as the pits of hell. Out there in the dark, I heard some sleigh bells. I figured that no one would be out there at that time of night unless they were running whiskey.

"I was right. It was a couple of mockie bastards with a sleigh full of whiskey. I pulled my old Betsy out of my pocket and I scared the pants right off them. I made them load their whiskey into my roadster and I drove it back to Winnipeg, where I resold it. I don't know how much whiskey I sold in my time but, personally, I never drank around the race track in daytime. I might drink until two o'clock in the morning but never after I stepped on the race track. A man needs to keep all his wits about him around the race track."

Bob Ramsey enjoyed a curious immunity from harrassment by the Winnipeg Police although his scallawaggery was more or less common knowledge among the gambling-and-drinking set. Possibly, the police officers subscribed to a widely-held belief that in the period of government-enforced drought bootleggers were merely providing a humanitarian service by relieving a national thirst.

"Back in the twenties I sprung a young American jockey out of the old Bond Street Jail," Ramsey told me. "They'd sentenced him to nine months for contributing to the delinquency of minors. They caught him messing around with a couple of young girls in St. Boniface.

"I smuggled him out of the jail house in a hamper of laundry. For four days I hid him in the Commercial Hotel, right across from the police station. Then I hid him in my sister's house. Finally, I shipped him back to the U.S. hidden underneath a load of bootleg whiskey. My conscience never bothered me. The kid had been framed – those two girls were just little St. Boniface chippies.

"I can't even remember the kid's name, now. I never heard

what became of him. The young bugger never wrote to me – maybe he never learned how to write."

Bob Ramsey is the classic example of the stubborn, hard-headed trainer who was certain to persist in the petit larceny of the turf until he was caught. By instinct and by habit he was dedicated to the circumvention of the stuffy rules of conventional behaviour. He won't even agree to enter heaven until he is assured that paradise is equipped with a race track which operates under Hudson's Bay Rules.

Speaking of Hudson's Bay Rules, the take-your-best-hold philosophy was rampant at the one-week meetings which, up until World War II, were conducted in the little town of Cochrane, about thirty miles west of Calgary. The Cochrane track was owned by Bumpy Rhodes and Dusty Rhodes, two charmingly offhand brothers from England who had emigrated to Alberta with the blessings – and, possibly with the energetic encouragement – of their families. In any event, the Rhodes brothers regularly received remittances of cash from the Mother Country. Officially, they were "rawnchers." There was an Alberta distinction between a "rawnch" and a "ranch" in the pioneering days when the polo-playing sons of British families decided to settle in the cattlelands. A "ranch" was a spread which yielded an annual profit to its owner – a "rawnch" was a speculative risk.

R. James Speers failed to share the general enthusiasm over the activities of those two middle-aged sprites, Bumpy and Dusty Rhodes. Each year, the Rhodes brothers waited until Speers publicly announced the dates of his Calgary Spring Meeting. Then, the Rhodes brothers would calmly announce that they would operate a meeting at Cochrane in the six days prior to the opening of Calgary.

Mr. Speers protested that it "wasn't cricket" for the Rhodes brothers to open directly before his Spring meeting. The Calgary bettors, after a week of precarious investing at Cochrane, were financially depleted before Speers got a crack at their bankrolls.

"Of course it isn't cricket, Speers old boy!" Bumpy used to acknowledge when they staged their annual argument in The Ranchmen's Club. "Cricket is a game which is played with a ball and a bat. Dusty and I simply are providing the natives with the opportunity to have a bit of a flutter."

In addition to the generally carefree attitude of the racing officials at Cochrane, there were no railings around the outer perimeter of the race course. The Rhodeses, who had a tendency to run short of money while awaiting their quarterly remittances from England, never did get around to building an outer fence. It was a deliberate oversight which occasionally provided some interesting racing.

One day at Cochrane, Guy Owens, who was embarking upon a training career with a one-horse stable, approached a veterinarian who was, under the appropriate circumstances, inclined to "give a little bit of help."

"I'm running my horse in today's second race, Doc," said Owens. "He needs some inspiration. Can you give me a speed-up pill for him?"

The doctor pulled a box out of his pocket, examined the pills therein and handed one to Owens, saying: "Give him this exactly thirty minutes before the race."

That afternoon, Owens sent his horse to the post for the second race. The horse bounded away from the start and opened a five-length lead. But when they reached the first-turn the horse was running so fast that he just kept on going, straight ahead.

Since there were no railings on the outside of the course, the horse didn't slow down. The jockey, frightened out of his wits, bailed out. The horse, running with inspired elan, vaulted the C.P. railway tracks and he didn't pull up until he stopped for a drink of water in a coulee, about one mile due south.

Later that night, the veterinarian, who had spent the afternoon visiting some equine patients on nearby farms, ran into Trainer Owens. "Did your horse win this afternoon?" the vet asked.

Owens told him in blasphemous phrases of the gallant steed's cross-country misadventures.

"Dear, dear," said the veterinarian, who was something of a local comic. "I forgot that your horse was going to race around two turns – I must have given you one of my straightaway-pills."

The average racetracker's attitude towards dope was basically casual. He thought of it in terms of horses, rather than in terms of human beings. Despite its easy accessibility around the tracks in the pre-saliva-test era, there were relatively few racetrackers who became hooked on the stuff. It was available, but its effects on the human constitution had been advertised so luridly, even in those days of comparative innocence, that there was no widespread disposition to seek the treacherous euphoria which it promised. Junkies really weren't welcome around the tracks and when they were detected they were expelled as pariahs.

Nonetheless, the possibilities of brief enlivenment for social purposes must have titillated my offbeat friend, Whittier Park Slim. I first saw Slim Howe when he arrived in Winnipeg, chauffering Don Cameron's yellow Packard phaeton. Cameron was later to achieve international fame when he trained Count Fleet to win the Triple Crown of North American racing. However, when he returned to his native Winnipeg on this particular occasion, he was training a strong of undistinguished platers.

In addition to chauffeuring Cameron's impressive yellow phaeton, Whittier Park Slim was Cameron's foreman, his groom and his court jester. Cameron, who had grown up in California and was eyeing the motion picture colony as a future source of affluent patrons for his racing activities, was a large, handsome man garbed in the height of fashion. His expensive suits and expensive shoes caused him to be an object of some suspicion among the Western Canada horsemen, most of whom looked as if their clothing had been provided by the Salvation Army. Whittier Park Slim was a chameleon and he adopted some of his employer's lordly demeanour.

During their visit to Winnipeg, Cameron was being entertained one evening at the home of some friends of his parents. Whittier Park Slim drove Cameron to the residence and then asked if he could keep the yellow phaeton for the remainder of the evening while he engaged in some of his personal social activities. Having made an impressive arrival for the benefit of his hosts, Cameron dismissed Slim and the car with an imperial gesture.

Slim drove back to the track where another healthy and eager young groom was waiting for him. They drove to a liquor store where they bought a bottle of rye and then drove to a grocery store where they purchased half a dozen bottles of the world's most widely-advertised cola drink. Then, with their eyes peeled, they drove slowly through the downtown streets of Winnipeg, appraising possible candidates for female companionship.

The yellow Packard phaeton proved an irresistible lure to impressionable young ladies who were strolling the streets in pairs. Furthermore Whittier Park Slim was an attractive chap, bright-eyed and full of gay bullshit, and the other boy in the car was Slim's counterpart in personality.

They selected a pair of likely-looking fillies; with a flourish, they ushered them into the yellow Packard, Slim taking the more comely of the two into the front seat with him. The other groom, who deferred to Slim as the senior partner in the stratagem, uttered no protest as he sat down beside the other girl in the back seat.

They drove into Tuxedo, the city's most opulent residential suburb, and Slim drove the car out onto the open prairie due south of Winnipeg. He pulled into an unfenced field one hundred yards from the gravelled secondary road, and with the practised sophistication of a man-of-the-world from California he stopped the car and turned off the engine.

It was a summer night in June. Whittier Park Slim opened four bottles of cola; he poured off an inch or so from each bottle and, working quietly and efficiently, he poured a hefty slug of rye into each bottle. The other three youngsters were engaging in pawky badinage while Slim, using the opened door of the glove compartment as a bar, busied himself with his decanting.

The first four bottles of the mixture disappeared quickly and, smacking his lips with evident satisfaction, Whittier Park Slim opened four more bottles and went through his cocktail-bar routine, again. Then the two couples settled down low in their respective seats and they engaged in whatever tribal customs healthy young human beings observe in a roomy open Packard on a hot prairie summer night.

The bliss of Slim and his compliant seatmate was interrupted by a cry of alarm from the back seat. Startled by the shout in the darkness, Whittier Park Slim popped up, extricated himself from his casual innamorata's warm embrace, and peered over the edge of the upholstery.

"Geeze-us," his racetrack friend was whinnying. "I don't know what's the matter with this dame but, she's passed out and she's foaming at the mouth."

"Well, it's my fault," Whittier Park Slim confessed lamely. "I thought that your girl looked a little dull – so I put a small shot of heroin into her first drink."

The young lady recovered consciousness after the two gentlemen had combined in five minutes of manual respiration, most of it in the area of her chest. She was able to walk without assistance by the time that they deposited her in front of her parental home, but as she slammed the back door of the Packard she announced that never again would she permit herself to be picked up by "a couple of crummy racetrack bums."

The last of the chemists who practised openly and unabashedly on western tracks was High-Ball Kelly. There may have been others who continued to administer assistance to horses surreptitiously long after Kelly had gone to limbo, but High-Ball was a man who was congenitally incapable of hiding his light under a bushel. High-Ball was extroverted and generous, and when he "sent" a horse, he broadcasted the information noisily, so that all his friends among the horsemen could share his anticipated good fortune.

High-Ball Kelly was also habitually improvident. There was another use of the word "chemist" around the race tracks. In this alternative definition, a chemist was a man "who turned money into manure." Kelly was thus the typification of the two-way threat, a chemist par excellence in two fields of ignoble human endeavour.. High-Ball didn't give a damn for money – his money or anyone else's money.

"There are two kinds of men: lenders and borrowers," he used to say. "I'm strictly a borrower."

High-Ball loved the finer things in life, and when he campaigned annually in Western Canada he insisted upon sleeping between clean sheets in hotel rooms rather than exposing himself to the rigours of a campcot in the barns. He was uncommonly careless in the matter of paying his bills and there were a few veteran hotel managers who, aware of his absent-mindedness, insisted upon him paying a week's rent in advance.

A new manager in the St. Regis Hotel in Winnipeg, who hadn't been apprised of High-Ball's little idiosyncrasies, was checking his current accounts and discovered that Kelly's bill was attaining monumental proportions while Kelly studiously ignored the little reminders which were slipped beneath his door at the end of each week. Furthermore, the manager never espied his mysterious guest. High-Ball was leaving and entering the hotel daily via the back fire escape which provided access to the parking lot. Furthermore, Kelly left the hotel for the track at five o'clock each morning and seldom did he return before Bob Ramsey's crap game had closed for the night.

The manager considered this situation carefully, and early on the morning after he had become aware of Kelly's steadily-mounting debt, he was sitting in his own car on the parking lot when High-Ball came clattering down the fire escape.

"Stop right there, Kelly," the manager shouted, leaping into High-Ball's path. "You owe me three weeks rent – I'm giving you exactly two days to pay up, in full!"

"Two days, eh?" Kelly cried gaily, clambering into his car and turning the key in the ignition. "Well, I'll take Easter Sunday and the Fourth of July."

R. James Speers had a very soft spot in his heart for High-Ball Kelly. For that matter, Jim Speers reserved a special soft spot for many of the genial improvidents of this world. It was impossible for anyone to dislike Kelly, who never lost his effervescent good humour, even in his moments of financial disaster.

Among his other social accomplishments, Kelly was able to imitate a stallion's whinny with startling realism. Mr. Speers never failed to be amused by Kelly's whinny. A couple of Mr. Speers' middle-aged friends – a lady and a gentlemen – had tarried overlong in the directors' private bar after the conclusion of an afternoon's races at Whittier Park. As dusk fell, they seated themselves on a bench on the Club House lawn, and although they were old enough to know better they were engaged in some rather silly small-talk. Mr. Speers who was watching them from his car in the adjacent parking-lot, sent an emissary to bring High-Ball Kelly into his presence.

High-Ball, after listening to Speers's whispered instructions, crept into the shadow of a bush, directly behind the mutually enchanted couple.

While they were engrossed in themselves, Kelly suddenly emitted the scream of an enraged stallion.

Without bothering to look back, the couple galloped to their cars in the parking lot, as speedily as their middle-aged legs would carry them.

Since he enjoyed such rapport with Mr. Speers, it wasn't surprising that Speers stood right at the top of Kelly's list of "lenders." At the conclusion of a Winnipeg autumn meeting, High-Ball went into the Speers office and confidently asked for a loan of a thousand dollars.

"You'll get this back as soon as I make a score, Mr. Speers," High-Ball said, stuffing the thousand dollars into his kick. "I'll see you at the front gate of Long Branch, in Toronto, right before the first race on opening day. You can count on me being there."

Two weeks later, I was having lunch with Mr. Speers and Lou Davies in the Imperial Room of Toronto's Royal York Hotel. It was the opening day of the Long Branch meeting.

"We'd better get out to the track," Mr. Speers said, calling for the bill. "High-Ball Kelly owes me a thousand dollars and he told me that he'd see me at the front gate, just before the first race."

As we descended from a taxi at Long Branch, High-Ball was standing there, smiling a happy greeting. He rushed up to Speers, pumped his hand warmly, and shouted: "I told you that I'd see you on opening day at Long Branch. Well, here I am. And now you'll have to excuse me because I'm on my way to New Orleans."

Waving his arms genially, Kelly strode away, leaving us open-mouthed. Kelly hadn't even mentioned the money.

"Well, High-Ball is a man of his word," Speers chuckled as we walked into the track. "After all, he promised only that he'd see me here before the first race."

Although Bob Ramsey frankly revealed that his favourite concoction for stimulating horses was the mixture of brandy, belladonna and heroin, High-Ball Kelly reputedly used some other exotic chemicals. There are a few oldtimers who sit in front of the fireplaces, cracking their knuckles in glee as they remember the slightly hilarious circumstances under which High-Ball "sent" one of his horses in a race at Chinook Park in Calgary.

History does not record what stimulant Kelly gave to his little mare that afternoon at Chinook, but she ran like a scared cat. She leaped from the starting-gate a full length ahead of her unstimulated rivals and she increased her lead with every jump. When they reached the finish-line, Kelly's mare won by fifteen open lengths.

It was an immensely popular victory because, as was his custom, Kelly had alerted his many friends that nothing less than an unanticipated Act of God would detain his mare from the swift completion of her appointed rounds on that particular afternoon.

High-Ball was standing in the winner's enclosure directly beneath the stewards' stand in the Chinook infield, awaiting his mare's return, after she pulled up slowly on the backstretch. The jockey experienced some difficulty in slowing her to a walk, because the mare was carrying enough high-octane fuel to send her all the way to the Rocky Mountains. As High-Ball awaited the mare's entrance to the winner's enclosure, he was waving his arms happily in acknowledgement of the cheers of his devoted admirers who, clutching bundles of pari-mutuel tickets in their hot fists, were gathered along the fences hailing his triumph.

The stewards, meanwhile, were out on the little open verandah which circled their stand. They were so close to Kelly that he could have reached up with one hand and touched their shoes.

As the little mare tiptoed onto the grass of the infield enclosure, she was sweating profusely from the combined effects of the drugs and her considerable exertions. Just as she was being wheeled into position for the traditional post-race photograph, she gave a slight quiver and, as the euphemism has it, she yielded to a call of nature.

It was no trivial call of nature. The mare spread her legs and she deposited a very large mound on the bright green grass.

A tiny sparrow was sitting on the white-painted fence rail of the winner's enclosure. The sparrow had been observing the victory scene with considerable interest and, when Kelly's mare relieved herself of her emotional and physical burden, the sparrows' eyes brightened and the bird poised for take-off.

As the sparrow circled briskly above the mound which Kelly's mare had deposited on the green grass, High-Ball was galvanized into alarmed action.

Ignoring the fact that the racing stewards were standing just a few feet from him, where they could overhear clearly even his most subtle whisper, Kelly took off his hat, waved it at the hovering sparrow, and shouted a warning:

"Little bird," he yelped, in apparently genuine consternation: "Don't touch that stuff – or you'll fly yourself to death!"

9

The Open City

The summer before I went away to university was probably my best season as a handicapper. It was sentiment rather than skillful deduction which assured my success. My favourite trainers happened to be enjoying a very good year and, loyally, I was backing their horses at every opportunity. Sentimental wagering usually leads to disaster on the race tracks, but this was one of those unusual seasons when dumb luck prevails over mathematical probability.

Admittedly, the summer wasn't an uninterrupted series of personal triumphs. After winning quite consistently at the Whittier Park and Polo Park spring meetings, our parents took my brother and me to Kenora for a one-month vacation in the lake district, while the horses moved west into the prairies for the four consecutive one-week meetings at the Calgary Stampede, Edmonton, Saskatoon and Regina. For me, the holiday was marred irreparably by my lamentably poor seamanship when I put Johnny Rogers' catboat onto the rocks during a sailing race.

Actually, the wind was much too strong for a sailing race that morning and many good skippers with more experience than I also took an unpremediated bath. My catboat capsized at the same moment when two thirty-two-foot scows, each carrying a crew of four, turned upside-down. The rescue launches, which were despatched from the docks, went first to the assistance of the thirty-two-footers. By the time that they got around to me, clinging to a lee-board of the upturned catboat, my craft had drifted onto some rocks. The battering which Johnny Rogers' boat took in the next ten minutes punched a couple of holes in the thin hull.

Wallowing in self-pity, I sulked when my parents reproved me for this maritime accident. I winced every time I was reminded that the repairs to Johnny Rogers' catboat would cost $150. The holiday had been destroyed for me and I suggested that I should go to Calgary, where the two-week racing meeting at Chinook Park was due to open.

I was even more crestfallen when all the members of my family agreed that this would be one hell of a good idea. I had an open invitation to stay at the home of Benton Mackid, a boarding-schoolmate whose family lived in a country house outside Calgary about a mile from Chinook Park. My father provided me with a round-trip pass on the railway. My stepmother, with almost too much eagerness, offered to buy me a berth on the train in addition to providing a generous sum for meals. Stiffening my trembling upper lip, I embarked on my westbound journey, feeling much like one of the early Christian martyrs.

I struck a bonanza at Chinook Park. The horses trained by Stub and Dooge Barnes were running home like well-trained pigs. Sir Lester Knifong and Dr. Levi Ronald were scoring with awesome regularity. Ada Whittier, a filly which Stub Barnes trained for W. A. Dutton, won twice at juicy prices and the members of the Mackid family began to suspect that they were harbouring Pittsburgh Phil.

My major triumph was scored by betting on a horse named Carpe Diem. I had a "whisper" on this gallant steed, which was trained by Guy Owens, a former jockey whose problems with increasing weight had forced him to end his riding career. Guy Owens and Ernie Green had been the only two jockeys around Western Canada who were sturdy enough to ride Son O Unc, a savage horse which Stub Barnes trained for Mr. Dutton. Although he was a gelding, Son O Unc literally was a man-eater. Early in his career, when he was a young horse of stakes calibre, he was reputed to have killed two Negro grooms. I was quite prepared to believe the story – the Barnes brothers kept a muzzle on Son O Unc, who permitted himself to be groomed only by Green and Owens, who had established a mysterious rapport with the maniacal old gelding.

Owens, who knew that I wouldn't broadcast the tip indiscriminately, told me that I could wager on Carpe Diem with confidence. I bet $10 win, $10 place and $10 show on the horse. Carpe Diem won and he paid $12.65, $4.80 and $4.60.

This coup led me directly to my only meeting with the greatest Briton of our times, Sir Winston Churchill. Although Sir Winston wrote voluminously of his personal recollections, he ignored our encounter in his published works.

Sir Winston (he was Mr. Churchill then) was in one of his occasional periods of political eclipse when he visited Calgary to address the Alberta Bar Association. Fate decreed that our paths should cross in the almost-deserted lobby of the CPR depot at Calgary.

The morning after Carpe Diem won, Benton Mackid drove me to the railway station, where I proposed to send $150 to my stepmother by telegraph. The $150 would pay for the repairs to Johnny Rogers' catboat. The anticipation of confounding my parents by discharging a debt of honour was filling me with keen anticipation.

I was scurrying across the station lobby with my head down as I counted the money in my hands and I crashed into a short well-upholstered gentleman who was being trailed by a small coterie of civic dignitaries. I glanced up at the victim of my careless assault and, to my horror, I recognized Mr. Churchill, whose newspaper pictures certainly were familiar to me.

Blushing, I stammered: "Excuse me, sir."

The great statesman didn't clasp me to his bosom, his eyes lighting with instant recognition. The great statesman merely glared at me and, unmistakably, he grunted. It was not the type of grunt which encouraged further conversation.

This momentous confrontation occurred on the morning of Saturday, August 24, 1929, even if Sir Winston didn't choose to mention the date in his memoirs.

Slightly intrigued, Benton Mackid and I followed Mr. Churchill's party at a respectful distance as they left the lobby of the railway depot, preparatory to climbing into a couple of open automobiles.

Apart from ourselves and two uniformed Canadian Pacific constables, the only persons to view the departure from the depot were two dusty cowpokes, who were draped over the hitching-rail outside the station. Obviously, the two cowpokes barely had survived a night of disaster. The story was pitifully evident in their wan countenances. They had come into town with a full poke; they had got drunk; they had been rolled by avaricious prostitutes. Now, financially and spiritually exhausted, they were moping in the comparative safety of the railway station's hitching-rail until the afternoon train to McLeod would take them home to the range lands.

Mr. Churchill, always the great actor, appraised the two hungover cowpokes as he walked towards the waiting automobile. Then, just before the car drove away, Mr. Churchill stood erect in the back seat of the car, turned towards the two human wrecks, raised his hat, and, looking at them directly, made a low bow. Without the trace of a smile, Mr. Churchill took his seat and the car drove away.

Benton Mackid and I had strolled behind the cowhands in time to appreciate the conclusion of the tableau.

One cowpoke raised his aching head from the hitching-rail and drawled to his companion: "Now, who the hell is that old dude?"

"Don't rightly know," his ailing companion replied slowly. "But sure as hell, he ain't Hoot Gibson!"

Came September and my parents despatched me to McGill University in Montreal. There was a general idea that I would study medicine and my parents were hopeful that I might become the greatest healer this side of Dr. Albert Schweitzer. As usual, my performance was to be a parental disappointment. My thick head did not provide fertile ground for professorial thought-seeding and my university studies were terminated after three years by mutual agreement with the Dean of the Faculty. It was just as well: thousands of Canadians, who still are living useful lives, might have gone to early graves if I had been permitted to practise medicine or surgery.

I was seventeen when my parents sent me off to McGill, escorted by Max Bell, a second-year student who lived in Calgary. Max's father, who published several western Canadian daily newspapers, was a close friend of my father. Since my long incarceration in boarding schools had left me pitifully ill-prepared for the bright lights of sinful Montreal, it had been agreed that Max, a steady, heady chap, was the ideal chaperon to establish me in suitable antiseptic surroundings at the university. Thus, I was waved aboard the same sleeping-car when Max's train passed through Winnipeg, en route from Calgary, and I recall that he appraised his personally-unsolicited ward with forced cordiality.

It was ironic that this was the same Max Bell who, years later, was to become an internationally famous owner of thoroughbred race horses. He was to own many celebrated thoroughbreds, including Meadow Court, who won the Irish Derby after finishing a good second to Sea Bird in The Epsom Derby. However, when he reluctantly assumed the duty of escorting me to Montreal, Max had never set foot on a race track and the only horses with which he was familiar were those which laboriously dragged delivery-wagons through the streets of western cities.

It was a case of the chaperon being seduced by his wayward ward. For reading material on the thirty-six hour train journey I had brought along, among other scholarly tomes, a copy of the *National Turf Digest,* a monthly magazine devoted largely to handicapping systems for horse-racing enthusiasts. The back section of the magazine featured the Montee Onliwon Ratings, which provided a speed rating for most of the horses currently running on North American tracks. In the past, careful perusal of the Montee Onliwon Ratings had enabled me to smoke out a few long-priced winners.

Observing my preoccupation with the magazine, Max Bell asked for elucidation of the figures I was jotting down on a piece of paper. Reluctantly, I complied. He was a very apt pupil. Within fifteen minutes he was asking questions which caused me to look at him with new respect.

I reached into my suitcase and pulled out my chart-book. This was a pocket-size, loose-leaf book, every page of which carried the form-charts for a seven-race program on the prairie tracks during the past summer. My daily charts had been given to me by Mr. Dutton and I always carried them in my jacket pocket for ready reference. Actually, it wasn't a very thick book; the prairie season had less than seventy racing days in those years. I explained the charts to Max and his face shone with the fervour of a religious convert. We sat up late that night, discussing the transient glories of horse racing while the train rumbled and clanked towards Montreal.

When we arrived in Montreal, we didn't go directly to McGill University to register for the coming year. We parked our bags in Max's fraternity house and we went to the Dorval track where Max could put his newly-discovered mathematical theories into practice. That day was his first exposure to a sport which, in all probability, cost him several millions of dollars. He bore me no grudge for that. We remained close lifetime friends although he became a multi-millionaire while I stumbled through the morass of financial mediocrity.

Montreal in those days was one of those cities where "you could do anything you were big enough to do." The city publicists advertised the French-English metropolis as the Paris of North America. Sailors from foreign ports regarded it, with gleeful anticipation, as the modern counterpart of Sodom and Gomorrah. The truth lay somewhere between the two extremes, but it was certainly a rather gaudy trap for any unsophisticated boy who had spent a sheltered life in strictly administered boarding schools. Max Bell, true to the trust reposed in him by our parents, made an earnest effort to guide me along the paths of righteousness, but his contract didn't call for him to maintain 24-hour-a-day surveillance. Apart from the fact that he accompanied me to the races and National Hockey League games – to the latter on complimentary tickets which were provided by W. A. Dutton's son, Mervyn "Red" Dutton, who was a wild-skating and terrible-tempered defenceman with the Montreal Maroons – Max wished me good fortune and went about his own serious business of acquiring a higher education. Neither tobacco smoke nor alcohol ever passed Max's lips, even up until today.

Montreal was probably the Canadian birthplace of thoroughbred horse racing, although the city of Trois Rivières ninety miles to the east staged the inaugural running of the Queen's Plate in 1836, twenty-four years before the haughty neighbouring province of Ontario inaugurated its own Queen's Plate, a race which has been run annually without interruption since 1860. The predominantly French population of Quebec never embraced the thoroughbreds with true passion, and with the exception of one brief, brilliant interlude under the aegis of Commander J. K. L. Ross in the 1920's, Montreal didn't challenge Ontario's racing supremacy until 1961 when the Blue Bonnets track was overhauled by brisk, aggressive new management.

By the time that Max Bell and I, all dewy-eyed western innocence, stepped timidly into the Dorval betting-ring, Commander Ross had disposed of his magnificent racing stables and his Montreal business interests and he had departed to live out the remainder of his life in Montego Bay, Jamaica. The loss of Commander Ross was a tragedy for Montreal racing. As president of the Montreal Jockey Club, he made Blue Bonnets one of North America's leading tracks. Blue Bonnets had a mile-and-one-furlong facing strip, topped with peculiar red loam. The grandstand admission price was $2.50, considerably higher than the admission price of New York tracks in that era and the Club House was restricted to members who could produce only the most impeccable social credentials. Blue Bonnets had that type of snob-appeal which was doomed to extinction in the coming depression. Needless to say, neither Max Bell nor I saw the inside of the Blue Bonnets Club House in that period – we just read about it in the Montreal *Gazette*.

Because each race track's charter permitted only fourteen days of racing each year, the thoroughbred sport in Montreal was being strangled by a proliferation of racing associations. There were seven tracks in the Montreal area, ranging from Blue Bonnets, at the top, down to Dorval, King Edward Park, Mount Royal, King's Park, Maisonneuve, Delormier Park and Kempton Park.

Something else had occured by the time Max Bell and I arrived in Montreal. The tycoons of the U.S. bootlegging industry had discovered that Canada provided sanctuary from the oppressive vigilance of the U.S. prohibition enforcement officers. When an employee of the big bootlegging syndicates became "hot" in New York or New Jersey, he was sneaked across the border into Canada where, in the argot of the illegal industry, he was "kept on ice." The French off-coast islands St. Pierre and Miquelon also provided sanctuary for gentlemen who were on the lam, but the mobsters had a distinct preference for Montreal where booze, broads and bright lights eased the tedium of enforced exile.

It was inevitable that with nothing but time and money on their hands these exiles should look for business opportunities in their neon-lit Elba and, some of the wealthier tourists hit upon the brilliant idea of buying up Montreal race tracks. Probably, they would have preferred to muscle in on the Montreal crap-games and the burgeoning game-of-chance known as *barbotte,* but although the civic administration was notably venal the constabulary made it quite plain that Montreal's night-time gambling would continue to be controlled by Montrealers. The constabulary also broadcasted the warning that any visitors who were detected carrying lethal weapons would be tossed into the bastille, to remain there until they rotted. The mobsters, who were enjoying their freedom in Montreal and had no real desire to precipitate a re-enactment of the War of 1812–1814, accepted the ultimatum in the spirit of true sportsmen.

Blue Bonnets and Dorval managed to continue operations without foreign assistance, but most of the other race tracks in the Montreal area were under the titular control of Tom Duggan, a widely-revered local Irishman who received some financial assistance from U.S. liquor interests. One of the men who bankrolled Duggan was William V. "Big Bill" Dwyer, New York's kingpin bootlegger. The Montreal race tracks did not prosper in the early days of the depression and when Tom Duggan died in 1933 he was broke. Duggan died owing Big Bill Dwyer a reputed $275,000. Although the repeal of the prohibition law in the United States was ruining Dwyer, he offered Duggan's widow a pension of a thousand dollars per month. The pension lasted only for a year, because by the end of that period Dwyer also was broke. Within another twelve months, this man who had controlled the largest share of the illegal liquor sales on the eastern seaboard was compelled to cadge ten cases of champagne for his own daughter's wedding reception.

Undoubtedly, the thoroughbreds enjoyed periods of sporadic prosperity in Montreal. Lou Davies, who has spent more than fifty years on Canadian tracks while running the gamut of activities from bettor through chart-caller to the general-managership of a western racing empire, recalls going to

Maisonneuve for the opening day of the meeting on July 1, 1923. The crowd was so immense that the management felt compelled to lock the main gates, twenty minutes before post-time for the first race. Those Montrealers who were left outside erupted indignantly upon being deprived of the opportunity to hazard their money. Reacting with typical Gallic fervour, they kicked down the gates and cheerfully swarmed over the wreckage to swell the mob which already was overtaxing the capacity of Maisonneuve. Davies also recalls his father taking him to King Edward Park, which was isolated on Ile Gros Bois. The only method of reaching the track was by ferry, which sailed from the foot of Pope Pie Boulevard. The ferry was no place for an impressionable child; a public crap-game was in progress on the main deck and the gamblers massed in such numbers that the captain was forced to order them to cluster amidships so that they wouldn't capsize the overloaded ferry.

Montreal's international reputation as a city where municipal cupidity went hand in hand with a high degree of moral tolerance probably removed any inhibitions which might normally have constrained visiting horsemen. In spite of the best efforts of Commander Ross and other highly motivated directors of the Montreal Jockey Club who strove vigorously to preserve the aura of probity at Blue Bonnets and Dorval, there were some very strange occurrences at other tracks. There was, for instance, the "ringing" of Westy Hogan at Kempton Park.

Westy Hogan was a horse of exceptional class. On one of his best days, he was beaten only a nose by Cudgel in the Schenectady Handicap at Saratoga, when Cudgel, ridden by Earl Sande, established a North American record of 1.56 for one mile and three-sixteenths. That was an All-Canadian nose finish. Cudgel was owned by Commander Ross and Westy Hogan was owned by Wilfred Viau, another Montrealer.

When Mr. Viau died of a heart attack at thirty-seven, his stable was dispersed. Westy Hogan briefly disappeared from circulation.

Westy Hogan was jet black. One afternoon at Kempton Park, a chestnut horse won a race which had shocking repercussions in the pari-mutuel department as well as in the headquarters of many bookmaking establishments in New York and Chicago.

In the great traditions of larceny, the plotters who had engineered one of the most successful coups in the records of Amercian gambling collected their swag and disappeared overnight. They tossed three quarts of oats in the chestnut horse's feed bucket and deserted him; leaving him untended in his stall at Kempton Park.

Next morning the stewards, who had been receiving some outraged telephone-calls from distraught bookmakers, went down to the stable area to investigate. The chestnut horse was led from his stall. A steward picked up a wet sponge and rubbed one of the horse's forelegs. As he rubbed, the chestnut hairs of the foreleg turned black. After an hour or so of vigorous rubbing with wet sponges, Westy Hogan stood revealed in his jet-black splendour.

Westy Hogan, deserted by the gambling group which had no further need of him, remained in Canada where he became a moderately successful progenitor of racing bloodstock.

Serious analysts of racing chicanery have always suspected that the camouflaging of Westy Hogan was the work of Paddy Barrie, a gay Irish scoundrel who left his mark on the American turf. Paddy never did get around to writing his confessions, but his rueful admirers insisted that some of his paintings were artistic enough to have been hung in the Louvre.

Paddy's specialty was disguising horses, causing them to resemble other horses. His frauds were so skillfully executed that on many occasions they would have escaped detection by anyone less astute than the curator of the Tate Gallery. He painted with astonishing rapidity. His masterpiece of speed and execution was the conversion of a horse, named Akhnahton, into another horse, named Shem, while they were travelling in a jolting horse-van on the short trip from New York to Baltimore.

After Shem won, and a disastrously untimely rainstorm caused his paint to curdle conspicuously before his handlers could get him back into his barn, Paddy was brought to book. The narrow-minded United States immigration authorities deported him to his native Ireland. They hung a rap of fraudulent conspiracy on the greatest British animal painter to wield a brush since the days of Sir Edwin Landseer. Paddy wasn't a fraud – he was a genius – but like many other genii he wasn't appreciated fully by his own generation.

During the late years of U.S. enforcement of the prohibition act, the gunzils and goons who were sitting out their exile in Montreal were victimized by the local citizenry. When he is removed from his native habitat where he has the tenuous security provided by his own mob, a hoodlum becomes childishly gullible in foreign surroundings. The U.S. hoods probably never felt at home in French-speaking Montreal and, in spite of their sinister reputations, they became eager "patsies" for any Montreal confidence-man who felt bold enough to gull them.

The touting area on Peel Street, a three-block strip from Burnside Street south to and including the Windsor Hotel, was staked by Jockey Fleming, a pioneer in amiable rascality. Fleming, a man who appears to be suffering from chronic anxiety neuroses, has patrolled that same beat restlessly for almost fifty years, loudly and profanely routing any other touts or hustlers who incautiously set foot on his territory.

Jockey Fleming would be the first to acknowledge that he is the world's worst handicapper: he couldn't pick the winner of a one-horse race. This lack of prescience in equine matters was over balanced by sheer gall, dogged persistence, and a spongelike ability to absorb insults. When The Jockey sidled up to a "mark" to lay the story on him, the only defence was a pair of swift heels. Fleming, who always has abhorred physical exertion, would never pursue a victim more than half a block. Running away from Jockey Fleming's clutching hands could be a mistake when he was younger and more powerfully-equipped vocally than he is today – pointing a quivering finger at his disappearing quarry, Jockey would curse him in language which would cause the ticker tape to yellow and wither in Peel Street brokerage houses.

When the vanguard of U.S. prohibition exiles arrived in Montreal, the wealthier among them lived, *en pension,* in the Mount Royal Hotel which was the northern boundary of Jockey Fleming's Peel Street beat. It was Jockey Fleming who first discovered that these well-heeled hoods were prospective suckers.

Fleming quickly ingratiated himself with the bored U.S. expatriates, who always were looking for a little bit of action. Through his labyrinthine connections Fleming provided them with feminine companionship, booze when the retail liquor stores were closed by the 11 p.m. bylaw, tickets to National Hockey League games, and transportation to the best crap games. In return for these services, the visitors tipped him quite liberally.

At that point, his own avarice got the better of him. The visitors liked to while away the afternoons in their hotel suites by betting on a few horses, and Fleming offered to place their wagers with a group of local bookmakers whom he recommended highly. Furthermore, Fleming claimed to be in receipt of daily feed-box information and offered to give them the names of horses on which they could bet with confidence.

It was one of the most transparent of old wheezes. The group of "local bookmakers," who were supposed to be accepting the bets, existed only in Fleming's nimble imagination. The horses on which he was touting the U.S. bootleggers were "stiffs" – horses which had no earthly chance of winning. Fleming was lining his own pockets although he insists, now, that he was piecing-off a percentage of the action to a couple of confederates who were in on the play.

Jockey Fleming made one almost-fatal mistake. Two of Bill Dwyer's rod-men, who had displayed unethical violence in disposing of the driver of a liquor truck which they had hijacked on the Jersey Meadows, were cooling off at the Mount Royal while Dwyer's lawyers squared the beef with the District Attorney's office in Jersey City. Jockey Fleming's early successes in his phoney bookmaking enterprise had made him incautious, and without weighing all the possibilities he permitted these two charming visitors to give him a $500 bet on a horse which he had selected personally.

The horse won, at odds of better than 10-to-1. Jockey Fleming almost swallowed his ill-fitting dentures when, standing in Moe Stern's little horse-betting parlour near the Windsor Hotel, he saw the winning price chalked on the results board.

Jockey Fleming had no intention of paying off $5,000. In fact, he couldn't have scraped up $5,000, even if he had put the bite on every other tout in Montreal.

Meanwhile, back at the Mount Royal Hotel, the two investors were awaiting Jockey Fleming's reappearance in mounting impatience. The hotel management was experiencing considerable difficulty in silencing the two gentlemen who were storming around the lobby uttering ugly threats concerning their plans for "that little bastard, if he doesn't turn up here pretty soon with those 5,000 clams."

Jockey Fleming had heard stories about U.S. rum-runners who, on becoming disenchanted with the unethical business methods of some of their associates, had encased such associates in quick-setting cement and had dumped them into fathomless waters.

Jockey Fleming decided that this was exactly the appropriate moment to take an overdue vacation. He disappeared from his Peel Street beat.

In fact, Jockey Fleming didn't surface again on Montreal streets until spies at the Mount Royal Hotel got word to him that Mr. Dwyer's two rod-men had returned to the United States. The charges against them had been dropped because, very significantly, all the witnesses to their alleged assault on their rum-running rival had disappeared. There were times when the management of the Mount Royal Hotel complained that the house was overcrowded with burly U.S. tourists who were refreshingly vague about the length of their proposed holidays.

Thereafter, Jockey Fleming confined himself to less hazardous occupations such as scalping tickets for sporting events. His survival as a hustler has brought him a certain amount of local celebrity in Montreal. Even today, if you walk along Peel Street or if you go into the drug store in the basement of the Mount Royal Hotel, you'll find him lurking furtively among the rows of shelved cosmetics and pharmaceutical goodies offering to sell you a ticket to a Montreal Canadiens hockey game at double the advertised price. When The Jockey, – who actually never rode a horse – goes to his final reward, the species of old time racing touts will have become extinct in Canada.

I missed the great days of Montreal racing, when Commander J. K. L. Ross campaigned his horses at Blue Bonnets and induced Mrs. F. Ambrose Clark, Ral Parr, Willis Sharpe Kilmer and other leading U.S. owners to ship their horses to Canada. I didn't return to Montreal with a couple of undistinguished horses of my own until six of the tracks had disappeared and the racing was concentrated at Blue Bonnets, which was being operated rather light-heartedly by Thomas Patrick Gorman, who was bankrolled by the heirs to the racing estate of Joseph Catternich. And I no longer owned a horse by 1961, when thoroughbred racing was revived at Blue Bonnets under vastly-improved auspices.

Thomas Patrick Gorman was born either twenty years too late or thirty years too soon to gain the sporting immortality which his colourful personality deserved. An Ottawa-born Irishman, he managed the Ottawa Senators in the National Hockey League, and when that club succumbed to financial anaemia he managed the New York Americans, who were owned by Big Bill Dwyer in his financial heyday. Gorman's travels also took him far afield to Mexico where he was the assistant general manager of the Agua Caliente race track.

Gorman, a man of immense personal charm, was always conceiving ingenious schemes for amassing a quick million dollars. After Phar Lap, the New Zealand wonder-horse, came to North America and scored an easy victory in the $100,000 Agua Caliente Handicap, it was Gorman who had the brilliant idea of taking Phar Lap on a tour of North America's major racing centres. Gorman was cursed with the type of luck which plagues imaginative Irishmen. Just when Gorman had finished signing a lucrative contract for Phar Lap to run exhibition races at New York, Chicago and Baltimore, the horse ate some paint-sprayed grass while grazing outside his barn at Menlo Park, California, and died, poisoned by arsenate of lead.

When he returned to Canada to manage Blue Bonnets, Gorman was full of expensive ideas, but the bankroll which was placed at his disposal was limited to the bare necessities. Consequently, he could offer only small purses; he attracted only horses of less-than-mediocre quality and many of the horsemen who rallied to his cause would have experienced some difficulty in obtaining admission to Royal Ascot. At a time when the major North American track-operators assiduously were courting a bright new public image of pristine purity, necessity forced Gorman to be indulgent. Many tracks were installing the film-patrol cameras to study the acrobatic activities of jockeys and horses in each race, but an expenditure was far beyond the limits of Gorman's budget. Although Gorman proclaimed stoutly that the saliva test would be enforced at his track, a search of the stable area at Blue Bonnets would have produced enough "joints" to provide electric street-lighting for the adjacent city of Lachine.

Unable to afford the salaries which were demanded by Stewards in other sections of the continent, Gorman installed friendly Montreal newspapermen in most of the official posts at Blue Bonnets. Gorman began his business life as a sports reporter on the Ottawa Citizen and, loyally, he never overlooked an opportunity to provide manna for his former colleagues in that underpaid profession. Coincidentally, while he was managing Blue Bonnets, Gorman also was general manager of the Montreal Canadiens in the National Hockey League. The Montreal Canadiens received excellent newspaper-coverage in the Gorman regime.

Several of the newspapermen whom Gorman appointed to official posts at Blue Bonnets were exceptionally competent racing observers and they performed their duties with commendable zeal. Others accepted their roles and their pay with wry cynicism.

My friend, Paul Parizeau, sports editor of *Le Canada,* occupied the post of patrol judge at the far turn, where the horses left the backstretch.

There was no telephonic communication between the patrol judges and the stewards' stand, and after one race Paul came hot-footing across the infield. When he was within hailing-distance of the stewards, he yelled: "I'd lodge a foul-claim against Number Seven."

After Parizeau had climbed the stairs of the stand and he was regaining his breath, the Presiding Steward demanded: "What's got into you, Paul You've been out on your patrol stand for three weeks and we never hear a peep out of you. Now, you want us to disqualify Number Seven."

"Well," gasped Parizeau, "Number Seven knocked Number Six right into the fence." Then he added indignantly: "Besides, I bet two dollars on Number Six."

Whether it was deserved or not, there was a widespread impression that there was considerable laxity in the officiating at Blue Bonnets when the judges' stand was occupied by sardonic newspapermen. I could vouch for the fact that a Blue Bonnets steward didn't scrutinize one particular race too carefully because, while the race was in progress, he and I were having a drink in the club house bar.

There was, perhaps, just a tinge of envy when horsemen who were racing at other Canadian centres spoke of Montreal's alleged permissiveness.

A dense fog shrouded the Woodbine track in Toronto one afternoon and I was standing on the Woodbine lawn with Gilbert Darlington, a friend who previously had raced his horses at Montreal.

The fog at Woodbine was so thick that it was impossible to see the racing horses until they were fifty feet from the finish-post. The possibilities for larceny were fantastic: a jockey could have racked up the entire field and the stewards couldn't have detected the foul.

"It's a shame to waste this fog on Toronto," said Darlington with a sigh. "If we could move this fog to Montreal, we could ruin every bookmaker in the country."

10

You Could Do Anything You Were Big Enough To Do

Before I got around to racing my father's horses and my own horses in Eastern Canada, there was to be a further period of indoctrination in the West. When the authorities at McGill University decreed that the completion of my education in medicine might imperil the entire Canadian community, I returned to our Winnipeg home in mild disgrace and, intent upon salvaging some parental respect, I was fortunate enough to get a job on the reportorial staff of the Winnipeg *Tribune*.

As a cub reporter, I worked a split-shift, serving as an over-eager errand boy for Victor Vereker Murray, the newspaper's distinguished police reporter and columnist. These working hours permitted me to renew my acquaintances at the race tracks during the early morning workouts, and I could escape from the police station each afternoon in time to see the last four or five races. It was this combination of personal interests which provided me with my first newspaper scoop.

On a warm summer evening, my second-hand green Ford touring car was parked on the open prairie south of Tuxedo, probably not more than two hundred yards from the spot where Whittier Park Slim administered a slight shot of hop to his companion's sparkless girl friend.

My companion of this occasion was a young lady upon whom I had evil designs but who always managed to thwart my advances. The young lady's father was the local partner in a firm of public accountants who audited the books of the

R. James Speers Corporation, which controlled the race tracks. Also, he was a close personal friend of Mr. Speers and he was a daily patron of the tracks, where he had access to all official secrets.

I was sitting behind the wheel, sulking because the young lady was being even less cooperative than the chaste Sabine women of legend, when she gave me a comradely nudge. "I heard something at the dinner table which may interest you," she said, smiling winsomely.

"Dad was telling Mother that a jockey at the track was caught carrying a battery today. Judge Schilling followed the boy to the jockeys' room after a race and found the battery hidden in the boy's right riding-boot. It's supposed to be a big secret because they don't want anything to get into the newspapers. The jockey's name is Brown."

All thoughts of romance forgotten, I dumped the young lady unceremoniously at the front door of her parents' home and I sped to the sports office of the *Tribune.* Although Judge Schilling at first was unwilling to talk, he capitulated when he realized that there had been a leak. He acknowledged that the facts were true, added essential details, and said that Jockey Billy Brown would be banned, thenceforth, from riding on any track in North America.

The next day, the *Tribune* carried an eight-column banner line on the first sports page, underneath which was a detailed story of the shameful conduct of Jockey Billy Brown. We scooped the pants off our rival publication, the Winnipeg *Free Press.*

For that feat of journalistic enterprise, I was awarded my first newspaper bonus: five dollars. The following winter, I bought the young lady a Ronson cigarette lighter as a Christmas gift. It cost me five dollars.

In the light of today's attitude, wherein racing associations go to great pains to publicize suspensions of jockeys and trainers who have committed various misdemeanours, it is interesting to re-examine the suspension of Jockey Billy Brown. If the Winnipeg *Tribune* hadn't stumbled on the story, Brown simply would have been shoved out of racing, very quietly, and the public never would have heard of him again. Back in the days of Jockey Brown, racing officials seldom if ever publicized suspensions in any but the most flagrant cases which had been easily discernible by the public.

Horse racing was endeavouring desperately to earn public approval in some of the more pious sections of this essentially Waspish continent and the track operators shrank from any suggestion of scandal. Accordingly, any racetracker caught in the act of cheating wasn't exorcised publicly. Simply, he was told privately to "pack his tack" and he disappeared, never to return to that particular city.

I watched thousands of races on Western Canadian tracks in my formative years and yet I can remember only one public disqualification of a winner. It occurred after a running of the Dominion Day Handicap at Whittier Park.

The favourite for the race was Rochester II, ridden by Buster McClair. Mr. Dutton started a two-horse entry of Shasta Rabbi and Shasta Sheik. As the field went into the final turn, Rochester II overtook the pace-setting Shasta Rabbi. Before they left the turn, Jockey Tod Leishman made his move on Shasta Sheik and he charged past Rochester II, on the outside.

As he saw the Dutton horse passing him, McClair reached out and grabbed Shasta Sheik's saddlecloth. Unknown to Leishman, Shasta Sheik was towing Rochester for approximately one hundred yards.

Suddenly, Leishman realized what was happening. Enraged, he stood upright in his irons and slashed McClair repeatedly over the head with his whip. They came to the finish line with Rochester winning by a short neck. The placing judges hung up Rochester II's number as the winner.

I had been sitting in Mr. Dutton's box. As the horses swept under the finish-wire, Mr. Dutton leaped to his feet and, with a surprising speed for a man of his age, he ran right across the track and stormed up the steps of the stewards' stand. His white moustache was bristling as he shouted his protest.

While the argument raged in the stewards' stand, Rochester II returned to the winners' circle and some innocent lady, who had been invited to preside at the customary stakes-race ceremony, placed a horseshoe of flowers over Rochester's neck. Mr. Dutton, who had descended from the stewards' stand, angrily snatched the flowered horseshoe from Rochester's neck, handed it to me, and ordered me to put it in his car in the club house parking lot.

I made the mistake of walking across the club house lawn, instead of taking a safer route along the race track. At that moment, the stewards were taking down Rochester's number and awarding the race to Shasta Sheik. Rochester II was disqualified into last place. Angry club house members, who had wagered on the disqualified favourite, ripped flowers out of the horseshoe as I scurried for the refuge of the parking lot. I don't believe that anyone was sufficiently ungentlemanly to aim a kick at me, but by then I was moving so swiftly that a tsetse fly couldn't have overtaken me.

Although I can remember him disqualifying only one horse in that early era, Judge George Washington Schilling was undoubtedly one of North America's most respected racing officials. There are horsemen still active who will tell you that Schilling wasn't merely an outstanding official – they insist that he was the greatest.

It was almost forty years after the Rochester II disqualification that I learned the secret of Judge Schilling's apparently tolerant reaction to foul riding. We were seatmates on a plane travelling between Vancouver and Edmonton.

"I had a personal rule," said the wise old judge, who at that time was still presiding at the Agua Caliente track at the age of eighty. "I gave every horseman – owner, trainer, jockey or groom – one free chance. The first time I caught them doing something, I warned them. If they tested my eyesight a second time, I told them to pack their tack.

"You've probably forgotten that Buster McClair never rode again after that Rochester II disqualification. That race was his second chance under my jurisdiction. In my time, I chased quite a few men and boys out of racing but it was a personal matter between them and me. I didn't want to give them a public black-mark, which might have deprived them of an opportunity to make a living in some other business. They knew that as long as they steered clear of the race tracks my lips were sealed."

George Schilling was the ideal man for his times. He could be supremely autocratic in his supervision of racing and he brooked no interference even from the track-owners, but he dispensed justice with mercy and compassion. He was born in San Francisco. In the houses on either side of his birthplace lived James J. Corbett, the former world heavyweight boxing champion, and T. A. "Tad" Dorgan, the celebrated newspaper cartoonist. Schilling knew every facet of human sportive frailty because he had been a San Francisco sportswriter and he managed a stable of prize-fighters before he became a racing official at Sunny Jim Coffroth's Tia Juana track in 1915. He ruled racing on the Western Canada prairies for thirty years and among his most formidable personal assets, which frequently proved embarrassing to touts and other renegades, was his photographic memory for faces, names and events.

He startled me, on our Vancouver-Edmonton plane trip, by saying abruptly: "You don't realize it but I have a pretty good past-performance book on you. You were the newspaper boy who broke that story about Billy Brown, in Winnipeg. Funny thing about Billy Brown: he was one youngster who couldn't get adjusted to life after I ruled him off at Winnipeg. A couple of years later, he came to me in San Diego and I got him a licence to work as an exercise-boy on tracks in California and Mexico, on the private understanding that he wouldn't re-apply for a jockey's licence.

"One morning, I was walking across the track from the steward's stand at Bay Meadows. A tractor was pulling a set of harrows down the track and I stood to let it pass. Because the tractor was making so much noise, I didn't know that Brown was working a horse along the inner rails. The boy saw me at the last instant and to avoid hitting me ran the horse right into the harrows. He damn nearly killed himself, but he may have saved my life."

That wasn't the only occasion on which death brushed George Schilling. He was sitting with another racing official in the front seat of their car at a track in the American south-west. A horseman who had been ruled off the previous day pulled out a gun and killed Schilling's seatmate with a single shot through the heart. Judge Schilling always promised admirers that he would write his racing memoirs, which would have rattled some skeletons, but he kept up such a pace throughout his lifetime that he never found the opportunity. He was on duty in the stewards' stand until three hours before he died in San Diego on August 14, 1969, at the age of eighty-three.

My scoop in the Billy Brown case was soon forgotten by the

editors of the Winnipeg *Tribune,* who despite my persistent wheedlings declined to move me into the sports department. With the blessing and relieved sighs of my parents speeding my departure, I moved to the Vancouver *Province* where, for the first time, I had the occasional opportunity to write about horse racing. Those opportunities were rare because the horse-racing beat was the exclusive property of Johnny Park, who wrote under the name of "The Little Colonel." Mr. Park's behaviour was at times slightly eccentric, and when he didn't turn up for work I was pressed into willing duty on the race track. Although this particular era wasn't the most prosperous in the history of B.C. tracks, it was certainly highlighted by an atmosphere of unbridled hilarity.

Bookmaking and bootlegging establishments were still running wide-open in Vancouver under the laissez-faire policies of Mayor Louis D. Taylor's civic administration. For that matter, there was generally no public stigmatization of the bookmaking profession in Western Canada. Tom Stone, who operated the Calgary Club, was a highly respected and warmly welcomed owner of thoroughbreds which raced over all western tracks. George Kendall, who handled the action of W. A. Dutton and other gambling-minded construction men in Winnipeg, raced his own horses under the name of the Scotia Stable and he was in charge of program sales at the Speers tracks.

Bookmaking was conducted with such engaging frankness in Vancouver that the larger operators banded together for mutual benefit under the unofficial name of "The Big Nine" and they took over a floor in one of Vancouver's principal office buildings near the city's main crossroads, the intersection of Granville and Georgia Streets. The Big Nine conducted their public business with all the decorum of a stockbroker's office. Their clients sat in comfortable chairs while they appraised the entries and results which were posted on wall-boards, in the manner of stock quotations. Whiskey was provided in case a well-regarded client suffered a mild relapse after blowing a $200-bet or, alternatively, in the event that a client wished to celebrate a victory. The Big Nine provided this whiskey, gratis, on the reasonable theory that alcohol stimulated a wagerer's enthusiasm.

The track operators viewed these bookmakers with mixed

feelings. The bookmakers, on a year-round basis, encouraged the practice of gambling among Canadians. Nevertheless, the track operators didn't wish to see the public betting with bookmakers while their own racing meetings were in progress – the track operators prospered only if that money was being wagered in their pari-mutuel machines.

No race track ever devised a foolproof scheme for stopping bookmaking, even on the track premises. The management of Vancouver's Lansdowne Park once hit upon the idea of providing two free boxes for the members of the Big Nine in the front row of the grandstand. They told the bookmakers that their presence was welcome as long as they would agree to sit in those two boxes, where they couldn't accept wagers from their wealthier clients who were in the habit of betting $100 or $200 on each race.

The Lansdowne management hired a Pinkerton detective named Morris Lane, who was given the job of supervising the two boxes, with strict instructions that the members of the Big Nine were not to be permitted to leave their seats.

Before each race, the bookmakers would make a few bets of their own. One would ask Lane to buy him a six-dollar combination on Number Five. Another would ask Lane to get him a five-dollar straight ticket on Number Four. Between them, they would give Lane money to buy tickets on five or six different horses.

The Pinkerton officer, who became pretty bored after spending a couple of afternoons standing watchfully behind the two boxes, accepted these betting assignments gratefully.

The bookmakers gave Lane bets of so many different denominations that it was necessary for him to spend five or ten minutes in the pari-mutuel department completing his transactions.

Naturally, as soon as they saw Lane disappear from his post of surveillance, the regular clients of The Big Nine would walk slowly past the two boxes, making their verbal bets in passing. The Lansdowne Park management abandoned the unequal struggle. There was no way that they could force the bookmakers to wear soundproof ear-muffs.

The usual concomitant of gambling is drinking, and Vancouver abounded in joints where, quite illegally, a thirsty wayfarer could obtain a glass of excellent spirits for thirty-five cents. A few of these establishments posed coyly as "clubs" but most were merely houses on downtown streets where the only requirement for admission was the strength to knock loudly on the front door.

It was in one of these booze-cans that I first met Jack Allen, the fight-promoter whose escapades were to intrigue me for the next thirty years. Allen, whose grave demeanour earned him the nickname "The Deacon," had begun his lawless career as business agent for a circus acrobat, The Great Herman. Making his debut as a manager, Allen booked The Great Herman into an open-air at Fresno, California. After their closing performance of the week, Allen was collecting the acrobat's tights and putting them into a suitcase. Then he went to the box-office to pick up their pay. The Great Herman had beaten him to the punch – The Great Herman had collected all their money and he had disappeared into the night, leaving Allen with his performer's tights and a two-dollar cardboard suitcase.

"That taught me an important lesson," Allen said years later. "Never get hooked up with anyone who can outrun you to the box-office." Recovering from that initial disaster, Allen became a bootlegger and occasional confidence-man in Skagway, Alaska, and he drifted into Vancouver as a manager of pugilists and a promoter of many ill-fated pugilistic extravaganzas. Vancouver, for twenty years, was the launching-pad from which he rocketed into New York's Madison Square Garden and, finally, he rebounded into the Walsingham Hotel in Toronto, where he spent his declining years, always dreaming of signing up a heavyweight who would win the world championship.

Deacon Allen had owned one of these Vancouver gambling-and-drinking clubs, but he had closed it before I met him. "It was a good money-maker but it was too hard on the health", he explained. "With all that drinking and gambling, I found that I was refereeing too many impromptu fights among my customers. One day, I just turned the key in the lock; I walked halfway across Granville Street Bridge and I threw the key into False Creek."

It was through Allen that, wide-eyed, I met Paddy Sullivan, another famous unlicensed publican. Paddy was renegade brother of John L. Sullivan, who later became United States

Secretary of Commerce in one of President Harry Truman's cabinets.

Paddy operated a club above a Granville Street restaurant, directly across the road from the original Vancouver Hotel. He was positively immune to the daily and nightly tumult in his joint. To maintain his reason, he concocted elaborate practical jokes with which he victimized the more pestiferous of his patrons.

One of the most irritating customers was a man named McCoy, a terrible-tempered Irishman whose fights with his wife were reputed to be considerably more stirring than some of the main events which Deacon Allen promoted in the Vancouver Auditorium.

McCoy arrived at Paddy Sullivan's poker table on a wet winter day. His angry countenance indicated all too clearly that he had come directly from his home after a noisy bout with his termagant wife. Sullivan took one look at McCoy and he went into his private office at one end of the club. Closing the door, Sullivan put in a telephone call to a baggage delivery company.

Mrs. McCoy had just recovered a modicum of composure after the violent family argument when a driver for the baggage delivery company knocked at her door. Reading from the notes on his order sheet, the driver blandly informed Mrs. McCoy: "Mr. McCoy has sent for his trunk – and ALL his clothes."

Mrs. McCoy erupted in Vesuvian splendour. She dragged McCoy's trunk out of a cupboard. She ripped his suits off the hangers and she hurled them into the trunk. She dumped his shirts, ties, underwear and socks atop the crumpled suits and slammed the lid. All the while, the patient baggageman was listening to some exceptionally unladylike language.

Half an hour later, McCoy was playing poker in Paddy Sullivan's club. His blood-pressure had subsided appreciably.

The baggageman lumbered up the stairs, hauling the trunk. Sullivan, who was awaiting his arrival, pointed to McCoy, who was engrossed in the card game.

"Mr. McCoy," said the baggageman, dumping the trunk on the floor beside the unsuspecting card-player, "your wife said to deliver your trunk – and ALL your clothes!"

McCoy dumped the poker table upside down when he

leaped to his feet, screaming with rage. He raced out of the place, cursing Mrs. McCoy and her ancestors unto the third and fourth generations and threatening dire reprisals. When McCoy finally discovered who had perpetrated the gruesome jape, he never set foot again in Paddy Sullivan's raffish establishment. Which, of course, had been a pleasant possibility which had flashed through Paddy's mind.

Vancouver, like Montreal, was a lotus land for an irresponsible and impressionable young newspaper reporter who was developing a thirst to complement his preoccupation with horses. With pre-race information which was provided for me by some of the prairie horsemen-friends of my childhood who had gravitated to Vancouver, I was tempted frequently to gamble far beyond my modest means. But God protects fools. I started downtown one afternoon, carrying forty dollars in my pocket. I was bound for the real estate agent's office to pay my forty-dollar monthly rent. Yielding to a perverse impulse, I stayed aboard the street car when it passed the real estate agent's office. The same street car carried me all the way to Hastings Park.

Heedless of any consequences, I walked into the race track waited until the afternoon's fifth race and bet the rent money on a nice little mare named Lady Gold.

She won and she paid $11.45.

Mind you, I "knew something." Lady Gold was owned by Jack Cole, with whom I had become friendly in my short-pants days in Winnipeg. Cole came to Winnipeg one summer; he was down on his racing luck and Frank Marks, the food-concessionaire on the tracks, gave him a job selling peanuts. Every afternoon, I bought peanuts from Jack Cole and we talked about horses. So, a few days before that race at Hastings Park, Cole had advised me to "have a little bet on my mare, the next time that you see her name in the entries."

The next morning, I paid my forty-dollar rent and I still had plenty of walking-around money. The next time that I went to the track, I confined myself to a total investment of four dollars.

At that time, they had two daily-doubles each afternoon. They had a daily-double on the first and second races and another double on the sixth and seventh races.

Before the first race, I bet two dollars on the combination of Margery Daw and Craiglee. Both horses won and the daily-double paid $26.40. I waited until the sixth race and I bet two dollars on the daily-double combination of Ynomis and Streamline. Again, both my horses won and the combination paid $486.50. I walked out of the track that night, radiating the affiuence of John D. Rockefeller as I kept my right hand in my trouser pocket, tenderly caressing fifty-one $10 bills. When you're working as a $40-a-week newspaper reporter, $510 buys a heap of groceries.

The irony of the situation didn't escape me. I was just lucky – I had a pocketful of money, only because I had remained glued to my streetcar seat when the train passed the real estate office, a few days earlier. Ah – a gambler remembers only his "hits." I'd like to have a dollar for every day in the intervening years when I've walked out of a race track, broke and dispirited.

Until I reached Vancouver, I had wondered, frequently, how the bottom strata of the race track fraternity – the grooms, the exercise boys and the hot-walkers – managed to maintain even a modicum of personal cleanliness. To be truthful, few of the ginnies seemed to change their clothing with any regularity. The ablutionary facilities on most tracks were primitive. There were a few privies or water closets but showerbaths were a rarity and bathtubs were non-existent. In the mornings you'd see the stablehands, stripped to the waist as they washed in tubs of water which had been heated over open fires beside the shedrows. Personal cleanliness was not regarded as a cardinal virtue among the lowly hot-walkers, and when two or three of them gathered around the same table in the track kitchen after wearing the same old dungarees and cardigan jerseys for a week or ten days, the combined aroma of horse manure and human sweat could be quite interesting.

It was The Flea who told me about the public steambaths in Vancouver. In the depression years, there were many of these steambaths in Vancouver – Swedish-type baths where cold water was sprayed on heated bricks. Friday was bath-night for Vancouver grooms, hot-walkers and exercise boys. They would repair to one of these bath-houses where $1.50 gave them access to a tiny cubicle with two cots. Any racetracker who was fortunate enough to have a compliant girl-friend would take her with him and they would sign the register solemnly as "Mr. & Mrs. Smith". The cashiers who issued the room-keys were world-weary dropouts who never bothered to examine the names in the register. Thus, for an outlay of three dollars a racetracker could hit the daily-double: shining cleanliness combined with healthy human diversion. Naturally, I investigated the steambath situation personally. They were everything that The Flea claimed for them.

The Flea's real name was Sidney Mole. He bitterly resented his nickname and he preferred to be addressed as Professor Mole or Sir Sidney. He was one of those characters who, somehow, become unofficial functionaries in race track press boxes. He ran errands for Massie White, who compiled the form-charts of each race, and he bolstered his income by engaging in a bit of discreet touting with two lively friends named Yum-Yum and Noodles. The Flea had been born within the sound of Bow Bells and his conversations were conducted in the perpetually plaintive and indignant accents of his birthplace.

The Flea was idiosyncratic in the matter of tea. On Sundays, many of us who weren't satisfied with only six days of weekly racing in Vancouver would clamber into automobiles and drive to the Longacres track, where they conducted Sunday racing in the neighbouring state of Washington. The Flea, who always joined in these jaunts, would be standing outside his Granville Street rooming house each Sunday morning, waiting to be picked up by one of the Seattle-bound cars. In one hand, he would be carrying a small paper bag.

In that bag would be sufficient English tea to sustain him through a day in U.S. territory. He insisted loudly that while Americans might be otherwise estimable human beings they didn't know a damn think about brewing a decent cup of tea.

All Vancouver racetrackers looked forward to the annual meetings at the Colwood and Willows tracks on Vancouver Island. Racing in Vancouver they regarded as a business, but the late-season weeks in Victoria were regarded as a sporting holiday. The purses in Victoria were small; the officiating was rather casual; the horsemen usually left their wives behind in Vancouver and everyone made the eighty-mile voyage across the inland sea with the express purpose of having a hell of a good time.

The overnight voyage from Vancouver to Victoria was an annual travelling carnival. Horses, men and tack were loaded aboard the C.P.R. night-boat which sailed from Pier D at the foot of Granville Street. There was little or no sleep for civilian passengers who committed the error of booking passage on that particular crossing.

Before the ship slipped its moorings, a crap game was in roaring progress. It was a very democratic crap game. Dr. W. J. McKeon, who became presiding steward at all the B.C. tracks, would be kneeling on the floor between two ginnies, vociferously demanding his turn with the dice. The ship sailed shortly before midnight and, travelling only at half-speed so that the revolutions of its twin propellors wouldn't disturb those passengers who were slumbering, it took six hours to travel through the inland passages to Victoria. The crap game usually continued until it was time to unload the horses at Victoria.

On one historic return-trip, at the conclusion of the Victoria race meetings, the usual crap game was terminated abruptly by a bloody altercation involving a trainer, Bill Canning and a groom named Bottles.

Bottles made three successive passes and Canning accused him of sneaking a pair of loaded-dice into the game.

Bottles was a man given to violent actions when his honesty was impugned. Pulling a knife out of his pocket, he carved up Canning with vigour and despatch. As a matter of fact, he put eleven holes in Canning before the ship's master-at-arms and some horseman, who had recovered their courage, succeeded in disarming him. The ship already had sailed from Victoria but, the Captain put back into port where an ambulance was waiting for Canning and the Royal Canadian Mounted Police were waiting for Bottles. Canning survived his hospitalization and Bottles survived his incarceration but, thereafter, he was denied the privileges of the race course and deported to the United States.

The favourite Victoria stopping-places for the horse racing set were the Strathcona Hotel and the Westholme Hotel. The partying was constant when the racetrackers were in residence in those two hostelries and only the sturdy and the brave among the visitors survived the prolonged wassailing with reasonably unimpaired health.

The Flea never was much of a drinker but he was a gregarious soul and dearly loved a party. Among his other accomplishments, he was a virtuoso harmonicist and no social gathering of the horsemen was considered to be truly a success until Professor Mole had made his appearance with his mouth organ.

The Flea arrived at a party in a suite in the Strathcona Hotel, escorting his current inamorata, a lady who worked in a Victoria steam-laundry. A particularly cosmopolitan group had gathered that evening. Deacon Jack Allen had come over from Vancouver to stage one of his fight-shows in the Tillicums' Hall and he arrived in the suite at the Strathcona late that night, accompanied by some of his alleged pugilists. Since it had been a poor night at the ticket-office in the Tillicums' Hall, the gladiators hadn't received very handsome purses for their evening's pummelling and they were hungry and thirsty. Scarcely waiting for an invitation, they plunged into the food and liquor with which the horsemen had stocked the suite.

Meanwhile, The Flea was sitting on the floor in one corner of the room, playing his harmonica softly as he serenaded the siren of the steam-laundry. The lady was enchanted – she sat in a chair, her hands folded in her ample lap, a blissful smile on her well-scrubbed countenance as she exuded soapy purity.

One of Deacon Allen's pugilists, who had dumped too much liquor into an empty stomach, rocked on his heels as he looked down on The Flea and the lady from the steam-laundry. The pugilist wasn't very bright – he bore a faint resemblance to Peter Lorre made up for one of his supporting roles in a Dracula film.

The pugilist tottered over to Deacon Allen and he extricated a conductor's ticket-puncher from Allen's jacket pocket. Allen, who was pouring a drink, didn't pay any attention to the pocket-picking. Allen had used the punching device at his fight show, to punch holes in the free tickets which he issued to newspaper reporters and civic officials, who always expected to be admitted to athletic events without charge.

The drunken fighter lurched back to the corner where The Flea still was serenading his inamorata. The Flea was engrossed completely in his music. The fighter carefully reached out with the ticket-puncher and, deliberately, clipped a hole clean through the soft lobe of Professor Mole's right ear.

Howling in pain and surprise, The Flea jumped to his feet. He raised his harmonica – which was almost as long as a cricket bat – and whacked the drunken pugilist on the top of the skull. The fighter slumped to the floor, unconscious.

The noise in the suite stopped abruptly, as the celebrants looked around in stunned surprise. Deacon Allen, slightly glassy-eyed, walked over and peered at the pugilist who, with a large lump beginning to protrude from his hair, was out like a busted light.

"This bum is a born loser," said The Deacon, his vision clearing sufficiently for him to recognize the body. "That's the SECOND time tonight that he has been knocked out."

11

Gentlemen of the Press

With the notable exceptions of Toronto and Vancouver, few daily newspapers in Canadian cities have employed full-time horse racing reporters. Surveying the possibilities early in my newspaper career, I realized quickly that the field of racing writers was filled to capacity, and the incumbent typewriter-thrashers were all vigorously healthy men who appeared quite capable of surviving for many more years. Squeezed out of contention by the established reputations of my older colleagues, I coveted and finally was given a job as a general sports columnist which provided me with journalistic leeway to write occasionally about horses and horsemen.

In the prairie provinces, the only man who wrote about horses on a year-round basis was Henry Louis Davies and, properly speaking, he wasn't a newspaperman. Actually, he published the past-performance programs which were sold daily on the tracks and he acted as a publicist for the R. James Speers organization. He made racing selections for daily newspapers in Winnipeg, Calgary, Edmonton, Saskatoon and Regina under the pseudonym of "Yorkshire Lad," and when the horses came to town he provided local newspapermen with most of their information about horses. He enjoyed a rare rapport with all sports reporters on the prairies and they leaned on him heavily. His encyclopedic knowledge of racing led him reluctantly into the managerial area and, after the death of

R. James Speers, he became general manager of the Western Canadian Racing Association.

It was his youthful passion for gambling which lured Lou Davies into horse racing. He was born in Montreal, where his father, Llewelyn Davies, was president of the Caverhill-Learmouth Company. His father first took him to the races at King Edward Park on Ile Gros Bois in 1917 and Lou became hooked almost instantaneously.

Eight years later, he was returning to Montreal from Ottawa on the evening train after scoring a modest coup on a horse named Drummond in the final race of the afternoon at Connaught Park. A gentleman who introduced himself as Herb Lister sat opposite him in the train's dining car. They talked about horses and Lister revealed that he had copyrighted the past-performance program which was about to be introduced to western tracks. Impressed by Davies' enthusiasm for racing, Lister offered him a job before they had finished their meal. Lou demurred, but a year later, when Davies won $1,500 in a Montreal crap game, he happened to bump into Lister again. Feeling uncommonly flush, Davies decided to accept Lister's repeated offer and he went out to Western Canada in 1926. He spent the next forty-five years of his racing-life on the prairies.

Until he was tapped for managerial duties, "Yorkshire Lad" was a bon vivant who spent much of his time with the heavy drinkers of the sports-writing profession. He gambled heavily, consistently, and with considerable success. When he was working at it, he was one of the best professional handicappers ever to walk onto a Canadian race track.

He lived handsomely when he was on the road, always staying at the best hotels, always eating at the best restaurants. Newspapermen who were fortunate enough to share his quarters on those trips still remember one of Lou's unfailing rituals. Before going to sleep at night in his hotel, he would telephone the room-service department and order a lavish breakfast for 8 a.m. Then he would instruct the hotel telephone operator to give him a wake-up call at 7:45 a.m.

When the phone rang in the morning, Lou would jump out of bed briskly and go to the bureau on which he had arrayed a bottle of gin, sugar, lemon juice, soda water and a few ice cubes which had survived the night without melting completely. Davies would mix two Tom Collinses, hand one of the drinks to his room-mate, and keep the other drink for himself.

Then he would get back into bed after re-arranging the pillows so that he could sit upright. As he awaited the arrival of the waiter with his breakfast, he would lift his glass high and toast the new day with the sardonic question: "Well, I wonder what the POOR people are doing?" The morning toast was an exercise in wry self-mockery. No one knew better than he the truth of the old racetrack adage: "All hoss-players must die broke."

Davies was a shrewd gambler who operated on a theory of controlled-losses. His personal gambling maxim was: "never lose more today than you can win back tomorrow."

Between his program-sales and his gambling, Lou usually saved enough cash during the five-month prairie racing season to keep him in comfort for the other seven months of the year. He and his wife, Carrie, maintained an apartment in Winnipeg, but customarily they wintered in Florida where Davies' genius as a handicapper paid their expenses. During World War II, when the U.S. Government ordered the cancellation of winter-racing in Florida and California, Lou permitted himself to be talked into going to Mexico City, to manage the local edition of the *Daily Racing Form* for one winter. Racing was new to the Mexico City area – the inaugural meeting at Hipodromo de Las Americas opened on March 6, 1943.

Lou selected horses for the *Daily Racing Form,* employing the pseudonym of "Sweep," and he was sitting in the office after the opening day's program congratulating himself on the fact that he had picked four winners in the paper. Without ceremony, two men burst through the door of his office and one of them demanded: "Are you *Señor* Sweep?"

"Indeed, I am, *señores,*" said Davies, preening slightly, under the impression that his visitors wished to congratulate him on his four-win performance.

"*Señor* Sweep," said one of the visitors, pulling a 38-calibre *pistola* from his pocket and tapping it significantly on the desk, "tomorrow, we will expect you to pick all seven winners!"

Señor Sweep decided, there and then, to assign the daily race-selections to his assistant, who was a Mexican national.

One winter in Mexico City was quite enough for Lou Davies who, although he still takes off-season holiday junkets to warm southern climes, never includes Mexico in his vacation itinerary.

When I arrived on the Vancouver scene, Alf Cottrell was the handicapper for the *Sun* and Wallace Kelk, a frail, deaf, genteel Englishman was writing for the morning newspaper which, struggling through the beginning of the worldwide depression, changed its name from the *News* to the *News-Herald*. The senior Vancouver turf writer was Johnny Park, the estimable and colourful Little Colonel, who presided at the *Province*.

As his nickname suggested, Johnny Park wasn't any taller than the average hundred-pound jockey, but years of sedentary occupation at the card tables had provided him with aldermanic contours. As far as gambling was concerned, he was an all-round athlete: he was a fantastically deft performer on the pool-tables or the billiard-tables; he had few peers as a poker player although his forte was actually contract bridge; he was a canny racing handicapper and he was equipped with an alcoholic thirst which encompassed all his activities. Even in his later years he had a round, smooth-skinned face which gave him an expression of childlike innocence, but behind that serenely cherubic countenance lurked the soul of a merry con-man.

As a matter of fact, the Little Colonel began his business career as an associate of two confidence-men. When he was barely out of his teens, Johnny already had won a reputation as the most promising young billiards-and-pool player ever to appear in Vancouver up until that date. Pool-hustling always has been one of the great skin-games of North America and the two con-men, who watched Park in action on the green baize-covered tables, hit upon a glorious enterprise.

Although he was almost twenty, the baby-faced Park didn't look any older than twelve or thirteen. So his two "managers" outfitted him in short pants, an Eton jacket and a stiff Eton collar with a fluffy bow-tie, and took him on tour of some unsophisticated towns.

Their technique was simple: They would prowl around the town pool hall, carefully setting up the take-off. They would promote a betting argument with the local pool champion and then they would insult him with the clincher: "You're no pool-player! We'll bet that this little kid in the Eton jacket can spot you ten points and whip you!"

The bets would be made. The local citizenry naturally would be eager to bet on their local champion. The Little Colonel, climbing on an apple-box to make his first few deliberately sloppy shots, would annihilate his bewildered opponent. The trio managed to clean out quite a few towns before the stories of "the little kid in the Eton jacket" received such wide circulation that Park decided that it would be wise to hang up his cue before some indignant opponent broke it over his skull.

The circumstances of his first employment on the Vancouver *Province* have been lost in the mists of antiquity, but certainly he was on the sports staff of that paper as early as 1912. His hole-card was Roy Brown, the non-drinking, non-smoking, non-gambling editor of the *Province*. Brown was one of those peculiar puritans who countenanced the presence of quite a few notable libertines on the newspaper's staff. Johnny Park made several excursions into the outer world, working as the chart-caller at the B.C. race tracks, engaging in a spot of bookmaking and other mildly lawless business enterprises, but invariably when John had worked himself into a financial cul-de-sac Roy Brown would rescue him and re-establish him on the staff of the *Province*. It was a relationship which mystified young reporters who, upon being granted employment, had been warned that immoderate use of alcohol was sufficient cause for immediate dismissal.

In my early years on the *Province,* after the racing season was concluded, Johnny spent the winters as night editor. Since the *Province* was an afternoon paper, this was not an arduous job and Park never exceeded his terms-of-reference for the position. He did very little editing; to the contrary, he did a considerable amount of entertaining around the horseshoe news-desk after midnight. He would summon three of his bridge-playing friends, one of whom was a prominent physician and another of whom was a construction tycoon, and he would order a couple of bottles of rye from a taxi company which engaged in bootlegging.

It was on this lobster shift, after his bridge players had decamped but a good portion of the rye still sloshed in the bottles, that Park regaled me with many of the details of his earlier gambling years. He had been, by his own admission, a very fast man with a buck.

He told me more than once of the afternoon at Willows Park when he ran a successful six-horse parlay. Gamblers dream of performing such a betting feat, but for most a six-horse parlay is as elusive as quicksilver.

Park was the chart-caller at Willows Park and before climbing to his tiny hut on the roof of the grandstand he carefully wrote down his personal selections for the afternoon's seven races. His clerk was Harry Harradene, whose name was truncated into "Harry Dean" by the racing fraternity. "Let's each put in a buck and bet on my selections. I feel hot today," Park said to his clerk, about twenty minutes before the first race.

Harry Dean obediently put a dollar in the pot and clambered down the ladder from the roof into the grandstand to purchase a two-dollar win-ticket.

The first horse won. "What'll we do now?" asked Harradene.

"Cash the ticket and bet the works on my horse in the second race," the Little Colonel commanded. Again, Dean went down the ladder and fulfilled the betting instructions.

As usual, the Little Colonel had carried a couple of bottles of rye to his rooftop aerie and he was nibbling judiciously.

After four races had been run, they had cashed four successive bets and Harradene was beginning to worry. "We have quite a bundle of money, John," he said nervously. "Shouldn't we pull up?"

"Let it roll," thundered the Little Colonel, who had lowered the level in one bottle of rye to an impressive degree and was feeling no pain.

Parks' horses won the fifth and sixth races. Harradene was weary from climbing up and down the ladder and the wad of money in his pocket was causing him to sweat. "We have more than $1,300, John," he pleaded, after cashing their tickets on the sixth winner. "Let's quit!"

"Piker!" roared Park, who was quite drunk by that time. "Bet the whole bundle on my horse in the last race. This is the biggest cinch of the entire afternoon."

Their horse didn't win the seventh race – he didn't even finish in the money. They blew the entire $1,300.

Talking about it, years later, the Little Colonel added an epitaph. "The thing that really burned Harry Dean," he said, "was that I wouldn't let him drag down his original one-dollar investment from the pot."

Johnny Park's ability to survive financial setbacks and the strictures of a succession of strait-laced managing editors was extraordinary. Aware of his nocturnal excesses, one or two of those managing editors switched him to day-jobs on the sports desk, threatening to fire him if he didn't turn up for work at 8 a.m. The Little Colonel was the first man of my youthful acquaintance – although, he certainly wasn't to be the last – who restored his tissues and his personal appearance by paying an early-morning visit to one of those barber shops where the white-haired proprietor combined the skills of tonsorialist, masseur and physician.

The Little Colonel would ease himself into the chair and the barber would spend the next fifty-five minutes shaving, combing, applying hot towels, administering occasional whiffs of smelling-salts and massaging the ailing racing editor with electric ticklers. The barber performed daily miracles of restoration.

Precisely at 8 a.m., Johnny Park would walk through the door of the newspaper's editorial department – powdered, pale and weak, but outwardly jaunty.

He began his newspapering on the *Province,* and although he broke his service frequently in the early days when he was aware that Roy Brown always would re-employ him, he was still active as the paper's official racing handicapper until 1959 when death finally overtook him. I last saw him at the Santa Anita winter meeting at Arcadia, California, in 1957. He had long since abandoned drinking, which he described sententiously as "a vastly over-rated sport." He was suffering from emphysema, albeit the distress of this disease did not prevent him from staying up all night playing cards. On that particular occasion he had been imported to California as a bridge-partner by one of those Vancouver construction magnates with whom he shrewdly associated himself. The Little Colonel confided to me that the construction magnate was paying the costs of their California vacation. Knowing that Johnny Park's skill with cards hadn't been impaired by the ravages of emphysema, I feel reasonably confident that Johnny's host and bridge-partner had a profitable holiday.

Toronto is the repository of horse racing's sturdiest traditions in Canada and as a consequence racing writers in that city have enjoyed a position of prominence in the daily newspaper profession. The racing beat was eyed with envy by other reporters, but once ensconced in the lotus land of sports-coverage the racing writer was seldom willing to be shifted to other editorial duties.

The two most durable and entertaining personalities among Toronto's many celebrated racing writers were Joe Perlove, of the *Star,* and Charlie Oliver, who wrote about horses for many years on the morning *Globe and Mail* under the improbable pen-name of Appas Tappas.

It would have been difficult to find two more dissimilar scribes working in any press box. Perlove was brash, extroverted and noisily convivial. Oliver was shy, introverted and sad-faced. Actually, Charlie had a merry heart, but he hid it behind a façade of lugubrious dolour.

Perlove was a hedonist, reckless with money, and he wagered as if he were the reincarnation of Bet-A-Million John Gates. Oliver was a cautious family-man, worrying continually over his debts, and when he bet his two dollars on a horse he did it with all the enthusiasm of a man putting his hand into a fiery furnace.

Oliver was a digger, conscientiously attending the morning workouts, painstakingly running-down stories and then writing them laboriously and fretfully. Perlove seldom bothered to move more than one hundred yards from the club house bar in search of a story. He relied upon publicity-conscious horsemen to seek him out, and this they did. He was easy to find – he would always be in the middle of the largest, noisiest group in the club house. And whereas Charlie Oliver sweated over his daily compositions, Joe wrote his stories carelessly and at breakneck speed. They had one thing in common – both were the bane of their sports editors' lives: Perlove because he cared not a whit for details, Oliver because his tortuous prose became so involved with detail that, occasionally, it defied editing.

Perlove was regarded initially as something of a curiosity

among his Toronto sports-writing colleagues, because he had been enrolled at the University of Toronto. However, he majored in squash and snooker at the university and he never permitted his exposure to the hall of learning to inhibit his dashing literary style.

After winning the University of Toronto snooker championship, Joe obtained employment in his father's cap factory on Spadina Avenue. He insisted always that he had been a cap-cutter, but any of Perlove's friends who later became aware of his complete lack of manual dexterity scoffed at the suggestion that even the most indulgent of fathers would permit Perlove to attack a piece of valuable cloth with a pair of scissors.

From the cap factory it was only a short jump to the daily newspaper, although he took a cut in pay to become a sports writer. The *Star* was notorious in that period for its turnover in personnel as new managing editors ruthlessly wielded the hatchet, but Perlove defied destruction.

Through sheer force of personality, Joe Perlove dominated the other writers on the Toronto racing beat throughout his lengthy and tumultuous association with the *Star*. He was a charming, immaculately groomed man and he sported a neatly trimmed moustache which, in company with the hairs on his head, became prematurely grey and then turned snow white when he was fifty. Always he wore expensive suits, dark blue or grey, and apart from his betting his one major personal extravagance was his wardrobe.

When he and I first became close friends Joe was married, but his wife, a very pretty lady, eventually became discouraged by his irresponsibility. When Joe wasn't at the races, he was out with his friends in the gambling-and-bookmaking fraternity playing stush, gin-rummy or pinochle. His wife divorced him and went home to live with her mother.

Without breaking stride, Perlove resumed the life of a gay bachelor, a role which suited him admirably, and thereafter he referred to his conservative wife and mother-in-law as McDougall & Brown, the name of an illustrious Toronto undertaking establishment.

In the final fifteen years of his life, a Perlove cult became apparent in the club houses on the Toronto tracks. He was a colourful raconteur, a wit, and laughter bubbled easily from him. Women found his company irrestible, even when he reached the age at which he treated them with avuncular courtesy. Each afternoon he was surrounded at his table in the bar by his salon of ladies, horsemen and younger reporters who hung on his words.

Joe dominated most conversations with a powerful voice. After a few drinks, his voice rattled glasses. A few of his intimates referred to him affectionately as "The Screamer." When Perlove fancied a horse's chances, he didn't merely speak about the possibilities of victory – he declaimed! In genially lordly fashion, he destroyed the arguments of anyone who questioned his judgement.

When Perlove was absolutely positive in one of his horsey assertions, his wiser friends ran from his presence before he overpowered them with his eloquence. Joe could be dead wrong; much oftener when he was right. Nevertheless, when one of his sure things was beaten, he regarded the result of the race as a horrendous upset, an unkind whim of the fates.

Dr. R. K. Hodgson, a widely respected veterinarian who trained horses, died and a group of reporters, headed by Perlove, left the Press Club to attend the funeral services, which were being held in a little church in rural Todmorden. No one was quite such where the church was – no one except Perlove!

"Just go the way I tell you," commanded Perlove, as he climbed into the front seat of a car, driven by one of our colleagues. Perlove refused to learn how to drive a car himself. He said that it would interfere with his drinking.

With Perlove shouting commands, the car twisted and turned along country roads. Eventually, the car reached a country church and Perlove led the group into the rear of the church. They sat down quietly, because the funeral service was already in progress.

They were jolted out of their personal reveries when, after five minutes of episcopalian prayers, the clergyman unmistakably used the words: ". . . our dear departed sister."

Perlove had given them another bum tip. He had guided them to the wrong church and the wrong funeral service.

When his own time came, Joe Perlove philosophically accepted the inevitable. For a year he knew that he was doomed by cancer, but the Perlove Cult still gathered in the racetrack club house bar each afternoon; he didn't drink; the laughter still tinkled around him; his old friends pretended that all was well.

Even when they dragged him off to Mount Sinai Hospital, where drugs could be administered to ease his pain, he was a debonair patient who was usually surrounded by nurses from other wards who dropped into his private room to bask in the radiance of that overwhelming personality. The only occasion on which he dropped his guard and acknowledged slight depression was the afternoon when the Mount Sinai officials informed him that they must send him to Riverdale Hospital because they required his room for "sicker patients."

The handwriting was on the wall. Cancer patients in the terminal stages of the disease are often transferred to Riverdale Hospital. Joe knew very well why he was being sent to Riverdale, but as usual the ultimatum provided him with the opportunity for a quip.

"You know that I have to go to Riverdale, and I know that I have to go to Riverdale," he said to Ray Timson, a Toronto *Star* sub-editor who had been sitting beside his bed. "But I don't WANT to go to Riverdale Hospital – because it's a very bad address."

On the afternoon he died in Riverdale Hospital, he wrote his will on a paper napkin which had been brought to him on his last luncheon tray. The nurse who was with him said that he insisted on writing it himself with a ballpoint pen before he lapsed into his final unconsciousness.

When he had finished, he told the nurse to give the paper napkin to his son-in-law and, satisfied, he closed his eyes. For a man who lived as Joe Perlove lived, the last words he wrote were his most poignant: ". . . I'm sorry that I can't stay."

Charlie Oliver's newspapering background was much more solid than Joe Perlove's. Charlie had been an office boy on the old Toronto *World* and rose to the eminence of police reporter on the Toronto *Globe*. There are long-memoried pensioners who insist that Charlie Oliver was the best police reporter in the history of Toronto journalism. To augment his meagre newspaper income, Oliver spent his afternoons working in the pari-mutuel department at Toronto race tracks, after which he would go to the police station to cover the crime-

and-accident beat for his morning paper. It was a gruelling daily schedule but Charlie had a wife and three growing sons to whom he was devoted.

When the *Globe* was amalgamated with the *Mail & Empire* under the new sports-minded ownership of George McCullagh, the racing writer for the amalgam was Douglas Eppes. After a lingering illness, Eppes died and Charlie Oliver was impressed into double-duty as racing columnist and police reporter. He occupied that dual position for fifteen years until a belatedly enlightened management decreed that he should devote himself exclusively to horse racing. Charlie, who enjoyed a persecution complex, professed to be unhappy on the racing beat and complained that he was losing his carefully nurtured contacts at the police station. When his failing eyesight and health impelled the compassionate newspaper management to recall him from the racetrack and they installed him in a little office where he continued to make his daily racing selections, he complained, again, that the newspaper deliberately was destroying the news sources which over the years he had developed in the shedrows. Charlie made an interesting career of personal chagrin.

Really, he had no reason to worry on either score. Long after he had left the police station, veteran law-enforcement officers who were in possession of newsworthy intelligence would telephone the *Globe and Mail* and demand to speak to Charlie Oliver. They would give their scoops to him alone: they declined to speak to younger reporters. Similarly, after he left the race tracks, horsemen still telephoned him when any important story was about to break in the equine world.

Appas Tappas insisted that he had been born under an unlucky star. Colleagues who delighted in Charlie's wryly comic daily descriptions of his personal betting misadventures were prepared to admit that he was, at least, accident-prone.

Charlie accompanied Jim Speers to Col. Sam McLaughlin's Oshawa estate to inspect a stallion named Blen Eagle which Col. McLaughlin proposed to present to Speers for shipment to the Speers breeding establishment near Winnipeg. It was one of those cases where Speers, who believed in obtaining the best possible publicity for racing, had telephoned Appas Tappas giving him an advance tip on the story. Because of its national morning circulation, horsemen always regarded the *Globe and Mail* as "the" racing paper.

Charlie, who never completely lost his awe of wealth, had dressed in his best blue suit and a new pearl-grey fedora hat for his meeting with the mighty men of the racing establishment.

The three men were standing in a grassy paddock at Oshawa, appraising Blen Eagle's conformation, when a large seagull flew overhead. The seagull took dead-aim on Appas Tappas and unloaded from a height of fifty feet. The seagull scored a direct hit. It was a high-explosive bomb which the seagull dropped, and not only did it ruin Charlie's new hat but Charlie's blue suit also felt the impact.

Returning to the *Globe and Mail* office in lamentable disarray, Charlie moaned to sympathetic colleagues: "I'm standing there with two millionaires and that gawddam seagull has to pick on me, in my only good blue suit."

Joe Perlove and Appas Tappas had one weakness in common. Both were expert handicappers, who picked a huge percentage of winners in their daily newspaper selections. When they went to the racetrack, they would forget about their own selections and listen to feed-box information from trainers who, for publicity purposes, wished to curry favour with them. These tips were well-meant, but frequently the horses lost.

On the other hand, Lou Davies, who made his selections on the basis of personal observation and mathematical measurement, rigorously declined to listen to any tips from friendly horsemen. It is significant that Lou Davies made money betting on horses, whereas Perlove ad Oliver lost much more frequently than they won. In his betting-years, Davies used to say coldly: "tips are for blind men."

Tips which went awry weren't the only curse of Charlie Oliver's betting activities. He exercised a strangely malign influence on the horses on which he wagered. Horses which appeared to be unbeatable lost races inexplicably when Charlie bet on them. Of course, he enjoyed talking mournfully of his losses – he seldom mentioned the fact that he had a few winners, too.

He bet two dollars on a horse at Dufferin Park, the little half-mile track in midtown Toronto. As the field turned into the short homestretch, Charlie's horse was leading by fifteen lengths. There was no way that the horse could lose, so without waiting for the finish of the race Charlie sprinted to a cashier's wicket to be sure that he was first in line for the payoff.

After the usual delay while the official result was being posted by the placing judges, Charlie plunked his two-dollar ticket in front of the cashier.

The cashier picked up the ticket and compared it with the results on the board. He threw the ticket at Charlie, muttering: "What are you trying to do to me? This horse didn't even finish in the money."

Stunned, Appas Tappas reeled away from the wicket.

His horse, which had been leading by fifteen lengths in the homestretch when Charlie last saw him, had bolted towards the outer rails. He leaped over the outer fence, dumping his jockey. The horse ran right through the track parking-lot and out into Dufferin Street. He didn't stop running until he collided with a trolley car on Bloor Street, a long city block from the track.

I was with him at the Hamilton Jockey Club one day when he had picked six winners and a second-place finisher in his morning paper selections. It was only a seven-race program that afternoon and, incredibly, Charlie, who had been listening to horsemen's tips, again lost $14, betting against his own selections.

The feature race of the afternoon was the Appas Tappas Handicap, which the tracker staged annually in his honor. The *Globe and Mail* paid for a pair of riding boots which Charlie presented publicly to the jockey who rode the winner of the race. On that particular afternoon, the winner of the Appas Tappas Handicap was Cease Fire, ridden by Pat Remillard.

As they stood on the track, posing for the official post-race photograph, Appas Tappas turned to Jockey Remillard and said reproachfully: "You and I are old friends, Pat. Why didn't you tell me that this horse would win?"

"Why didn't I tell YOU?" Jockey Remillard echoed incredulously. "You picked him in the paper this morning as your best-bet of the day!"

12

The City Was Swinging

When I settled in Toronto, Whitey the Pest had left, by request, but the city was swinging. The crap games, which hadn't yet been outlawed by the provincial government, were going full blast and the bootlegging joints were operating as if they had been licensed by God Almighty. The Ontario Government didn't get around to authorizing the public sale of spirits-by-the-glass until 1946 and through the previous twenty-five years, the only place where an ordinary citizen could buy and sit down to a drink of hard liquor was a bootlegging establishment.

Whitey the Pest was gone, but the town was afloat in gambling characters whose nicknames suggested that they were fugitives from the pages of one of Damon Runyan's fantasies. Within the first year after my arrival in Toronto, I was on cordial speaking terms with Alabama Sam, Maxie Chicago, Joe the Goof, Bobby the Punk, Charlie Snakes, Johnny Come Lately, Jockey Tubby, Toothpick Tommy, The Dictator, The Beast, The Gorilla, Roughneck, Hots Nuts Louis and The Good Kid.

Whitey the Pest was gone, but no one loudly lamented his departure. Whitey the Pest's disposition had been quite nasty, at times. During a poker game in the Prince George Hotel, when he had lost twenty or thirty consecutive pots, Whitey took umbrage at a canary owned by the occupant of the hotel suite in which the game was being played. The canary was simply chirping cheerily every time The Pest lost a pot. Whitey reached into the cage, pulled the canary from its perch, and bit the bird severely. Shortly thereafter, Whitey had a slight argument with a bookmaker. Whitey was sitting behind the wheel of his car and the bookmaker was standing on the roadway as they exchanged insults. Whitey took his foot off the clutch and ran over the bookmaker. Then he put the car into reverse and backed over the recumbent bookmaker.

The bookmaker wasn't particularly popular but the concensus among the Gambling Set was that Whitey had transgressed the code of sportsmanship when he ran over him the second time. So, Whitey blew town.

The night of my arrival in Toronto, Ralph Allen took me to Benny Stockley's Gymnasium. It was perhaps, the most appropriate place for a newspaperman to entertain an unsophisticated incoming colleague. Sir Benjamin Stockley's Gymnasium occupied an old, abandoned church one block north of Maple Leaf Gardens, and within this dilapidated structure Benny served physical culture and drinks on a 50-50 basis. As soon as a client had sweated himself into exhaustion in the gym, Benny would permit him to enter the Stockley family living quarters in the vestry, where he could buy a soothing drink for thirty-five cents. I realized immediately that Stockley must have some connection with horse racing, because a racing sulky was hanging from the roof of the church sacristy.

Of all the sporting-drinking spots in Canada, Sir Benjamin Stockley's Gymnasium was unique. The walls were decorated with a fantastic assortment of oddments: swords, rifles, flint-lock pistols, old sporting prints, faded sepia photographs of long-forgotten female pugilists, riding crops, horseshoes, sets of boxing gloves, engraved silver trays, framed caricatures from the *Tatler* and the *Bystander,* and even a couple of long-haired shrunken human heads which had been donated by a diplomatic envoy from a South American state where head-hunting hadn't been stamped out completely.

When Stockley dipped his nose into the sauce, it was his habit to attend auction sales where he purchased additions to his collection of useless junk. After one such safari, he staggered back into his church carrying three polo mallets, for which he had outbid all competitors.

As he was nailing the polo mallets to the overcrowded wall

of the vestry, one of his drinking clients asked stupidly: "Why in the world would you bother to buy three polo mallets?"

"My boy," Benjamin replied solemnly as he hammered home another nail, "I'm preparing for a rainy day. You never know when a polo mallet might come in handy."

After exposing me to Toronto nightlife at Stockley's, Ralph Allen took me out to Woodbine the following day to give me my first view of the Ontario horse-racing scene. Allen, who had already established his reputation as the most stylish and erudite sports columnist in Canada, had been one of my playmates on the Winnipeg *Tribune* before he was lured to Toronto by the *Globe and Mail.* He knew that I was a devotee of the thoroughbreds and he knew, too, that my father was thinking of transferring his own modest racing operations to Eastern Canada, now that I was joining the staff of the *Globe and Mail.* My father, who never lost faith that I would abandon my Morning Glory role, thought hopefully that the time might come when I could supervise these equine activities.

Woodbine was a revelation to me, after my years on the tracks of Western Canada. Visually, it was magnificent with its immaculately manicured lawns, its luxuriant grass infield, the towering elm trees and the majestic sweep of its one-mile racing strip. In its time, Woodbine probably was rivalled only by Saratoga as the beauty-spot of the North American racing circuit. Nevertheless, the stable area at Woodbine was a distinct disappointment to me. The rickety stables were shamed by comparison with the neatly painted green and white cottage-barns at Jim Speers' Whittier Park and Polo Park in Winnipeg. The manure and discarded straw was piled high between the shedrows, a situation which wouldn't have been tolerated on even the half-mile tracks at Calgary, Edmonton, Saskatoon or Regina. Woodbine provided opulent comfort for club house members, but life on the backstretch was messy and dirty.

I learned quickly that there were two distinct strata of society in Ontario racing. Some of the great stables were still in existence but the Hendries and the Seagrams, traditionally the two most prominent racing families, were operating on a drastically reduced scale. Commander Ross had disappeared from the Canadian turf; Col. R. S. McLaughlin, Harry Hatch and Col. Jack Smallman were still racing, but the sport was in a transitory state. E. P. Taylor hadn't burst onto the scene at that juncture although, speculatively, he was campaigning a few horses under his first nom-de-course: the Cosgrave Stable.

There were good horsemen and good horses in abundance, but the atmosphere wasn't as happy or as carefree as it had been, in my experience, on the tracks of the West. The deplorable circumstances in which some of the horsemen laboured could have been blamed on the federal government of Canada. Back in 1921, when the federal government authorized pari-mutuel wagering in Canada, it was decreed that no track could have more than fourteen days of racing in any calendar year. There were seven tracks within a ninety-mile radius of Toronto. With heavy investments in real estate, grandstands, and club houses, the individual tracks simply couldn't make enough money in fourteen days to provide such amenities as shower-baths and toilets for the lowly ginnies. The club houses were kept spick and span for the members and their guests; the grandstands were painted occasionally to provide a spurious atmosphere of cleanliness for the paying-public, but the generally unenlightened racetrack management of the period turned a blind eye and a deaf ear to conditions on the backstretch.

The situation was to be improved dramatically within ten years of my arrival in Toronto; first, by the formation of a Canadian branch of the Horsemen's Benevolent & Protective Association; secondly, in 1952, by the emergence of E. P. Taylor, who bought up all the existing racing charters. The federal government was persuaded to amend its restrictive legislation; Taylor consolidated all of Ontario's thoroughbred racing into three tracks and built handsome racing facilities, in which the horsemen were provided with quarters which were as good as, or better than, those which were provided for club members and the betting public. The fifteen-year transformation was astonishing. From a tumbledown empire of seven weather-beaten tracks, Taylor created a new world for the horsemen and the public, three tracks which became models for future thoroughbred racing development in North America.

When I made my first timid incursion on the hallowed Woodbine turf, I was suspect on two grounds: I was a newspaperman and I was a Westerner. Newspapermen were barely tolerated at Woodbine, where the Ontario Jockey Club still maintained a highly restricted membership. When a newspaperman was issued with a club house pass to Woodbine, he was reminded gently that he was expected to wear shoes. Fortunately my employer was George McCullagh who, in addition to owning the *Globe and Mail,* maintained a string of race horses which were stabled at Woodbine. McCullagh wielded a fairly large editorial stick in Toronto and the directors of the Ontario Jockey Club eyed him with additional misgivings because he failed to wear the traditional grey topper, tailcoat and striped trousers when his colt, Archworth, won the Queen's Plate. A nonconformist who was always eager for battle, McCullagh wore a grey business suit when he sauntered up to receive the royal gift of fifty guineas from Their Majesties, King George VI and Queen Elizabeth. Their Majesties didn't blink at McCullagh's informal attire, but the directors of the Ontario Jockey Club, choking in the clutches of their own starched wing collars, were scandalized.

Westerners still were eyed a bit warily around Woodbine when I arrived. To be truthful, Westerners were regarded with apprehension by the home guard of Ontario horsemen. After the racing season concluded on the prairies and in British Columbia each year, a few western trainers were in the habit of selecting their better horses and shipping them to Toronto for the autumn meetings. The western invaders won quite a few races – usually at juicy prices – and with the long nonproductive winter approaching the Easterners didn't take kindly to being deprived of those purses. Torontonians, then, were the most insular of all Canadian horsemen and they resented encroachment upon their private preserves.

Major Palmer Wright, the punctilious secretary of the Ontario Jockey Club, was plagued by nightmares, resultant from one earlier visitation by Westerners. Seldom were westerners granted stall-space at Woodbine; usually, they were assigned stabling at the less-imposing Thorncliffe and Long Branch tracks and if they entered a horse in a race at Woodbine they shipped the horse across the city in a van. Major Wright, on one occasion when he decided to relax the senseless discrimination against western horsemen, had accepted a stabling application which had been submitted by Chatahoochie Smith, a Calgarian.

Even when judged by the free and easy standards of Western Canada tracks, Chatahoochie Smith was something of a character. He operated a barber shop on Calgary's Eighth Avenue but horse racing was his passion. His failing eyesight eventually forced his retirement from the tonsorial profession; only death could remove him from the list of horse trainers and he still was a familiar figure around the Calgary stable area in 1971, at the age of seventy-two.

Major Wright was blissfully unaware of the possible results of his unprecedented gesture of interprovincial goodwill when he agreed to permit Jack Smith to stable four horses within the sacred precincts of Woodbine.

The Major had retired for the night to his private bedroom on the second floor of the Directors' Building at Woodbine, when Chatahoochie Smith's raffish outfit was vanned through the stable-gates, after being unloaded at a downtown railroad siding. The watchman at the gate merely directed the van-driver to the assigned barn and then, in all probability, he resumed his nap.

After his horses had been unloaded and placed in their stalls, Chatahoochie Smith examined his surroundings. It was a moonlit evening and, as he stared across the track, he could see all that lush green grass in the Woodbine infield.

Many months had passed since Chatahoochie's horses had seen green grass. He decided that, after their rigorous summer racing campaign, and after their long train ride from Calgary, they deserved a change of diet. One by one, he led his four horses from their stalls, led them across the track, unsnapped his shank from their halters and turned them loose to gambol happily on the greensward. Little did he know that he was trespassing on holy ground – he was permitting his shaggy cayuses to romp on Woodbine's carefully-kept steeplechase course, which was Major Wright's particular pride and joy.

The Major was awakened at the crack of dawn by a distraught watchman banging on his bedroom door. While the watchman pointed and babbled, the Major peered from his bedroom window. The Major always had a rather low boiling-point, but on this occasion he almost burst a blood vessel when he saw Chatahoochie Smith's scruffy animals desecrating his beloved infield.

That was the last occasion on which Chatahoochie Smith

was granted stabling accommodation at Woodbine. In the ensuing few years, other western horsemen were seldom granted stall at Woodbine, unless their credentials had been personally vouchsafed by R. James Speers.

The Ontario horsemen's suspicions of me thawed gradually after Appas Tappas volunteered to introduce me personally to all those older trainers who were acknowledged to be the resident grousers. It is axiomatic of life on the backstretch that the best horsemen are usually those who do the most bitching about conditions. There were grounds for considerable bitching around such Ontario tracks as Dufferin Park, Fort Erie and Stamford Park, a fly-infested, leaky-roof operation at Niagara Falls. I subscribed to the complaints and when the Horsemen's Benevolent & Protective Association was formed, I was one of the thirteen charter-signators and became unofficial publicist for the malcontents. I make no apology for the fact that I used my daily newspaper column shamelessly to espouse the horsemen's cause.

Before the formation of the H.B.P.A., the Ontario trainers could be divided into three groups: the Establishment, consisting of those men who trained for the directors of the Ontario Jockey Club; the Anti-Establishment, which consisted of almost everyone else – and Jim Fair!

Jim Fair formed a group by himself – because Jim wore no man's collar; in fact, he wore few collars of his own.

Jim Fair always described himself proudly as "a poor dirt-farmer from Brantford." Although he feigned disreputability, he had a keen mind and, occasionally, he bred and developed a very good horse. He was noisy and frequently outrageous, but I developed a vast affection for him, possibly because he reminded me of some of those old western horsemen who had influenced my youth.

Fair delighted in ruffling the staid directors of the Ontario Jockey Club. I never discovered his hole-card, but invariably he had an entire barn assigned to him at Woodbine for his undistinguished homebreds while other owners, who had much better horses, couldn't get a stall at Woodbine. He appeared to both fascinate and repel the fastidious Major Wright who always winced perceptibly when Fair shouted a noisy and often salacious greeting to him when the Major, trailed by his minions, made his daily morning inspection of the stable area.

Old Jim lived in his tackroom at the end of the barn, and he dressed deplorably. He would swagger around in front of his barn, his boots unlaced, his fly unzippered, his shirt open to the waist and he would scratch his crotch vigorously as he shouted commands to his cowed stableboys. His employees were the source of his running feud with the H.B.P.A. after it was formed. Jim's stable-help consisted of skinny teen-aged boys whom he brought to the race track from the Brantford area after dazzling them with stories of the vast fortune which could be won on the racetrack. Regrettably, Jim often was low in funds and a few of his bolder grooms complained to the H.B.P.A. about their overdue back-pay. Jim always paid up, but only after he had managed to insult every member of the H.B.P.A. committee who approached him in the matter.

When short of funds, Fair impressed one of his young stablehands into duty as chef and the entire outfit cooked their meals on a rickety old wood stove outside the tackroom door.

One morning, after routing Major Wright with a few coarse jokes, Jim, scratching his crotch even more vigorously than usual, bawled at one of his grooms within my hearing: "Son! What have we got for breakfast this morning?"

The boy scurried into the tackroom; a couple of seconds later, he stuck his head out the door and reported in a piping voice: "Just three eggs, boss!"

"Just three eggs, eh!" Jim chortled. "Well, fry two for me – and scramble the other one for the rest of the gang!"

A general sports columnist cannot confine himself entirely to the race track and, in my first few years in Toronto, other local gentry kindly assisted in furthering my education in kindred pastimes. The crap games weren't closed until George Drew's Conservative party gained control of Ontario politics, and in the interim I had an opportunity to study the dice operations. The compulsive Toronto racetrack gambler was usually also a patron of the crap games, although my own newspaper income wasn't large enough, in my opinion, to permit me to engage in games of chance where you could blow a week's salary on one roll of the dice. If I was going to lose money, I preferred to lose it slowly – in two-dollar bets at the racetrack. There wasn't much secrecy connected with the Toronto crap games in their final lush years before George Drew padlocked them. There was a strong-armed guard on the front door, screening the clientele to weed out undesirables and – if necessary – to press the alarm bell in such a very unlikely emergency as a police raid.

Newspapermen were welcome, although the gambling operators had a relatively low opinion of newspapermen's credit ratings. It was in Manny Feder's Brookside Club that I had the good fortune to make the acquaintance of the Good Kid.

The Good Kid was a tubby little man, a carnival-hustler who had toured every corner of North America with such outdoor entertainment outfits as Johnny J. Jones, Rubin & Cherry, Conklin & Garrett and Royal American Shows. Although he was a carnie, his avocation was horse-betting. He was equipped with a mental past-performance chart on every off-beat character in Canada and, in ensuing years, he was to prove to be an invaluable source of fascinating trivia.

Later that night, I asked Joe Perlove, who had taken a mild bath at the roulette table: "What's the Good Kid's real name?"

"Damned if I know, although he has been around for years," replied Perlove. "The only thing I can tell you about him, for sure, is that he has a brother named Percy Piffles".

It transpired that the Good Kid's real name was Louis Drillick. It was years later that I met his brother, Percy Piffles. Early abandoning the itinerant life of a carnie, Percy Piffles had settled in a midtown New York where he became a successful tout, specializing in harness-racing.

The Good Kid contributed notably to my slowly increasing knowledge of Canadian folklore. On our second meeting, in an all-night Chinese restaurant after the crap games had closed, he was telling an interminable story about a gentleman named Pushcart.

Completely bewildered, I interrupted him and asked: "Who is Pushcart?"

"Aw, you must know Pushcart," said the Good Kid incredulously. "He's Squinchy's brother-in-law."

Appas Tappas was the only racing-writer who was regularly sent out of town in those days to cover the meetings at Niagara Falls and Fort Erie. Since George McCullagh was a racing enthusiast, it wasn't very difficult to persuade him that the general sports columnist should accompany Appas Tappas on those foreign assignments. There's nothing quite like a newspaper expense account to assure the completion of a well-rounded education.

The Queen Elizabeth Highway from Toronto to the American border city of Buffalo, N.Y., hasn't always been a multi-laned autobahn. Horsemen who were compelled to drive their vintage automobiles from the western outskirts of Toronto to the Fort Erie Jockey Club did so with some trepidation and only after considerable thoughtful planning. The road was paved from Toronto as far as the Niagara Falls cut-off; the next eighteen miles into the Fort Erie track were loosely gravelled. In midsummer, dense clouds of dust arose from the hot, dry gravel as the passing cars rocketed over the rough roadway. There were quite frequent head-on collisions as the drivers were blinded by one of the most massive smoke-screens since the Battle of Jutland.

When a horseman had completed the trip from Toronto to Fort Erie, he was usually content to remain in the environs of the Niagara Peninsula for at least a week before venturing onto the highway again. There was one jehu, Spats Duffus, an employee of the pari-mutuel department, who recklessly drove back and forth between Toronto and Fort Erie every day of the fourteen-day Fort Erie meeting. He would drive from his Toronto home in the morning and he would drive back from Fort Erie following the afternoon's final race. He drove so swiftly that horsemen declined to ride with him unless they were paralyzed by drink. Either Spats was a masochist or he had something very special going for him in Toronto.

Such an arduous journey scarcely could be contemplated until the illegal watering-holes along the route had been encircled in red ink on the road-maps of the intrepid motorists. There was no real problem associated with obtaining a restorative drink once you had arrived safely in Fort Erie; the pleasant bistro operated by Fort Erie Johnny was just a couple of miles down the road from the racetrack, shaded by towering trees and scenically situated with a lakefront vista.

Many a horseman, after availing himself of Fort Erie Johnny's bottled stock, enthusiastically divested himself of his garments and, as naked as a jay bird, waded out into the milky lukewarm waters of Lake Erie. If you had experienced a calamitous day at the races, it was almost impossible to drown yourself, because Lake Erie was so shallow that you'd have to walk almost all the way to Buffalo before you could find water which was deep enough for total submersion.

The facilities for suicide were much better during the Niagara Falls meeting at Stamford Park. Any disgusted wagerer who elected to dive over the Falls was almost certain to end all his problems. Few racetrackers yield to suicidal impulses. The man who bets on horses is essentially a romanticist, always dreaming that he'll hit the jackpot on the following afternoon. The horsemen and investors who spent the Niagara Falls meeting in the General Brock Hotel, the Foxhead Inn and other less impressive oases, were intent on prolonged roistering rather than immediate self-destruction.

Ideally situated, almost midway between Toronto and Niagara Falls, was Irish Davy's, which must have been the best-known unlicensed bar in Southern Ontario. When you negotiated the traffic circle on the Queen Elizabeth Highway at Stoney Creek, you turned right at the first stoplight. Less then one hundred yards up the dusty sideroad, on the right-hand side, there was a pretty two-storey white cottage nestling in an apple orchard. In this bucolic setting, David Ambersely, who had come from Ireland with his entire belongings in one medium-sized carpetbag, provided firewater and laughter for thirsty wayfarers. He bootlegged in approximately this same area, always within eight or ten miles of downtown Hamilton, for thirty years and not more than ten per cent of his clientele ever discovered that he had a legal surname; simply, he was known far and wide as Irish Davy.

Irish Davy's clients were a cosmopolitan group. In addition to the parched horsemen who thronged his cottage during the racing season, there were nightly gatherings of politicians, pugilists and wealthy sportsmen from nearby Hamilton. There were, to be sure, some other rather rowdy interlopers, but Irish Davy usually gave them short shrift and they became silently inhibited by the occasional arrival of Irish Davy's spiritual advisor, Father Dan, in clerical garb. Father Dan was a dear man, an enlightened priest, impressively orotund of speech, with a habitually jolly face, centred by a proboscis which gave him a resemblance to Rudolph the Red Nosed Reindeer. When Father Dan dropped in to bless the gathering, he was usually accompanied by a young Irish tenor who later married the heiress to a chocolate bon-bon fortune.

Both Father Dan and Irish Davy were lavishly sentimental and easily moved to tears. When the young Irish tenor would put one foot on a kitchen chair and wave a half-filled glass in his hand as he emitted the throbbing notes of "A Little Bit of Heaven," a hush would fall on the drinkers. Father Dan and Irish Davy, moved to the very roots of their Irish souls, would sit there weeping happily.

"A God-given voice!" Father Dan would shout happily, wiping away the tears as the applause shook the little house. Fortunately, the nearest neighbour was fifty yards down the road.

Regrettably, I arrived in Ontario too late to have more than a casual acquaintanceship with Irish Davy's other dearest friend, Matt Hayes, an enormous publican who operated the International Hotel in Hamilton. Matt Hayes weighed close to four hundred pounds in his prime. I happened to drop into Irish Davy's one afternoon, just after Father Dan and he had returned from burying Matt Hayes in a Hamilton cemetery. Davy was white-faced, in shock.

"Poor Matt just wasted away in the undertakers'," Davy was muttering, as he busied himself around the kitchen sink. "He didn't weigh more than two hundred pounds in the box – the other two hundred pounds must have been liquid."

"Dear man! God rest his soul!" Father Dan was murmuring. "Matt was a fine Christian man – he never watered the drinks he sold to the good people of Hamilton. God rest his soul."

I can attest to the fact that Irish Davy, when his own time came, didn't lose weight appreciably during the post-mortem ministrations of the undertakers. I was one of six pallbearers at his funeral and it was the heaviest casket I ever assisted in carrying. I learned later that one of his sentimental clients, desirous of Davy being properly outfilled for his trip to Valhalla, had secreted the better portion of a case of rye whiskey inside the velvet lining of the casket.

David Ambersley conducted all his conversation in a nasal Irish screech. He was a walking sports-record-book and he delighted in settling the arguments of his clients who deferred to him as the definitive authority. He was a misogynist and a compulsive gambler and he fancied himself as a chef.

Undoubtedly, he earned culinary fame with the gigantic stews which he prepared, when the mood was on him. He made his stews in a thirty-gallon cauldron; he guarded the secret of his recipe and, usually, the stew simmered on the stove for three or four days before he decreed that it was ready for eating. Meanwhile, the word that "Irish is building a stew" would be circulated throughout Southern Ontario and his hungry clients would converge on his house from miles in all directions. Walter McMullen, the revered Hamilton *Spectator* sports editor who had lost a leg to the surgeon's knife, was accused of using his artificial limb to stir Davy's stews, but such unsanitary activities were denied stoutly by both principals. On one occasion, a swan flew away from a millionaire's estate near Oakville and it was felled by a shot from ambush at Van Wagner's Beach, near Davy's home. Irish Davy was suspected, but no charges were laid because the Provincial Police were unable to produce the *corpus delicti.* Nevertheless, some of the clients complained about unusually large bones which they found in Davy's stew later that week.

One night, when he was well-foxed with the grape, I managed to extract from him the recipe for his "Turtle Mulligan Stew." These, according to the Escoffier of Van Wagner's Beach were the ingredients of his thirty-gallon concoction:

The meat of two twenty-five-pound turtles. (Stripped down, they aggregated approximately thirty-two pounds.)

Six cans of tomatoes.
Six cans of corn.
Six cans of peas.
Two dozen potatoes.
One parsnip.
One turnip.
Six stalks of chopped celery.
Two bunches of parsley.
Ten pounds of ox tails.
Four garlic beads.
One pound of butter.
One pound of barley.

Thirty pounds of shredded chicken.
One tablespoon of summer celery.
One bottle of Bovril.
Two bottles of tomato ketchup.

The "Turtle Mulligan Stew" was Matt Hayes' favourite dish. One evening in Irish's cottage Matt knocked off fourteen bowls of that stew. On the way home, much, much later that night, he stopped into a wayside beanery for a little snack of ham-and-eggs. Matt held most of the Southern Ontario records for catch-as-catch-can gourmandizing.

Davy claimed the distinction of being the world's unluckiest horse-bettor, and no one who knew him well questioned his claim. His bootlegging establishment produced thousands of dollars each month, but apart from the small percentage of his take which he devoted to his personal living-expenses, he lost every dime of it to bookmakers.

Ambersley insisted that he was the only man ever to lose a bet on a one-horse race.

When he came first from Ireland, he lived briefly in Chicago. He went out to a Chicago track one afternoon and the third race on the program was a steeplechase. However, the steeplechase was going to be a walkover because there was only one entrant – a horse named Big Bear.

Simply for laughs, the bookmakers in the main betting-ring posted a price of 1-to-100 against Big Bear completing the course. Ambersley, who couldn't let even a one-horse race go by without making a bet, walked up to a bookmaker's stand and he wagered ten dollars on Big Bear. The bookmaker accommodated Irish Davy, only because they were drinking-friends. The most that Irish Davy could win was ten cents!

Big Bear started out at a slow canter. He negotiated the first five jumps gracefully and then he hobbled at the sixth fence. Big Bear made a bad landing; he broke his right foreleg and – naturally – couldn't complete the course. Irish Davy lost his ten dollars.

When the horsemen were returning from the closing day of the Stamford Park meeting one September evening, there was the usual gathering in Irish Davy's unlicensed estaminet. The boniface was shouting and lamenting his luck – he bleated that he had lost his last twenty-two consecutive wagers on horses which had been running at Stamford Park.

"You can break your losing-streak next week," said Johnny Passero, a former jockey, interrupting Davy's tirade. Passero had just begun his training career with a small public stable and he was doing very well.

"I'm going to start Tropics at Woodbine next week," said Passero. "If the track is fast, forget about him. But if it comes up muddy, you can mortgage this house and bet the wad on him. In mud, he'll win all the way from here to Pocalottee."

The conversation took place in my hearing on a Sunday evening. Tropics was entered in a race at Woodbine the following Wednesday. On Wednesday afternoon, one of those sudden, violent electrical storms deluged the northern shoreline of Lake Ontario. Irish Davy went to his side window and he looked across the lake towards Toronto. The lightning was flashing, the thunder was roaring, and the rainclouds pressed low and angrily over the Toronto area. Woodbine, which was right on the lakeshore, was certain to be a muddy slough.

Knowing that his losing-streak was about to be ended, Davy walked over to the telephone, to give his bookmaker a $200 bet on Tropics.

At the precise second when Davy lifted the telephone-receiver from its hook, a lightning-bolt hit his house. The shock travelled right down the telephone cord. Ambersley reeled backwards; he fell, striking his head on the stove and he was knocked unconscious.

When he came to, his house was in darkness. The electric power had been knocked out; he joggled the telephone-hook and the line was dead. Groping around the kitchen, he found a small battery-operated radio which he used in emergencies. He switched on the radio and, after it warmed up, he was just in time to hear the announcer giving the race results from Woodbine.

Tropics had won the race – and he paid $27.

It could happen only to a star-crossed gambler such as Irish Davy Ambersley.

(Racetrackers being notably superstitious, Chapter 13 hereby is omitted from this book.)

14

How To Win A Fortune

The time had come for me to win my fortune on the race track. Fortunately, greed was one of the very few vices which escaped inclusion in my multi-flawed character and, even in my wildest dreams, I never contemplated acquiring riches. All my life I have HEARD of men who became wealthy as a result of betting on horses but, strangely enough, I never met one of those elusive midases. The only persons I have known who could actually produce evidence that they won money consistently through horse-betting, were bookmakers. Most of those, after they became rich and pious, abandoned their lawless ways and spent their declining years comfortably as hotel-owners and playing-members of the better private golf clubs.

There were times, admittedly, when I dreamed of making enough money to buy "that little place in the country," the fifty-acre farm with the trout-stream winding its way under the lofty elms, the little barn with accommodation for two or three decent horses, and a nice paddock with white rail fences. Mind you, I was living on a newspaper salary which escalated slowly from $3,500 per year to $10,000 per year, but over that same twelve-year period ten different horses raced in my colours and I didn't lose any important money. Certainly, I didn't make any money from my racing ventures – but I didn't lose much either, and I had a hell of a lot of fun. For that singular feat of almost-breaking-even over a period of twelve years, I'm convinced, now, that I deserve belated election to the Racing Hall of Fame at Saratoga.

The first horse which won a race in my colours on an Ontario track was a two-year-old gelding named Broom Time. After a family visit to Saratoga the previous summer, my father had telephoned me from Montreal to Toronto to tell me that he was going to make me a gift of a thoroughbred yearling. A few days later, he sent me the pedigrees of three of Jim Speers' yearlings, on which he had taken an option. I was told that I could choose any one of the three.

The two other yearlings in the group were fillies. I spent hours, carefully examining the pedigrees and the photographs which had been mailed to me. Eventually I chose Broom Time, because he was a gelding and I preferred his breeding: he was sired by Brooms and he was out of a Craigangower mare named Rise. The following Christmas Morning, my father presented me with two certificates, one issued by the Jockey Club in New York and the other issued by the Canadian Livestock Records in Ottawa; both certificates testified that James A. Coleman was the registered owner of Broom Time, a chestnut gelding with a white blaze-and-snip on his nose and a very small patch of white hairs on the coronet band of his left foreleg.

Broom Time had been broken with the other Speers yearlings by Andy Robinson, a distinguished pioneer of the western racing circuit and then my horse had been turned over to Duke Campbell for training. Campbell trained the Speers runners and, additionally, he was handling some older horses for my father.

Shortly after the New Year, I persuaded the *Globe & Mail* to send me to Winnipeg, on the flimsy pretext of writing some hockey columns. My real purpose was my first meeting with my first horse.

I was sick with disappointment when I saw Broom Time in the flesh. The photograph which had been sent to me, before I selected him, was a side-view. When he was led out of his stall at Whittier Park for my inspection, I saw immediately that he was badly cow-hocked. When he walked, his hocks clicked against each other like a set of castinets. Furthermore, he was sleepy-eyed and lazy, and when we put him back in his stall he crossed his front legs, leaned against the wall and, sneering at me with curled lips, went fast asleep. Aware of my disappointment, Andy and Duke hastened to assure me that Broom Time's hind legs would straighten up when he attained full growth and they assured me further that his apparent lethargy would disappear the first time an earnest jockey tanned his hide.

They were right on both counts although I doubted them at the time. Broom Time didn't even buck his shins as a two-year-old and it never was necessary to expose his unusually sturdy legs to the heat of the firing-iron while he was in my possession.

I returned to Winnipeg at the end of June to see Broom Time make his racing debut at Polo Park. Again, I had an excellent excuse for asking the *Globe & Mail* to pay my expenses. Officially, I went to Winnipeg to cover the annual running of the Canadian Derby which, on that occasion, was won by my father's very nice colt, Western Prince.

My debut as an owner wasn't exactly a howling success. I was over-anxious to make a triumphant return to the tracks where first I had been intrigued by horse racing. I asked Duke Campbell to give Johnny Craigmyle the mount on Broom Time and, furthermore, I told him that I would give Johnny a bonus of $100 if he won the race. This was an unnecessarily large bonus since the winner's share of the purse was only $500. Horse racing is a sport of trial-and-error: if you are wise, you profit eventually from your own mistakes.

Craigmyle would hammer the hips off a horse to earn a bonus of $100. Broom Time was hooking a highly-fancied colt, Ompalo, which Harry Hatch had shipped in from Toronto. Ompalo was a fit horse and Broom Time was making only the first start of his life. Craigmyle gunned Broom Time out of the gate on Ompalo's heels and they ran one-two all the way to the finish-wire. As I watched Johnny wielding his whip energetically, I winced with every swing of his arm and I feared that my over-eagerness to win a purse might have ruined a decent colt while he was still a baby. To my surprise, Broom Time lapped up all his oats that evening and, apart from walking in the manner of an aged arthritic for two or three days, he survived his baptism admirably. Never again did I make the mistake of importuning a jockey to ask too much of a green two-year-old.

Campbell and I were to continue to be warm lifelong friends, but already I was overlooking some excellent advice which my father had given me. My father had said: "Never interfere with your trainer – when you reach the stage where you want to tell him how to run things, you'd better be ready to train the horses yourself." Of course, I had a tendency to forget many of my father's words of wisdom. Years earlier, he had told me: "Most of the bettors who walk through the gates of a race track leave their brains in the parking-lot." I should have remembered that one.

After Western Prince won the Canadian Derby, Campbell allowed quietly that he was going to turn out the horse until September when he would take him to Toronto. In the meantime, he said smoothly, it would be silly to leave Broom Time in Western Canada. Campbell suggested that Broom Time should be shipped east immediately, if I could find a trainer to handle him. Duke mentioned trainer Gordon McCann – in fact, by a remarkable coincidence, he had already been speaking to McCann by long-distance telephone and McCann was willing to take over my two-year-old. Campbell was pretty bright – essentially, he was an easygoing man who had tabbed me as an incipient nuisance.

Gordon McCann is the same Gordon McCann who, in a later decade, was to achieve considerable fame as the trainer of E. P. Taylor's many great horses. When he was in the process of getting his bearings as a conditioner of thoroughbreds, McCann charged me only four dollars per day to train and feed Broom Time. I imagine that later he commanded a considerably higher fee from E. P. Taylor.

McCann really wasn't overjoyed by the prospect of training Broom Time. Eastern horsemen still had a generally low opinion of two-year-olds from the prairies and Broom Time's only recommendation was his second-place finish, behind Ompalo. Broom Time still was cow-hocked, sleepy-eyed and lackadaisical, and when McCann watched the colt being unloaded from a railway car at the Hamilton Jockey Club he was far from favourably impressed by the appearance of my sterling steed.

Reluctantly, McCann entered Broom Time in a race at Hamilton six days later. I sat in Mr. Harry Hatch's box that afternoon and, as the two-year-olds paraded to the post, Mr. Hatch said to me in kindly fashion: "Don't be disappointed, son, if your colt is outrun this afternoon. I'm running a first-time-starter, Acara, in this race and I suspect that he's going to be one of the fastest horses I've ever owned." Mr. Hatch was quite correct: Acara won in a common gallop and Broom Time was far up the racetrack. Sitting next to me in the box while I stifled my disappointment was an Argentinian adventurer whom I met for the first time that afternoon. His courtly international manners were much admired by Mrs. Hatch, but I didn't pay too much attention to him. The Argentinian gentleman's name was Horatio Luro and he had brought a couple of selling-platers to Hamilton on his first invasion of Canadian tracks. He turned out to be a pretty fair horseman later: he won the Kentucky Derby with Decidedly in 1962 and he won the Derby, again, with Northern Dancer in 1964.

I was beginning to be weighed down by the thought that Broom Time was doomed to go through his entire life without winning a race. Then, after the horses had moved along to Stamford Park, I was sitting at my typewriter in the *Globe and Mail* one night when McCann telephoned from Niagara Falls. McCann, who seldom became enthusiastic over any horse's chances in a race, surprised me by saying: "It might be worth your while to catch a ride over to Niagara Falls tomorrow. I don't know for sure – but it looks as if I may have found the right spot for your colt."

A horse has even a heartier appetite than an automobile and, naturally, I couldn't own a car as well as a horse. I hitched a ride to Niagara Falls the next morning with Charlie Hemstead, a hotelier-horseman who wore a diamond stickpin as large as a locomotive headlight, and we stopped at a few bootlegging joints along the highway for sustenance. We gaily spread the time-honoured warning: "The Big Horse Runs Today!"

We took quarters in the General Brock Hotel before we went out to the race track. On rubbery legs, I went into the paddock to watch Gordon McCann saddling Broom Time. McCann had commissioned the riding services of Chris Rogers, a cocky young Canadian jockey who, up to that point, had ridden less than one hundred winners in his three years of striving. The combination of a maiden two-year-old and a brash jockey who treated my trainer with back-slapping condecension did not fill me with confidence, particularly when Rogers complained to me that my racing colours of blue-and-ivory stripes weren't quite dashing enough to match his own flaming personality.

My enthusiasm, which had been mounting steadily through the preceding eighteen hours, was suddenly drained from me as I trudged back to the press box to watch the race. A few horsemen, who knew that I still hadn't broken my maiden as a horse-owner, were kind enough to wish me good luck and I responded with limp civility. Really, I was preparing myself for another disappointment.

I sat staring straight ahead of me until I heard the track announcer, Buck Dryden, shout "they're off" into his open microphone. I ventured a peek across the track and my mouth went dry – my blue-and-ivory colours were in second-place as the two-year-olds rushed down the backstretch. I closed my eyes and I opened them again when Appas Tappas clouted me between the shoulder blades and rasped: "You're on the lead – and really running!" I lurched to my feet and, sure enough, Broom Time was in front as the field turned into the homestretch. I tried to yell, but no sounds came from my open mouth. Suddenly, people were banging me on the back and wringing my shaking hands and I confess that I couldn't see because my eyes were full of tears of happiness. Remember, please – nothing like this ever had happened to me before!

There is nothing which can match the thrill of winning your first horse race; particularly if that race is won by a horse which you have bred; or a horse which you selected personally as a yearling. Every win is exciting – but the first win brings ecstasy. I was so excited, laughing and shouting in sudden release, that I didn't even get down to the winner's circle to have my picture taken with Broom Time. I could see McCann and Chris Rogers waving to me from the track, but I simply couldn't make it. I sat down again, shaking like an aspen leaf. I must have been pale, too, because Appas Tappas peered at me curiously and he said: "Boy, you need a drink!!" Someone in the press box produced a full bottle of rye and I tilted it and glugged thirstily until I could hear my heart begin to beat again.

Two things crossed my mind immediately: I must thank McCann and Rogers, and I must telephone my father in Montreal. I rushed to the paddock and caught the trainer and the jockey just as they were coming off the track. McCann was a bit embarrassed by my effusiveness; Rogers, who sniffed the raw liquor on my breath appreciatively, merely recognized a kindred spirit. I went to the office of P. G. Demetre, who owned Stamford Park, and he permitted me to use his telephone. I can still hear my father's voice and remember his words, warm and paternal although I had interrupted him in the middle of a business conference: "That's splendid – I hope that you'll have many more of them."

Then I walked across the infield to McCann's barn, which was located close to the six-furlong chute, and spent the remainder of the afternoon staring at Broom Time fondly, attempting to act as if winning was no novelty to me. Broom Time really was the one who didn't find it necessary to feign an indifference to the thrill of winning; he cleaned up his evening feed-tub in record time and then, crossing his front legs, he leaned against his stall-wall and he fell asleep. He was a horse with a truly Professional Attitude.

Radio stations in Toronto and Hamilton made a practice of broadcasting race results from Ontario tracks every afternoon and by the time Charlie Hemstead dropped me off at the General Brock Hotel that evening, an unofficial Broom Time victory party was already in full swing. Irish Davy, who had finally won a bet, padlocked the front door of his estaminet at Van Wagner's Beach and persuaded one of his clients, Johnny Cappelli, to drive him to Niagara Falls where he had been assigned the room directly opposite mine in the General Brock. His door was open when I returned from the track; the din was terrific and the house detective was already pleading for quiet. Irish Davy pulled me into the room and, proudly, he opened his suitcase to show me the "luggage" which he had brought on his impromptu holiday. The suitcase contained one clean shirt, one clean pair of socks, one can of dental powder for his false teeth, eight bottles of rye – and nothing else! It was quite a party. The house detective resigned from the hotel staff shortly after midnight and joined in the choral cacaphony. I recall that he had a melodious but untrained baritone voice. When I struggled out of bed the following morning and pulled the lid off my portable typewriter to sweat over my daily column, I was suffering from what my newspaper friend, Carl "The Great" Shatto used to describe as "one of those hangovers with a double-yolk."

Every horse owner learns that life isn't an easy procession of triumphs. After bringing Western Prince to Toronto that autumn, Duke Campbell temporarily retired from training horses as he had been induced to take over the more important job of supervising the Pine River Ranch, Mr. Speers' big spread at Carberry, Manitoba. Coincidentally, my father decided that the time had come for me to immerse myself more deeply in the horse business and he left it to me to acquire a new trainer. Through the next eleven years, I had the good fortune to be associated with three notably successful trainers: Douglas Ness, Dr. R. K. Hodgson and, finally, Morris Fishman.

It was said of Doug Ness: "If you turned Ness loose in an open field with one hundred horses he never had seen before, he could pick out the best horse of the lot within half an hour." This may have been a slight exaggeration, but he was certainly the most knowledgeable all-round horsemen I had met up to that point. He had spent his earlier years around show-horses and he had forgotten nothing that he had learned among that sharp-eyed fraternity. Compared with the oldtime show-horsemen, racetrackers were mere babes in the woods.

Doug Ness had enjoyed a year of tremendous success on the race tracks as the trainer of a public stable when I placed our horses in his charge. I confess that I made some pretty thorough investigations before, timidly, I asked him to take over our horses. My father once had warned me: "The only way to become unpopular around a racetrack is by winning too many races." Ness had been winning too many races and there were many of his less successful rivals who already were frothing with ill-concealed envy. Nevertheless, three veteran horsmen whose opinions I respected above all others, James J. Heffering, Harry Hatch and Harry Giddings, told me that I never would regret placing myself in Doug's eminently capable hands.

Nor did I regret it. Those two years in which Doug Ness trained our horses were full of exhilarating experience and considerable success although some instinct told me that this brilliant horseman was heading for disaster. For one thing, he bet too much: although Doug Ness acquired a couple of modest fortunes from his horsey activities, he bet it all in the pari-mutuel machines and he was in poor shape, financially, when he died. More importantly, the envy which was aroused by his success as a trainer resulted in his being ruled off at the very peak of his racing career, and although he was reinstated thirty months later he never regained his winning stride.

Doug Ness was a stout man with a broad, bland face and he walked with the rolling gait of a newly-beached mariner. One gimpy leg and a façade of childlike innocence were the products of his early training in the devious ways of the show ring. He had been kicked by an indignant horse which objected to having a wad of ginger stuffed into its anal orifice, an ancient practice which inspired show horses to give particularly spirited performances in the ring. And Doug had learned early that when you're buying and selling horses, it is necessary to keep your face completely expressionless. The merest flicker of interest, betrayed by a gleam in one eye, could cause a horse's price to jump twenty-five per cent.

There were many theories concerning Ness's sudden spurt to pre-eminence among the trainers on Canadian race tracks. From the show ring, Ness simply brought new practices and a wealth of personal experience to the race track. He had a distinct edge in all-round horsemanship over many of the disgruntled rivals who resented his success.

For one thing, Ness was a "better feeder" than any other trainer to whom I had been exposed, up to that point. He fed his horses three times a day; ignoring the standard race-track practice of feeding only in the morning and evening. Ness would often drive out to the track at midnight to see that his horses were given a third feeding. Also, he used experimental food-additives before other trainers were willing to give chemically-reinforced provender to their horses. Ness's horses always were apple-fat and, certainly, they ran in a manner which suggested their lavish diet agreed with them.

Ness brought equipment and ideas from the show ring. Western Prince was a stud, and when Ness began to train him for us he equipped him with a jock-strap before each race. Good old Western Prince had a set of testicles which were as large as grapefruit, and when he ran under Ness's direction those formidable glands were tucked into a neat, soft leather bag fitted with a strap which passed over the horse's back.

"The reason that he won't extend himself in some races is that those testicles get knocked by his hind legs," Doug explained. "Didn't anyone ever give you a good kick in the nuts when you were playing football?"

He had another quaint little wheeze which he used with Western Prince and other entire male horses in the barn. Ness would have a groom carry a bucket of ice water to the paddock before a race. Just as the horse was ready to leave the paddock for the track, Doug would produce one of those bulb-sprays which housewives used when they were dampening clothes, before ironing. Doug would fill the bulb with ice water which he would squirt on the stud's testicles. As soon as the bitterly cold water hit them, the horse's testicles would retract into the abdominal cavity.

"Just like diving into the cold Atlantic Ocean," Doug would say cheerfully as he appraised his handiwork. "This son of a buck won't be interested in anything except running for the next ten or fifteen minutes."

Ness was much too smart to mess around with drug stimulants, but he had a fatal admiration for hand-batteries. He never used a "machine" on a horse in my presence, but I wasn't completely stupid and I realized that there must have been frequent occasions when he "warmed up" a horse in the barn before the horse went onto the track.

He had one flighty mare, Musical Mood, whose addiction to electrical shock-treatment was notorious. In fact, her groom used to refer to her affectionately as the Presto-Lite Kid.

Doug took the stable to campaign one autumn at Thistledown Park, near Cleveland, and Musical Mood covered herself with glory. In the closing week of the meeting, she won three consecutive races. Her first win was scored at a distance of one mile and one-half. Three days later, she came back and won at the considerably shorter distance of one mile. Then, on the last race of the meeting's final day, she won again at a distance of one mile and one-half.

Two hours after that final race of the meeting, the Thistledown grandstand mysteriously burst into flames and it was consumed completely by fire.

The origin of the fire was never explained officially, but Canadian horsemen who were present on the occasion opined facetiously that "when the jockey got off Musical Mood after that last race he threw his battery into a trash can under the grandstand."

The suggestion that Musical Mood was even an innocent party to incendiarism was, I believe, an unjust calumny on a very good racing mare. Nevertheless, I must acknowledge that Musical Mood was quite spooky for several months after she was shipped home from Thistledown to winter with the other Ness horses at the J. C. Fletcher farm on the northwestern outskirts of Toronto. Up until the following February, she was likely to climb the walls of her stall in alarm when she heard a groom using a pair of electrical hair-clippers to trim the pelt of one of her equine neighbors. As her own groom said: "if you stuck a light-bulb in her mouth, she'd still provide enough glow to read a newspaper – and she's been away from the track for four months."

Ness's hole-card was his natural gift for perceiving the latent ability in horses which were running poorly for other trainers. When Ness saw such a horse running in a claiming-race, priced considerably below its potential racing value, he would deposit his money with the Racing Secretary, and without the slightest compunction he would claim that horse. Doug was no sloppy sentimentalist – he would have claimed a horse from his own mother, if he thought that she was making the mistake of under-pricing the horse.

Ness acquired a great many winners through the claiming-box and in the process he acquired some enemies. A trainer who had lost a horse to Doug for a claiming-price of $1,000 would be slightly embarrassed when, a few weeks later, Doug would be winning races in the $2,500 to $3,500 class with the same despised thoroughbred. Around the race track, there are the needlers who can always be counted on to fan mere embarrassment into active indignation. Inevitably, one of these needlers would approach the dispossessed trainer, offering such jocular counsel as: "You'd better take a few training lessons from Ness. Your old horse sure has improved since he claimed him."

Certainly, most horses showed a sharp improvement after they had been in Doug's barn for a few weeks. Rival trainers watched his continuing triumphs with grudging admiration, but beneath their public protestations of admiration there was a gathering groundswell of bitterness. Old-fashioned established trainers didn't enjoy being out-trained by a man whom they regarded as a johnny-come-lately to the tracks. It was particularly galling to see Ness winning races with stock which they had discarded contemptuously.

This bitter-sweet relationship was emphasized when Doug parked his big Buick sports-phaeton outside the Racing Secretary's office at Stamford Park one morning. While he was inside the office, another trainer, Leo Grogan, removed all the spark plugs from the Buick.

It was the morning of July 12 and, in memory of the Battle of the Boyne, Grogan decorated the Buick with orange lilies. Doug was all smiles when he emerged and he saw the decorated car. However, his smile was erased gradually when he stepped on the starter and there was no response from the Buick's engine.

When Doug opened the hood, he discovered that all the spark plugs had been removed and he also discovered a printed sign resting atop the engine block. On the sign, the following message had been lettered carefully: "Let's see you make THIS one run!"

He who lives by the sword is reputedly fated to be skewered in reprisal and there were a few angry trainers who, eventually, began to claim horses from Ness. I was an innocent victim of this internecine warfare and, while Doug was my trainer, I lost Broom Time and a good filly named Alpine Astarte to the righteous haltermen. Coincidentally, I sold Western Prince to a friend, Joe Tomlinson, and I had shipped another cheap horse, Alberta Broom, to Ottawa in the custody of a quiet little trainer named Turk Watts.

Although I was very fond of Doug Ness, all my instincts warned me that he was heading into big trouble. He had incurred the enmity of the Establishment by claiming a mare from a director of the Ontario Jockey Club and he compounded this sin by elevating the mare into handicaps, in which she performed with astonishing success. Since I was in the habit of assaulting the Racing Establishment two or three times weekly in my newspaper column, I realized that they would be quite happy to nail me to the mast when they got around to settling their score with Ness. The day of reckoning was coming just as surely as God made little apples, but Doug wouldn't listen to my warnings and he ignored the dire prophecies of his other well-meaning friends.

"What the hell!" Doug snorted amiably. "They can't do anything to me. I'm not doing anything that's illegal."

Nevertheless, it was only a matter of months before they lowered the boom on Ness. Through the previous weeks, undercover agents had been haunting the vicinity of Ness's barn. One afternoon, just when a groom was leading one of Doug's horses to the paddock for a race at Old Woodbine, a detective rushed into Ness's tackroom and, triumphantly, pulled a hand-battery from the pocket of an old raincoat which was hanging from a nail on the wall.

Later, on the basis of the detective's evidence that an illegal device, the battery, had been found in the barn, Ness was suspended from racing and "denied all privileges of the course."

To this day, I've never been satisfied that Doug Ness wasn't framed. It would have been a simple matter for anyone who wished to be rid of him to sneak into Ness's tackroom and plant a battery in the pocket of that old raincoat.

Unavailing, I espoused Ness's case in my column in the *Globe and Mail,* a circumstance which titillated our publisher, George McCullagh, who was always a bit sardonic on the subject of the Racing Establishment. Before I charged recklessly into print, I called on Ness and said: "There's one thing I want you to tell me truthfully, Doug, before I get involved in this business. The battery that they found in the tackroom – was it your battery?"

"Of course, it wasn't mine," Doug retorted in pious indignation. "MY battery was locked in the glove compartment of the Buick."

15

The Good Doctor and the Good Ex-Jockey

The next trainer with whom I had the good fortune to be associated was the eminent veterinarian, Dr. Robert K. Hodgson. In at least one respect, Doc Hodgson was the direct antithesis of Doug Ness; whereas Doug was a compulsive patron of the pari-mutuel machines, Doc wouldn't bet ten cents that the sun will rise tomorrow morning. If Dr. Hodgson ever bet as much as a two-dollar bill on one of his chargers, that singular splurge escaped the attention of turf historians.

"Madness! Sheer madness!" The Doc would mutter when, after consulting him in the paddock, one of his wealthier patrons would rush away to buy a bushel of tickets on the race. The Doc would tug his long nose and he would grumble about the high incidence of idiocy among human beings. Although he was a convivial man, Dr. Hodgson usually managed to convey the impression that his respect for horses was higher than his respect for people who bet on horses.

Dr. Hodgson was an exceptionally easy-going veterinarian with a large practice. He had been coerced into training race horses, against all his normal inclinations. A few of his veterinary clients had talked him into training jumping-horses and, because steeplechases and hurdle-races were limited to approximately thirty events each season on the Ontario tracks, the same horse-owners eventually importuned him into training their flat-runners. The Doc's sales-resistance was shockingly low; he became the trainer of a large public stable, chiefly because he was incapable of saying "no" when prospective horse owners sought his services. He was one of Canada's best horsemen and he was one of the world's most disorganized businessmen. I am sure that when he died I must have owed him at least a small amount of money for training and veterinary fees but the task of unravelling his tangled financial accounts baffled the best minds in the federal government's Estates-Tax Department.

Instead of sending out monthly bills to his clients, Dr. Hodgson would send out bills on an annual basis – if he thought of it. Sometimes he would let two years slip past before he sent out his bills. I devised my own method of staying more or less even with him. Whenever I received a cheque from the racetrack after one of our horses won a race, I'd endorse the cheque and hand it to him quickly. I received only one sketchy financial statement from him in the entire course of our association, and on that occasion he had assembled a jiggery-pokery collection of figures which indicated that *he* owed money to *me*. Where money was concerned, Doc Hodgson was a character straight out of the pages of Alice in Wonderland.

I had met Dr. Hodgson around the Ontario tracks, soon after my arrival from the West, but I had become considerably more familiar with him as a fellow-patron of Sir Benjamin Stockley's unlicensed estaminet. The Methodist merchant princes who owned the church property in which Benny bootlegged in downtown Toronto had evicted him when he was in a period of temporary financial embarrassment and he had transferred his operations to his country estate, a little farm on Leslie Street where his nearest neighbours were E. P. Taylor and Dr. Hodgson.

I remember well the tragic day on which the bailiffs conducted the auction sale of Benny's precious collection of curios in the old church. The city's leading second-hand dealers were out in force to bid on the relics, and their trucks were parked at the front door of the church. As soon as a dealer bought an item, he would order an assistant to take it out to his truck.

Meanwhile, Stockley had employed the services of some grubby urchins who lived in the neighbourhood. These urchins were stealing the merchandise from the trucks and bringing the items back into the church through a rear door. In this manner, Stockley managed to salvage many of his most prized heirlooms.

At the conclusion of the bailiff's sale, Stockley made a purchase which in the circumstances was slightly unusual. The evicted boniface contracted with one of the second-hand dealers for the purchase of a safe which had caught his fancy on a recent visit to the dealer's premises. It wasn't just an ordinary fireproof office safe, it was a monstrous safe – large enough to service the offices of a partnership of corporation lawyers. Benny arranged to have the safe shipped to his country estate where, until his death, it occupied approximately fifteeen per cent of the available floor space on the main floor of the house. The safe was used for only a single purpose – it contained Benny's stock of whiskey, gin and rum.

The Squire of Stockley Manor became discretionary in his selection of drinking clientele in his declining years in the countryside. Stockley Manor wasn't just a drop-in spot for any thirsty wayfarer; it was necessary to be a friend of the proprietor, preferably an old friend with horse-racing or pugilistic antecedents. Even with these established friends, Benny could be cavalier in dismissing them from his establishment when he was out of sorts. The Squire had been a fighter until he came to Canada – a booth-fighter in those oldtime English travelling carnivals – and his face, particularly his nose and his ears, had been much battered. When Benny decided to dismiss his guests because the evening had become boresome, no one bothered to argue with him – despite the fact that he was short-statured and aging, Benny had kept himself in remarkably good physical condition. His biceps resembled the thighs of yearling steers.

Accordingly, one night when I invited Gabby Hartnett to accompany me to Stockley Manor for a few soothing libations, I had the forethought to telephone the Squire a couple of hours before our descent on him, to ascertain whether he was in a humour to greet guests. Benny was excessively jovial on the phone – he bade us come in our good time.

Mr. Hartnett, the well-nigh immortal catcher of the Chicago Cubs who was subsequently elected to the Baseball Hall of Fame, was visiting Toronto on a baseball mission and, before we repaired to Stockley Manor, it was necessary for him to scout an International League game at Maple Leaf Stadium.

This mission consumed several hours and, when we arrived at Stockley's country estate, the mood of our host had changed dramatically. He had banished all his patrons – with the sole exception of Doc Hodgson, who was classified as a family friend and, more importantly, a neighbouring laird. There were no welcoming lights on the porch; the blinds were drawn and Stockley and The Doc were having a private philosophical discussion in a dimly lit room.

Not to be put off after a fifteen-mile drive into the country, I shoved Mr. Hartnett ahead of me and we knocked thunderously on the back door. After a decent interval, the door was flung open and Benny glared up at the huge Hartnett, whose perpetually red face was beaming cheerfully.

"And oo the 'ell might you be?" Benny roared at unwitting Hartnett.

I jumped into the breach and said quickly: "Benny – this is Gabby Hartnett."

Sir Benjamin was unimpressed. He peered at Hartnett again and rasped: "'e's an 'ealthy looking bawstid. 'E 'as a face like a piece of raw salmon."

"No, you don't understand, Benny," I piped. "This is Gabby Hartnett, the great catcher."

"Chroist, I was a great catcher meself. Just look at them ears," retorted Benny, pointing to his own handsomely cauliflowered lugs.

At this juncture, Dr. Hodgson, who had been aroused by the uproar, appeared in the doorway and advised: "Let them in, Benny. If they get out of line, you can look after the big one and I'll whip the tar out of the little one."

It was in these chummy circumstances, approximately half an hour later, that I summoned the boldness to tell Dr. Hodgson that I needed a trainer to handle a very promising yearling, Leonforte, which had been purchased a few weeks earlier from Jim Speers. I hemmed and hawed and I looked at Dr. Hodgson pleadingly. He was a very kind man and, as usual when he was cornered by a persistent petitioner, he found it impossible to say "no". He tugged his nose; he grumbled and finally he said: "Oh, hell. I guess I can make room for one more horse. Tell Speers to ship him down from Winnipeg and arrange with the van-man to drop him off at my farm."

This same curious inability to say "no" had resulted in Dr. Hodgson becoming trainer for Willie Morrissey, a famously irascible Irishman whose feuds with the Racing Establishment led to his founding the Canadian branch of the Horsemen's Benevolent & Protective Association. Morrissey had claimed a mare, Mintwina, on an American track, and in her first start in Morrissey's colours at Hamilton she fractured a sesamoid. Morrissey decided to ship Mintwina home together with another of his ailing horses, Sol Gills. Through sheer coincidence, the van, carrying the two horses, was passing Hodgson's farm when Sol Gills became desperately ill. The van-driver quickly turned into Hodgson's place and unloaded Sol Gills. While the veterinarian was ministering to the sick horse, the van-driver also unloaded Mintwina and led her into a stall in Doc's barn. It was typical of Hodgson that, simply, he never bothered to ask Morrissey to remove the unexpected equine guests. Subsequently, Mintwina was bred to Ladder and she produced Bunty Lawless, one of the truly great horses in the history of Canadian racing.

The first thing he knew, Hodgson had become trainer of the Morrissey racing stable.

The Morrissey-Hodgson racing arrangement flourished for many years, despite the deep gulf separating the personalities of the two principals. Morrissey was a fiery little Irishman who had been born in Toronto's gas-house district, known as Cabbage Town, and he had single-handedly fought his way to a comfortable financial plateau. He was a non-drinking, non-smoking bachelor, he was a gambler and a hotel-owner, he was scrupulously honest, but his strong character was flawed by an Irish passion for nurturing lifelong grudges. His hatred for his enemies – or for those friends who, even unwittingly, managed to offend him – was truly monumental.

Willie was a dedicated hater. He never forgave a slight. A prominent Toronto bookmaker who was a mutual acquaintance died suddenly, and the following morning at the race track I asked Willie if he was going to the funeral.

"No," Morrissey replied sharply. "I didn't like him while he was alive – and I don't like him any better now that he's dead."

Doc Hodgson was dominated completely by Morrissey,

although he never appeared to resent Willie's dictatorial attitude. Doc didn't dislike anyone – violent antipathies were foreign to his nature. Essentially, the veterinarian was a gentle man and there were many occasions when he chafed under Morrissey's unreasonably provocative goadings, but Doc had great resources of emotional serenity. I am quite sure there were frequent occasions when Hodgson considered ending their trying business relationship, but he shrank from the bitter Irish recriminations which his resignation would have occasioned. Morrissey's attitude was that you were "his man" until death ended the contract.

It is probable that his association with Morrissey placed the Doc in his curiously ambivalent position. Hodgson's original patrons, when he was training jumpers, were some prominent members of the Racing Establishment.

Congenitally, Morrissey was the foe of the Establishment. In his later years, he permitted the normal resentments of an Irish boy who had been born into poverty to be magnified out of all true proportion. Willie had an extremely prickly disposition, and when he waged war against the Establishment, it became total war. His fifteen-year battle with the racetrack operators was triggered by an incident which verged on the ludicrous.

In the racing season of 1946, Morrissey had a filly, Casa Camara, and a colt, Hi Bunty, which were Canada's best two-year-olds. Casa Camara and her stablemate were head and shoulders above their juvenile rivals, and when Willie nominated his pair for the Diamond Ring Stakes at Long Branch, the track owner, Fred Orpen, took a peculiarly evasive course of action.

Orpen knew that with Casa Camara and Hi Bunty in the field for the Diamond Ring the public would undoubtedly back them off the boards and he would be faced with a minus-pool in the wagering. Orpen was very fond of money, and the thought of having a minus-pool on one of his races filled him with horror.

So Orpen decided to offer another two-year-old race on the same day as the Diamond Ring. Casa Camara and Hi Bunty had finished one-two in the Cup and Saucer Stakes, a couple of weeks earlier. Orpen named his alternative race for two-year-olds "The Gold Cigarette Case," and he effectively barred the Morrissey juveniles from the Gold Cigarette Case by announcing that the race would be confined to "horses which did not finish first or second in the Cup and Saucer."

In the eyes of the public it was a sleazy stratagem, but the Gold Cigarette Case was run with a field of nine starters. The Diamond Ring was run with Casa Camara as the only starter.

Casa Camara simply galloped casually around the one-mile-and-seventy yards course while the crowd applauded her.

Thereupon, Fred Orpen, who dearly loved to make public speeches, clambered upon a platform in front of the Long Branch grandstand, grasped a microphone attached to the public-address system, and called aloud for Willie Morrissey to come to the platform to be presented with the diamond ring which was awarded annually to the owner of the winning horse.

Morrissey was seething in his grandstand box. He was absolutely livid over the manner in which Orpen had deprived Casa Camara of an opportunity to humble her juvenile rivals. While Orpen entreated him on the microphone, Morrissey just sat there, glaring straight ahead of him.

Orpen was becoming embarrassed and the crowd was becoming derisive. Doc Hodgson walked down the track until he was opposite Morrissey's box and he, too, urged Morrissey to come out to accept the diamond ring. Morrissey stonily ignored his trainer.

While the crowd offered helpful comments, the blushing Orpen strode off the platform. He said that he was going to lock the diamond ring in the track safe and he vowed never to give it to Morrissey until Morrissey personally asked for it.

It is difficult to say who was the more childish performer in this farce – Morrissey or Orpen. Nevertheless, this unseemly misunderstanding had long-lasting repercussions in the world of Canadian horse racing.

The next season, Morrissey emerged from training quarters with a string of new two-year-olds bearing strange names. Morrissey had a new filly named Gem Thief. He had another juvenile named No Ring. The implications were quite obvious and – in case the public missed the point – there was another colt named Red Nosed Fred. Certainly, Mr. Orpen's proboscis was prominent and it was rubicund.

Wealth had not covered all the scars of Morrissey's rough childhood in the gas-house district and he could be a dirty fighter when he was enraged. A couple of other two-year-olds bore names which gratuitously insulted Orpen's only daughter.

There was no way that the horses could be barred from running on Ontario tracks. The names for all thoroughbreds which raced in North America were approved by the registrar of the Jockey Club in New York City. The registrar was blissfully unaware of the sizzling feud in Ontario when he approved the names for Morrissey's juveniles.

Morrissey was an implacable foe. Once aroused by the incident of the diamond ring, Willie decided to clip the wings of *all* Canadian track operators. He induced the Horsemen's Benevolent & Protective Association to spread its activities to Canada and he became president of the organization which, really, was an equestrian labour union. The H.B.P.A. soon managed to raise such a pother that the Ontario Government was forced to arbitrate the war by appointing the first Ontario Racing Commission, a move which sharply curtailed the powers of individual race track operators.

Most men would have been satisfied by this sweeping victory over the Establishment. Willie Morrissey, however, was no ordinary mortal. Morrissey never forgot a grudge!

Ten years after the Diamond Ring Incident – and, indeed, three years after Fred Orpen had disappeared from the Canadian racing scene – Morrissey was unwilling to end the feud. Morrissey came to the races in 1957 with another filly which he named Stole The Ring. The newspapers gleefully reopened all the old wounds. Again, the public was titillated. Morrissey stubbornly resisted any suggestions that, for the sake of peace, he should change the filly's name. The story took on added fillip when Stole The Ring was undefeated as a two-year-old, winning all her five starts.

Horse racing is a sport which abounds in ironies. Potentially the best of Morrissey's opprobriously named horses were Gem Thief and Stole The Ring. Both fillies were fated to have their racing careers ruined by the misadventure.

Gem Thief was one of the "Winter Book" favourites for the Queen's Plate in her three-year-old season. In a trial race, a week before the Queen's Plate, she bolted when the starter was marshalling the field. She dislodged her jockey, crashed into the inner rails, and sustained a deep gash in her left shoulder. She never recovered completely from that injury and she was forced into premature retirement.

When the two-year-olds went into winter quarters at the end of the 1957 season, Stole The Ring was regarded as a platinum-plated cinch to win the Queen's Plate of 1958. She had outclassed all the colts and the other fillies while scoring her five consecutive victories in 1957.

Fate stepped in again. During her spring training for the Queen's Plate, Stole The Ring became ill. She missed four weeks of all-important conditioning and, additionally, she didn't have the opportunity to run in any preliminary races.

Nevertheless, Morrissey stubbornly insisted that Stole The Ring would start in the Queen's Plate – a run of one mile and one-quarter – without a single tune-up race. Morrissey even imported Johnny Longden from California to ride the filly. The public was deluded, too – the combination of Stole The Ring's juvenile record and the presence of Longden, who was at the peak of his fame, impelled the public to bet the filly into favouritism.

Longden did his best. He took Stole The Ring into the lead and, running gamely, she led through the first mile. She was running on her heart alone through the final quarter-mile as she staggered home in third place. That race ruined her – never again was she to enter the winner's enclosure.

Doc Hodgson wasn't on hand for the Stole The Ring denouement. Doc had died, and a few years before his death he had retired indignantly from the training profession. The stewards had given him a brief suspension and, quite inadvertently, Willie Morrissey had been the agent of Hodgson's misfortune.

Morrissey had a friend, Norman Heise, who owned two thoroughbred full-sisters, Willegivit and Fifty Seven. The fillies were almost identical in appearance, although Willegivit was a four-year-old and her sister was a year younger. Heise had a disagreement with his trainer, and in his dilemma he turned to Morrissey for advice. Morrissey told him to send the two fillies to Dr. Hodgson's farm. As usual, the strong-willed Morrissey persuaded his reluctant trainer to add two more horses to his overloaded stable.

Doc disliked the two mares cordially and never bothered to examine them carefully. His carelessness in this regard cost him dearly – he became involved in a ludicrous case of mistaken identity. When Willegivit was unloaded from the van at Hodgson's barn, she was led into a stall and a groom tacked a card with the name "Fifty Seven" on the stall door. Then, Fifty Seven was led into the adjoining stall and the name "Willegivit" was tacked on *her* door. Such a mistake couldn't occur on a North American track today, when all thoroughbreds are tattooed on the upper lip before they are licensed to race.

The following summer, Willegivit won a couple of races, running under the name of "Fifty Seven." The Doc wasn't the only man who was shortsighted: the paddock judge, who is supposed to inspect each horse carefully before every race, never detected the fact that "Fifty Seven" actually was her older sister.

In fact, no one around the race track realized that the two fillies had exchanged identities. There were many red faces among the racing officials when the innocent deception was disclosed. I can vouch for the fact that no one around the Hodgson barn profited by betting on "Fifty Seven" in her two winning starts. To the best of my knowledge – and I seldom was far from the stable in those days – not even her groom bet as much as a two-dollar bill on her.

It wasn't until an afternoon at Long Branch that Heise's former trainer, who had been compaigning in Montreal, wandered into the paddock just as "Fifty Seven" was being saddled for a race. This former trainer, overcome by a flush of piety, rushed to the stewards to report that Dr. Hodgson was running a "ringer."

The stewards, acutely embarrassed because their own paddock officials hadn't detected the deception, were forced to impose a short but salutary suspension on Dr. Hodgson. Knowing Hodgson's unquestioned probity, and weighing the additional fact that Hodgson never bet on horses, the stewards went to great pains to issue a statement in which they expressed the conviction that the respected trainer "was not guilty of any mal-intent."

Nevertheless, Dr. Hodgson was humiliated by his own carelessness; he felt that his personal integrity had been impugned. Despite the coaxings and blandishments of the entire racing fraternity, Doc stubbornly declined to renew his trainer's licence the next year and devoted himself exclusively to his large veterinary practice. I've always felt that, secretly, Doc was rather glad that the stewards had provided him with the opportunity to retire from training: he was becoming increasingly irritable under the load of responsibility imposed by Morrissey's horses. And, of course, the suspension of his widely-respected trainer provided Morrissey with fresh ammunition for his relentless battle against the Racing Establishment.

Having been involved successively with two trainers who got themselves ruled off, I began to have an uncomfortable feeling that I was the jinx. Certainly there was no possibility of my spreading my malign infection to my next trainer, Morris Fishman; Morris had received a lifetime suspension from horse racing, fifteen years *before* I met him.

It should be explained that Fishman had received his lifetime suspension when he was a jockey. Judge Francis Nelson was a man of much wisdom. He suspended Jockey Fishman and then he kept his eye on him. When Morris became too heavy to contemplate a return to the saddle, Judge Nelson rescinded the suspension and gave Fishman a trainer's licence. His confidence was justified: Morris became a very successful trainer, who studied the rule book with scholarly zeal.

It should be explained further that Morris was a rider in the days when jockeys "rode to orders." If a trainer told a jockey that he did not wish his horse to win any particular race, the jockey was very careful in following the trainer's instructions. Most really good jockeys of that era could restrain even the most enthusiastic horse. There were some jockeys whose techniques were studied by the engineers who designed the Westinghouse Air-Brakes which were installed on American railroad trains. A trainer could become very surly and unreasonable if a jockey permitted a horse to win a race in contravention of instructions. Such a careless jockey was seldom employed again by that trainer. Trainers were betting-men in those days – or their patrons were betting-men – and a trainer would frequently arrange to have his horse beaten in two or three races until he built up a nice juicy price.

For that reason, a jockey who could "pull" a horse without

exciting the curiosity of the stewards or the patrol judges was regarded by trainers as, indeed, a gem of great price.

There were some trainers who arranged for their horses to be "pulled" in six or seven consecutive races before permitting a jockey to "turn him loose." When they bet their money, they seldom made a mistake.

In the seasons when Dr. Hodgson was training our horses, we were stabled close to Fishman at Woodbine. We became friendly and I began to hear stories from other trainers concerning Fishman's prodigious equestrian feats. There was a good deal of early-morning drinking around Fishman's tack-room and alcoholic lubrication at that hour of the day frequently produces exaggerations. Accordingly, I decided to seek an impartial opinion of Fishman's horsemanship from a veteran trainer who avoided our matutinal wassailing. I approached Bill Campbell, who had been around Canadian tracks for thirty years.

Mr. Campbell was sitting on an upturned apple box gnawing a cigar when I approached him. After a few of the customary pleasantries I asked him bluntly: "What kind of a jockey was Morris Fishman?"

Mr. Campbell removed his cigar from his mouth and stared into space reflectively for approximately thirty seconds. Then he turned to face me and said, without the trace of a smile: "Morris was the strongest jockey I ever saw – he could stop an elephant going for a bale of hay".

Fishman had done most of his riding for a reticent, tough-minded Irish trainer named Jimmy Boden, who campaigned a stable for several wealthy owners. Boden raced his horses in Maryland and on the major tracks of Eastern Canada and his patron-owners were heavy bettors. Under Boden's stern tutelage, Fishman had learned very quickly that it is often much more expeditious to lose a race than to win one. Boden was the type of trainer who permitted a rider to make no more than one mistake. Fishman was smart – he never made that first mistake and he stayed in Boden's employ for many years.

Fishman stepped into the breach when Dr. Hodgson was suspended and he offered to take my colt, Leonforte, to Detroit where he planned to campaign his public stable. It was the beginning of a long and very satisfactory friendship.

Remembering all the stories of Fishman's riding assignments for the crusty Jimmy Boden, I asked him one day "What was the best day you ever had as a jockey?"

"Well, I rode six horses one afternoon at Bowie," Morris replied thoughtfully. "I won on four of them: I pulled the other two – but I could have won all six."

Fishman's unfailing candour was one of his most refreshing characteristics.

A nosey newspaper columnist can obtain access to privileged information and, in the process of doing some research work on a journalistic project, I was handed the voluminous personal files of Judge Francis Nelson, in which he had recorded all the official decisions which he had made during his career on North American tracks. It is essential to remember that in those days Judge Nelson was his own court, jury and hangman – there was no appeal from his decisions. In the files, under a Montreal dateline in Judge Nelson's own handwriting, I found the following intriguing item: "Jockey M. Fishman. Suspended for life. FOR ATTEMPTING TO DECEIVE THE STEWARDS."

This, to me, sounded like a rather flimsy pretext for imposing a lifetime suspension. Attempted deception scarcely could be classified as a capital offence, even under the strict provisions of the Criminal Code of Canada.

The morning after I read Judge Nelson's long-forgotten ruling, I went out to the track and, over our second eye-opener, I revealed my discovery. I asked Fishman for his version of the suspension. As usual, Morris was engagingly frank.

Fishman had been riding at Montreal. Frankie Slate, a former jockey who was serving a lengthy suspension for some racetrack larceny, was living in an apartment in that city. One night, Fishman went to visit Slate.

The next morning, Judge Nelson summoned Fishman to his presence. Morris was no fool; he realized immediately that a private dectective, hired by the race tracks, must have followed him to Slate's apartment. When Judge Nelson put the question to him, he admitted promptly that he had visited Slate. It was only when Judge Nelson asked whether there was anyone else in the apartment that Morris felt impelled to tell a small lie. Actually, another jockey – a Cuban – had been in the apartment when Fishman arrived. Not wishing to involve the Cuban rider, Morris said that he and Frankie Slate had been alone, having a social chat.

Morris should have realized that his falsehood was eminently transparent. Judge Nelson employed the services of more than one gumshoe – another detective had been shadowing the Cuban jockey. It was this seemingly trivial lie which resulted in Jockey Fishman being deprived of the right to ride anywhere in North America, through the remainder of his lifetime.

I was aghast when Fishman told me his story. The enormity of the punishment appeared to be out of all proportion, when scaled against the crime. I exploded in indignation.

"How the hell could Nelson give you a life suspension for telling a lie?" I yelped. "You really hadn't DONE anything!"

"No," agreed Morris with a shrug and a tiny grin. "But Slate and the Cuban and I were PLANNING to do something! Judge Nelson beat us to the punch."

Fishman and I were racing partners until E. P. Taylor hired me to work for his newly-formed Jockey Club, which comprised all the thoroughbred tracks in Ontario. At that juncture, unwilling to have a conflict of interests, I felt that it would be judicious to retire gracefully from the ranks of horse owners.

Actually, there was a third partner, Yonnie Starr, who had been Fishman's agent when Morris was a jockey. Regrettably, their long friendship and their business association was dissolved in a senseless and noisy argument which had nothing to do with their racing activities. Starr went his own way and became an eminently successful trainer. Fishman, who was the Hebrew counterpart of Irish Willie Morrissey, refused to speak to his former amanuensis for many years after the unhappy disruption of their partnership. As a bewildered innocent party to the explosion, I risked Fishman's wrath, and to this day I have managed to remain on extremely cordial terms with both men.

It was in partnership with Morris Fishman that I became, briefly, a breeder of thoroughbreds. We bred a colt which was foaled on St. Patrick's Day. To commemorate the memory of the snake-scourging saint, in addition to satisfying the prickly racial pride of the formidable Mr. Fishman, I petitioned the Jockey Club in New York to grant the horse the name of Irish Moe. Miss Brennan, in the offices of the Jockey Club, must have been in one of her jovial moods when my application papers arrived on her desk because she approved the name promptly.

Irish Moe was cut out to be one hell of a good race horse. In retrospect, I believe that he could have become the money winner who would have lifted the mortgage from my humble homestead. He might have been the horse who provided the wherewithall to buy that long-sought "little place in the country." He won three races as a two-year-old and then Morris took him to Florida to prepare him for his three-year-old campaign. I couldn't afford to travel to the Florida tourist resorts with our horse and I spent the winter dreaming big dreams in the frozen northland. Dreams – that was all they were – because they dissolved with the coming of daylight.

Daylight came bleakly on a morning in April when the horse-van from Florida creaked to a halt in the Woodbine stable area. As soon as I saw the expression on the face of Montreal Red, one of Fishman's travelling grooms, I knew that there was serious trouble: Irish Moe had contracted pneumonia on the 1,700-mile ride from the hot Everglades into still-chilly Ontario.

A dying horse is a pitiable sight. Poor little Irish Moe was led into his Woodbine stall; he was swathed in blankets and an infra-red heat light was installed in the socket directly above him. The veterinarians ministered to him hour after hour, and his groom never moved far from the stall door. Despite the heat generated by the blankets and the infra-red lamp, he stood there shivering for two days – his mute agony clearly evident in his feverish eyes.

On the third day, he slumped into the straw and no longer could he lift his head. Morris summoned the veterinary to put the colt out of his misery, and before the doctor swung around the end of the shedrow Morris shoved me into his car and we left the track.

Halfway downtown, I was staring dully through the car's windshield when I heard Morris's voice from the driver's seat. "The day before I left Florida," he was saying, "a man came to our barn and offered us $10,000 for Irish Moe. I didn't bother to telephone you, because I knew that you wouldn't want to sell him. So you've just blown $5,000."

I felt much too sad to laugh.

16

Well, It Was a Good Idea at the Time

I wasn't the first impecunious newspaperman who was daft enough to attempt to win the Queen's Plate. Several years before my arrival in Ontario, a group of bedizened reporters in the employ of the Toronto *Star* had pooled their slender resources to purchase a lamentably ill-equipped steed which they entered in Canada's richest horse race. Even if I had been aware of their disaster, I doubt that I could have been dissuaded from my own brash decision to Shoot For The Moon.

There is ample historic evidence that the major races of the world are seldom won by small-time owners. There are Lords of the Realm who have dissipated vast family fortunes in their attempts to capture an Epsom Derby. Even the Whitneys and the Vanderbilts, with all their inherited millions, have suffered frequent frustrations when they coveted the Kentucky Derby. It is axiomatic in racing, however, that the major prizes are usually won by horsemen of considerable wealth. It is only in the realms of fiction or old-fashioned motion pictures that white-goateed Col. Beauregard Martingale, ennobled by shabby, genteel poverty, brings an unheralded colt out of the canebrakes to score a stunning upset in the Dubby, suh! The winning jockey in such cases usually is the Cunnel's granddaughter, Elizabeth Taylor or Judy Garland, disguised as a boy. Not a few of us wet our pants in excitement during that big scene when Elizabeth or Judy doffed her jockey's cap, permitting her long dark tresses to cascade all the way down to her comely buttocks.

It was in 1936 that the Toronto *Star* hired a highly unusual reporter named A. D. "Cowboy" Kean. Admittedly, The *Star* had acquired a reputation for hiring unusual reporters; through their revolving doors, in the immediately preceding past, had passed such gentry as Ernest Hemingway, Morley Callaghan and Pierre Van Passen.

Cowboy Kean's reportorial credentials were sketchy. He came to the *Star* from Western Canada where he had been recently employed by the federal government as a buffalo hunter. It was one of those eras in which governmental policy changed directions abruptly. Previously, in order to save the bison from extinction, the government had collected all the remaining herds in a vast reserve known as Wood Mountain Park. However, the bison had reproduced with the splendid zeal of rabbits and the bison population had grown so rapidly that it became necessary to thin out the herds before the country was overrun by the fur-collared beasts. Accordingly, Cowboy Kean was one of a group of wranglers employed to shoot a daily quota of bison. The meat was shipped to major North American hotels and, for a time, buffalo steaks were featured on the menus of some of the continent's most opulent hostelries.

A. D. Kean professed to know a good deal about horses and, indeed, he had the bandy legs to substantiate his stories of a youth spent in the saddle. He was barrel-chested and his craggy face looked as if he had been weathered by prairie blizzards. He was an extraordinarily gentle-mannered man and his newsroom colleagues were charmed by his unquenchable, almost childlike optimism.

Kean came into the *Star* editorial department one day after an early-morning visit to Woodbine and announced that he had discovered a bonanza. He had come upon a nine-year-old thoroughbred named Hurry Fox, which had never started in a race. He importuned his reportorial colleagues to form a syndicate to purchase this mysterious animal, which could be bought for $200. Kean said he would train the horse personally and enter Hurry Fox in the Queen's Plate, which at that time had no age restrictions for entrants. Kean argued persuasively that – in view of the fact that the horse had never raced before in public – he would win the Queen's Plate at astronomical odds and his journalist owners would become filthy rich.

Kean was a very vigorous man, although he was well along in years. He professed to drink animal blood to keep himself tuned-up physically. The members of the Star's reportorial staff weren't notably squeamish, but none of them felt strong enough to check on their colleague's rather unattractive diet. Kean also must have been amazingly persuasive because the purchase of Hurry Fox occurred in the depths of the Depression, when journalists were lucky to have enough money to keep themselves respectably clothed. Nevertheless, he induced ten or fifteen reporters and sub-editors to join the syndicate, purchased Hurry Fox, and set about training the animal for its sensational racing debut in the Queen's Plate.

There are oldtimers around Toronto who still talk wonderingly of Cowboy Kean's training methods. These oldtimers insist that, since Kean couldn't afford to buy a stopwatch, he actually timed Hurry Fox with a kitchen alarm-clock. As it transpired, Hurry Fox ran so slowly that Kean could have timed him with a sun dial.

Came the day of the Big Race and the members of the Star Syndicate went en masse to Woodbine to watch their noble charger run in the Queen's Plate. Kean had been bringing in glowing reports of Hurry Fox's training moves and the members of the Syndicate went into hock to scrape up another $200 for betting money.

In a moment of utter insanity, Gordon McCann had agreed to ride the nine-year-old maiden. When the entries had been drawn the previous morning, Hurry Fox had won the dubious distinction of carrying the unlucky number thirteen. Perhaps it was this unpropitious omen – or possibly Kean lost his nerve – but he scratched the horse from the race, shortly before post-time. Officially, his excuse for withdrawing was that his horse needed a muddy track – and it hadn't rained in the Toronto environs for five days.

As the crestfallen members of the Syndicate surrounded him, Kean announced that he would start Hurry Fox in the Hendrie Memorial Handicap, five days later.

He was as good as his word. Hurry Fox went to the post

for the Hendrie Memorial, but Jockey Gordon McCann wasn't on his back. McCann had recovered his sanity and he went into hiding on the morning of the race. Undismayed, the trainer sweet-talked Jockey Frank Dougherty into accepting the mount.

"I was hiding behind one of the steeplechase-jumps in the infield, watching the race," McCann said, many years later. "I never saw a horse get beaten so badly. The winner was crossing the finish-line when poor old Hurry Fox came around the final turn. He was beaten more than an eighth of a mile."

None of the members of the Star Syndicate committed suicide. Kean, however, was crushed by his embarrassment. He resigned from the *Star* shortly thereafter, and became the editor of a horse magazine. None of the survivors of the incident recalls what became of Hurry Fox. He was never seen on a race track again.

Although many years have passed since I ran a horse in the Queen's Plate, my stitches still hurt when I laugh and the scars still are dimly visible, white streaks on my psyche. The absurdity of a working newspaperman competing against millionaires in the horse-racing business dawned on me only after my post-race nausea subsided and, perspiring profusely, I forced myself to sit down with the tattered bills. By a conservative estimate, the experiment had cost $7,000, and I was lucky to get off so cheaply.

The affair began innocently over a luncheon with R. James Speers, on a visit to Winnipeg. Mr. Speers told me that he had a chestnut yearling, by Brooms out of Donna Julia, which I could have for $1,000. The breeding was impeccable: Brooms had won the Hopeful Stakes at Saratoga and Donna Julia in her racing days and had established track records at Woodbine and Thorncliffe Park. Furthermore, Mr. Speers offered to take me out to Whittier Park the following morning to watch the colt being "breezed" for the first time.

I committed the cardinal sin of horse racing – I fell in love with a horse at first sight. I was sitting in the old abandoned grandstand at Whittier Park the next morning when the colt tiptoed through the gap from the barns. He stood stock-still for at least two minutes, sniffing the gentle morning breeze. His ears pricked as he looked around him, alertly, intelligently and full of confidence. Then he went about his business calmly and sedately. The boy on his back jogged him once around the track very slowly, and when they came to the head of the stretch the boy settled himself low over the horse's withers and clucked to him. The chestnut colt fairly flew through the stretch. As I watched him, I felt my eyes smarting with excitement and I was puffing furiously on an unlit cigar. I turned to Mr. Speers, who was sitting beside me, and I said one fatal word: "Sold!"

Two weeks later, the colt was shipped to Toronto, to be placed in the care of the estimable Dr. R. K. Hodgson. The colt was named Leonforte, as a filial salute to my bellicose and horse-hating younger brother. Leonforte is a mountain town in Sicily, captured by the combined action of two Canadian regiments, the Princess Patricia's Canadian Light Infantry and the Loyal Edmonton Regiment. My brother had been a company commander with the Patricias at the time of the assault on Leonforte, and as a result he had been decorated by Field Marshall Montgomery.

Doc Hodgson whistled appreciatively when he had his first sight of Leonforte, and breezed him once at Thorncliffe Park before he put him into winter quarters.

It would be stretching the point to say that Leonforte was the sensation of Canadian racing when he made his two-year-old debut but, in looks, he was a genuine smasher. He was brilliantly speedy, too, although he had a tendency to run wide on the turns until we discovered that he was bothered by "wolf teeth." When those painful dentures were removed, he settled down to business admirably.

Doc raced Leonforte very sparingly as a juvenile and he raced him only against the very best colts in the country. Leonforte started five times and he won two of those races. His fifth race was run at Fort Erie and he won with such ridiculous ease that the clockers were touting him as the probable winner of Canada's two richest stakes for two-year-olds, the Coronation Futurity and the Cup and Saucer.

I suppose that I am one of those persons who was destined to work for a living: in any event I didn't collect either of those two big purses. I was sitting in my office at the *Globe and Mail* one night, labouring over my hot typewriter, when Doc Hodgson telephoned from Fort Erie.

Leonforte had injured a knee. It wasn't a serious injury, but Doc recommended that the colt should be retired for the remainder of the season. After all, he reminded me, our principal target was the Queen's Plate; it would be folly to ruin a decent colt by rushing him back into action after his knee injury had healed.

Sitting there with the telephone receiver pressed against my left ear, I felt as if someone had kicked me in the solar plexus. I recognized the wisdom of the trainer's advice, although my disappointment was almost overpowering. I reached into my desk drawer and, thoughtfully, took a long, neat drink from a bottle which I kept for moments of grimmest emergency. For once, the liquor had no palliative effect. I was nauseated, and I contemplated nine more months of restless waiting before I could lift the mortgage.

Actually, the nine months passed rather speedily although my physical health and spiritual serenity were impaired seriously by my excessively industrious attempts to burn both ends of the candle. I spent much of my time glowering at Leonforte in his box stall on Hodgson's farm and I wasted many sleepless nights cavorting with some of my sturdiest playmates: Deacon Allen, the battling Colcloughs, and a Chinese taxi-driver named "Nine Dollar Charlie."

The Deacon, who was the most indestructible of human beings, held court nightly in his room in the Walsingham Hotel – or the Dancing Pig, which it was more commonly called. Whenever we called for a taxi to take us on one of our nocturnal missions, it was our invariable bad luck to discover that the taxi was driven by Charlie, the wily Oriental. No matter where we went, and no matter how long or how short the trip, Charlie always demanded a fare of "nine dollars."

In an effort to reduce Charlie's standard charges, the Deacon would frequently invite the taxi-driver into his room at the Walsingham when we reached that sanctuary and he would ply Charlie with great lashings of whiskey. Charlie had a considerable capacity for bottled spirits and, also, he contributed to the entertainment. After two or three drinks, Charlie would express his gratitude by standing on his head on the seat of a kitchen chair.

However, the alcohol never impaired his single-minded

devotion to taxi fares. After drinking half a bottle of the Deacon's whiskey, he would stand on his head for a few minutes, descend from his inverted perch, smooth his clothing, and say pleasantly: "Well, I've got to go back to work. That'll be nine dollars, please, Mr. Allen."

It was one of those nights when "Nine Dollar Charlie" was standing on his head in a corner of Deacon Allen's hotel room that I sold a mare named Isaldwana to Wally and Nellie Colclough. I wasn't content to be an improvident horse owner – I wanted some of my friends to share my misfortunes.

Isaldwana was an unraced mare which had been languishing on Doug Ness's farm while he was sitting out his suspension. Doug had asked me to sell her for him. The Colcloughs had been intrigued by my backstretch stories and their eyes were glinting with the anticipation of buying a horse. Without qualm, I told them to buy Isaldwana.

There was some ironic justice in this transaction. Wally Colclough was an old friend of mine who had spent his early life selling rather dubious mining stocks to unsophisticated clients via the long-distance telephone. Nevertheless, he was a charming hustler and he boasted proudly: "They'll have to admit one thing about me – I never sold one of those damn stocks to a friend or a relative."

I knew that Isaldwana was a bum; Wally Colclough knew that Isaldwana was a bum. Wally simply wanted to buy a horse so that he and Nellie could mingle with their stockbroker friends in the club houses on Ontario's race tracks.

The Colcloughs were real characters. Wally, like myself, was a native of Winnipeg, and he had spent a carefree youth travelling the world in the general proximity of such celebrated confidence men as Titanic Thompson and Bye-Bye Brown. Nellie had been a hoofer in her youth and she had been a beauty. Regrettably, Wally was much given to drink and he was a very poor driver. His inexpert driving had left its mark on Nellie's face.

On at least three occasions, Wally had run into immovable obstacles in his big Cadillac and, on each occasion, Nellie had been catapulted through the windshield. She used to refer to her scars genially as "souvenirs of my early career, when I was testing windshields for General Motors."

Nellie was one of the warmest-hearted ladies in the entire world but her husband aroused her vigorous animosity when she partook immoderately of the demon rum. She was a very strong lady, equipped with a left hook which would have been envied by Jack Dempsey or Joe Frazier, and Wally would always flee in terror when she lined him up for a rocket-trip to the moon. Additionally, Nellie had the memory of an elephant and she brooded over imagined discourtesies; particularly, she brooded over the completely unintentional gaucheries of her portly spouse. In those black moods, Nellie was capable of giving the startled Wally an artistic fistic lacing.

One Christmas Eve, Wally and I were sitting in Deacon Allen's room drinking with a couple of huge and uninhibited professional wrestlers. Completely unknown to the rest of us, Nellie had been busting her gusset in preparing an extravagant Christmas Eve dinner and she had given Wally strict instructions to be home by 7 p.m.

It was midnight when Wally snapped out of the alcoholic trance and he remembered his dinner date at home. In a burst of genius, he invited the two wrestlers to accompany him to his home for a few more drinks.

Nellie, meanwhile, was completely furious. Her turkey dinner had burned to a crisp. Nellie had taken to the bottle and she was awaiting her husband's arrival in mounting rage. However, when Wally ushered the two gargantuan wrestlers through the door ahead of him, Nellie realized that she was outnumbered and went off sulkily to her bed, to fall into a deep, deep sleep.

She didn't say anything about the incident the next day. In fact, she didn't say anything about it for almost three months.

Then, on a morning in March, Wally was shaving, preparatory to making a trip to Niagara Falls, N.Y., to sell some of his moose-pasture stock to a couple of American suckers. He was in high good spirits and he was singing to himself as he regarded his friendly lathered face in the bathroom mirror.

At that precise juncture, Nellie called from the adjoining room, "Stick your head in here for a minute, dear."

Wally opened the bathroom door and stuck his head into the bedroom.

Nellie was standing there with a huge cut-glass pitcher

raised high over her head. She swung her arm and the pitcher shattered as it struck Wally's unprotected skull.

Wally stood there, wobbling, as the blood from several cuts dribbled into the lather on the face. With surprising mildness, he asked: "What was that for, dear?"

Nellie glared at him and she snapped: "That, you son of a bitch, was for Christmas Eve!"

Doc Hodgson must have been the most patient of men. Constantly, he was at the beck and call of the irrepressible Willie Morrissey and, as the owner of a prospective Queen's Plate entrant, I was adding to his burden. On the days when it was impossible for me to inspect my colt personally, I was on the telephone, demanding reports from the trainer. No matter how late the hour when I routed him out to answer my questions about Leonforte, Dr. Hodgson was unfailingly courteous and he would reply soothingly: "He's doing champion, Jimmy – just champion."

My indulgent employer, George McCullagh, maintained an efficient intelligence service in the social and political areas within the *Globe and Mail*'s circulation zone, and he was well aware that my nocturnal conduct left something to be desired. Compassionately, he decided that a change of scenery would cool my fevered blood and he despatched me to Europe on a three-month roving assignment. No one ever could question George McCullagh's generosity to his employees: he equipped me with an expense account which provided leeway for a good deal of extra-curricular entertainment.

It was a noble experiment on the part of George McCullagh and, although the trip certainly broadened my journalistic horizon, it also provided me with an international palate for alcoholic stimulants. More than a normal share of my reportorial assignment was devoted to investigating the wagering possibilities at such celebrated race courses as Royal Ascot, Longchamps and Auteuil.

I regarded direct communication between me and my North American headquarters as an unnecessary expense, but I was astounded one night to be called from the bar of a Paris hotel by the concierge, who announced with hand-wringing obsequience that the transatlantic operator had a call for me.

Fearing the worst, I picked up a lobby house-phone with

trembling hands, only to discover that Deacon Allen was calling me from the Dancing Pig in Toronto. He felt impelled to give me a transoceanic report of two momentous events: "Nine-Dollar Charlie," financially fat from his over-charging tactics, had signed up for an Arthur Murray course in ballroom dancing, and Wally had catapulted Nellie through the windshield of his Cadillac, again. This time, Wally hit the jackpot – he had crashed into the rear end of a parked police car, and the constabulary had taken a very narrow-minded view of his advanced state of inebriation. Wally was in the market for the services of an outstanding criminal lawyer, with friendly police-court connections.

Undoubtedly, the phone call gave me a delayed attack of homesickness. A few nights later, I was sitting alone in an Amsterdam bistro, moodily munching smoked eels and washing them down with egg-cup-shaped glasses of Bols gin. A trio of Netherlands musicians were grouped at my back, playing that old western ballad, "Don't Fence Me In," and they were singing the words in English. With tears streaming down my face, I tipped them generously, at the expense of George McCullagh, and I hurried back to my hotel to put in a couple of telephone calls to Canada – the first spoken words which had been heard from me in several months.

With an effort, I relegated Leonforte to second place on my list of telephone calls. It was the middle of the night in Canada, but as always Dr. Hodgson was too polite to tell me to take a big jump into the Zuider Zee. From far across the Atlantic, I could hear his voice repeating the familiar phrase: "He's doing champion, Jimmy – just champion." Although I hadn't spent all of George McCullagh's money, I went down to the lobby and arranged for the concierge to book me passage on the first available plane to North America. Woodbine was beckoning – and the Queen's Plate was only a few months away.

A racing problem awaited me in Canada. In my absence, Willie Morrissey had appointed himself to manage my horse. His motives were unselfish, but he acted without my invitation and in his usual impulsive fashion. Without consulting anyone, he had commissioned Herb Lindberg, a California jockey, to ride Leonforte in the Queen's Plate.

I was appalled when this intelligence was whispered to me by Doc Hodgson. Before leaving Canada, I had promised the mount to George Courtney, an honest but undistinguished Canadian jockey who had ridden Leonforte in all his two-year-old races. Furthermore, Courtney was the colt's regular exercise boy, in all his morning workouts. I had a moral obligation to Courtney, although in the interests of Dr. Hodgson's sanity it was necessary for me to handle the impetuous and well-meaning Mr. Morrissey with exquisite tact.

Only one course was left open to me: I told Courtney that he would receive the jockey's customary bonus of ten per cent of the winning purse, even if he didn't ride Leonforte in the Queen's Plate. In return for this, Courtney would continue to gallop the colt in the mornings and ride him in the Plate Trial, a week before the big race. Already, I could see that it would be necessary to reduce the size of my little dream-house in the country. With ten per cent of the purse for Lindberg, ten per cent of the purse for Courtney, and another ten per cent for Doc Hodgson, the purse was disappearing quickly. I'd be lucky if I emerged from the race with enough money to buy a haircut and a shoeshine.

My natural misgivings about the entire affair evaporated as soon as I took my first look at Leonforte on a spring morning at Woodbine. Gad, but he was a handsome rascal. He had filled out beautifully in winter quarters and his bright coat was dappled with healthy vigour.

Even old Tom Bird, who had clocked every prospective Queen's Plater in the previous forty years, was impressed. The first time he peered at Leonforte in action, in my presence, Tom turned to me and he said judiciously: "He has a nice big King James ass on him, son." That, from old Tom, was the supreme accolade.

The emotional rigours of preparing a horse for the Queen's Plate have broken the health of more than one good trainer. There was a good deal of tension around the southwestern corner of the Woodbine in the two months before the race. We were stabled next to Morris Fishman, who was training Kanlee for two high-rolling financiers, Harry Lahman and Louis Chesler. Fishman's two well-heeled patrons stood to win $50,000 in "winter book" bets if Kanlee captured the Plate.

Fishman, who had a gnawing sense of personal responsibility for the excessive wagering by Lahman and Chesler, soothed his taut nerves by taking early-morning doses of neat whiskey. Fishman detested drinking in solitude, and throughout April and May his tackroom was jammed with rival trainers and nervous horse-owners in need of sedation. There were some mornings when an entire case of whiskey would be consumed in Fishman's barn. Looking back on it, I realize now that we staged a reckless and continuous two-month party. Lahman set a tremendous pace as a shedrow host and those spring mornings took their toll: he was dead, two years later, at the age of thirty-nine.

I had dreamed of making my own killing with Leonforte in the "winter book." However, when I returned from Europe, I was appalled to discover that the Toronto bookmakers were quoting my colt at the ridiculously low price of 10-to-1. I had expected to get odds of 25-to-1. Ruefully, I scraped up $200 from the bottom of my piggy-bank. My prospective winnings of $2,000 would be only sufficient to pay the traditional bonuses to my two jockeys: George Courtney and Herb Lindberg.

The directors of the Ontario Jockey Club had made some considerable alterations in the conditions for the Queen's Plate by the time that I made my bid for glory and riches. No longer were nine-year-old maidens – such as the ignominious Hurry Fox – permitted to enter the race.

In Leonforte's season, the Queen's Plate was confined to three-year-olds which had been foaled in Canada. The Jockey Club had imposed other pecksniffian restrictions: a Queen's Plate candidate had to be trained on Canadian soil. This rule meant that your horse had to be in Canada continuously from January 1 in the year of the race: in other words, you couldn't take your horse to Florida, California or any warm climate where the training conditions were infinitely superior to those in Canada.

Furthermore, the candidates were permitted to run in only *one* race prior to the Queen's Plate. This preliminary race – known as the Plate Trial – was run exactly seven days before the Queen's Plate. And to make the situation even more ridiculous the Plate Trial was only a six-furlong sprint. It was a hell of a poor conditioner for the nine-furlong Queen's Plate, with only a seven-day interval. Many good horses were ruined by this strange scheduling of engagements, before The Ontario Jockey Club relaxed the impositions several years later.

Leonforte had been out of actual competition for eight months, which meant that we were going to ask him to run the nine-furlong Queen's Plate with only one short sprint under his belt. Nevertheless, there were other owners whose horses were under the same handicap. It was madness, sheer madness! In those years, there were very few Queen's Plate-winners who were durable enough to continue racing successfully until they reached the age of four or five.

Obviously, there were many owners and trainers who were quite as recklessly hopeful as Dr. Hodgson and I – because twenty-four horses were entered in the Plate Trial. The directors of the Jockey Club deliberated solemnly and they decided to split the field into two races, with twelve starters in each division. The luck of the draw decreed that Leonforte should start in the first division.

The day before the Trial, Willie Morrissey stormed into the barn, fuming with indignation and sputtering apologies. He had been unable to locate Jockey Lindberg, who was reported to be in New York City.

This solved one of my financial problems. Doc Hodgson couldn't hide his smile as he told Morrissey: "To hell with Lindberg. Forget about him – we'll ride George Courtney."

Leonforte and George Courtney combined their talents and their courage to lift me to ecstatic heights the following afternoon. As the field for the first division of the Plate Trial lunged out of the starting-gate, Leonforte was in a bit of a tangle. There was a good deal of banging and bumping among the front-runners and Leonforte was quickly shuffled back into sixth place along the inner rails. Courtney did not yield to panic in those awkward circumstances. He restrained my colt lightly and stayed on the rails, waiting for his opportunity.

As the field left the backstretch and they went into the turn, Courtney clucked to Leonforte. The colt, still skimming the inner rails, moved onto the heels of the leaders.

I held my breath because I realized what Courtney had in mind – he was going to attempt to go through a narrow hole when the leaders went slightly wide, at the head of the stretch.

I saw Leonforte heading for that narrow gap and, instinctively, I closed my eyes.

I heard a great roar from the crowd and opened my eyes. Leonforte had made it – he came through the gap like a champion and Courtney gave him the gun. There he was – my colt – running in front of the field!

A couple of late finishers made a bold charge at Leonforte through the final furlong, but he was in command of the situation. He was the winner by a long neck, with Courtney hand-riding furiously.

Doc Hodgson and I didn't bother to go into the winner's enclosure for the customary picture-taking ceremony. To be truthful, I was weak with excitement and I suggested that we should repair to the tackroom for a long, quiet drink which might settle my jangled nerves. On our way to the barn, we detoured through the Woodbine paddock where Dr. Hodgson signed the official saliva-test papers. As we walked away from the paddock, and when we were out of earshot of the unofficial well-wishers, the old trainer said warningly: "I don't want to disappoint you, boy, but I'm not certain that your colt is ready to run a mile and one-eighth next Saturday. We'll take a look at him after he cools out."

Thirty-five minutes later, we were sitting on two camp chairs in front of the tack room when we heard the roaring which signalled the finish of the second division of the Plate Trial. Another five minutes passed before a groom came past the barn, leading one of the horses which had raced in the second division.

"Who won it?" Doc and I shouted in unison.

"Tularch – by as far as you could throw a rock!" the groom growled over his shoulder.

Dr. Hodgson and I exchanged wry glances. Tularch was owned by George McCullagh – who owned me!

Here was the classic confrontation, so beloved by the scriptwriters of old fashioned movies: the raggedy-assed reporter with the temerity to challenge the wealthy autocratic newspaper owner in the country's leading horse race. George certainly was a millionaire; and, certainly, I represented the economic proletariat.

And, strangely enough, I was destined to beat him!

With so much at stake for me, the next six days were agonizingly suspenseful. I went through the motions of writing my daily newspaper columns, although I was preoccupied with the coming race. George McCullagh, in his daily visits to the *Globe and Mail* cafeteria to hobnob democratically with his slaves, never failed to single me out for a few verbal shafts. He vowed loudly that he would fire me if Leonforte won the Queen's Plate. George was a fine man, genuinely concerned with the welfare of his employees and no one was ever fired from the *Globe and Mail* unless they committed some ghastly crime, such as raping the mayor's daughter. Nonetheless, my sense of humour was being eroded by the pressure of uncertainty and I had difficulty joining in the general laughter which greeted his ham-handed jocularities.

Dr. Hodgson's pessimistic remark after the running of the Plate Trial had conditioned me for disappointment. It is essential, though, for a horse-owner to be a perpetual optimist if he wishes to survive in the racing business.

I listened to Dr. Hodgson and nodded sagaciously, but I was clinging to hope. Without hope, life simply isn't worth living. And because I clung to hope, I lay awake at night dreaming of the possibility of success – and dreaming of the manner in which I must be prepared to accept such success. I was reaching for the moon and I dared to believe that it was within my grasp.

As I lay in bed at night, I could see myself leading Leonforte into the winner's enclosure. Laughing at myself in the dark bedroom, I planned a modest little speech with which I would answer the questions of my colleagues in the media who were assigned to interview the winning owner. I would pay tribute to Dr. Hodgson for his patient handling of the horse; I would pay tribute to George Courtney for the manner in which he had ridden the horse; I would say a few words about Jim Speers, who had finally realized a lifetime ambition when a colt bred by him won North America's oldest racing fixture; and, above all, I would pay tribute to Leonforte, who had done most of the work.

I was ready for the Queen's Plate – now it was up to Leonforte.

The Saturday morning of the Queen's Plate dawned overcast and muggy. I wore a new suit for the occasion. It was only a grey flannel suit, appropriate attire for a daily newspaper columnist. It was customary for the owners of Queen's Plate entrants to array themselves in grey toppers, claw-hammer coats and striped trousers on the day of the race. Not only would I have looked mildly ridiculous in such habilements, but my clothing budget couldn't be stretched to cover such an impractical investment.

For once I was thoughtful enough to refrain from intruding on Dr. Hodgson's final preparations at the barn. When the Queen's Plate runners were called to the paddock, I stood silently in the stall while Dr. Hodgson saddled our colt. When he gave a leg-up to George Courtney, I gave George an encouraging pat on one arm. George didn't get too many Queen's Plate mounts during his riding career, and when he had an opportunity he could be counted upon to do his very best. As the horses left the paddock for the post parade, Dr. Hodgson and I walked into the Woodbine infield, where we had planned to watch the race.

There were sixteen runners in the Queen's Plate that year and Leonforte had drawn the number two post position. The colt had lost weight during the preceding week, but he hadn't lost nearly as much weight as his owner, who had become positively gaunt from sleepless anxiety. "He looks pretty good," Doc Hodgson said, as the three-year-olds went into their starting-gate stalls, just a few yards east of the furlong-pole. "We've done all we could do. This is the payoff for eighteen months of training."

As he spoke, the stall-gates opened and the three-year-olds debouched in a disorderly cavalry charge. Leonforte was crowded badly in the first few strides and he was shuffled back into the pack. However, Courtney kept his cool; he found running-room on the inside and he had Leonforte in a contending position as the field thundered into the first turn. When they straightened out for the long run down the backstretch, Leonforte was in fifth place and his action was smoothly rhythmical.

Then, as the field swept into the final big turn with a half-mile to go, Leonforte gave me my thrill. He rushed up on the outside of the four leaders. I tried to shout encouragement, but

I don't believe any sound came from my parched mouth.

One split second of elation – and then, dismay.

At the head of the homestretch, Leonforte simply flattened out. Gamely, he attempted to keep running, but he lost all his action. He floundered and struggled, but he couldn't keep pace. As the leaders rushed for the winning-post, I realized that my colt was beaten. I forced myself to watch the finish of the race but, really, I was hoping that the infield grass would open suddenly, permitting me to fall silently into a very deep hole. I was numb; I had expected too much.

But wait – there was one note of wry consolation.

As the stragglers crossed the finish-line, I noticed that my own blue-and-ivory racing silks were far in front of a familiar set of orange-and-black silks. Those orange-and-black silks were carried by Tularch, the two-to-one favorite in the Queen's Plate wagering.

I had beaten George McCullagh!

There's one thing about owning race horses: eventually you're forced to learn how to play the role of the Gracious Loser. I managed a smile and, as we followed the crowd which was re-crossing the track from the Woodbine infield, I thanked Dr. Hodgson for all that he had done for me. I meant it, too. Doc had trained some race horses which approached greatness but none of those ever received more tender loving care than he gave to Leonforte.

I went into the Club House and stayed long enough to engage in the customary post-race pleasantries. Then I went to a downtown bistro to ponder the extent of my folly. I had blown my bankroll; my rash persistence in running Leonforte in the Queen's Plate had probably ruined a potentially good horse; I had over-matched myself.

As I was absorbing these lessons over my first drink, I glanced idly at the Woodbine program which I was still carrying in my hand. The Queen's Plate had been won by a gelding with the improbable name of Moldy. Moldy was owned by Col. R. S. McLaughlin, the multimillionaire Canadian automobile manufacturer.

Oh well, I said to myself, it's nice to see Col. McLaughlin win another big race – he needs the money!

17

You Remember Only the Good Days

I would be lying if I said that it was solely my somewhat dilettante ownership of horses which kept me enamoured of the racetrack in my adult years. Obviously I would be lying, too, if I said that I was motivated by a desire to win money. Betting was one of my lesser compulsions: if anything, it was a controllable minor vice.

No! As it was in the beginning, so it was to be to the end. I was hooked on "characters." I was fascinated by almost every man and woman who was part of the racing world. It was the horsemen and the horses who had enmeshed me originally but, as the years passed, the touts, the bums and the drifters eventually caught and held my attention. I suppose that every man whose fate compels him to labour on the commercial treadmill yearns for a different type of existence. I found my spiritual home on the racetrack – I soaked up the warmth of even those casual friendships offered by the men who worked around horses. I felt I was happier on the racetrack than I could have been in any other environment. I hadn't been born with the intellectual and emotional equipment to become wealthy. The members of my immediate family hold another theory: they believe that I am just plain damn lazy. Since the censurious connotations of the latter theory have usually been softened by good-humoured tolerance, I am prepared to acknowledge its validity although I do not glory in its truth.

I would be lying, too, if I said that I hadn't been offered the opportunity to win big bets. I was offered the betting privileges in a "boat race" at Sportsman's Park in Chicago when I was visiting Doug Ness, who was freshening up our horses at the Illinois track on their way home after a winter campaign in New Orleans.

The result of the "boat race" was guaranteed personally by Mr. Golf-Bag Sammy Hunt, who was stabled next to us. Mr. Hunt, a rather charming man if you weren't aware of his connections, was one of the heirs to the dismembered empire of Al Capone. Mr. Hunt was able to guarantee the result of the race because he happened to own all but one of the starters – although his name didn't appear as an owner on the Sportsman's Park program. That one unsuspecting horse which wasn't owned by Mr. Hunt had about as much chance as a snowball in hell.

I didn't bother to bet on the race – not, I confess, because I was restrained by any noble scruples. As a newspaperman, I was nervously aware of Mr. Hunt's reputation for occasional outbursts of blood-chilling indignation and I did not wish to be in the vicinity if the "boat race" proved to be a maritime disaster. I needn't have worried – the race was a model of successful larceny – but I was aboard a train en route to Toronto when the horses went obediently about their appointed rounds.

There were numerous other occasions of which my backstretch friends gave me feed-box information. From some of these tips I prospered quite handsomely, though always I was restricted by my weekly income, by caution, and by the lack of what gamblers term "the killer instinct."

My newspaper earnings in the years when I owned horses never surpassed $10,000 annually. For all my acknowledged self-indulgence, I didn't neglect my family financially. My weekly pay envelope from the *Globe and Mail* – minus the income taxes which had been deducted at the source – went directly and intact to my family. It was my much smaller earnings from radio broadcasts and magazine writing which financed my extra-curricular activities.

My wagering normally stayed within the limits of the amount of money which I was carrying in my pocket. There were times when I bet with bookmakers on credit, and I feel quite sure that I have managed to overlook a few minor but nonetheless outstanding debts to a few of those gentlemen. They *are* gentlemen – bcause they never bothered to reproach me for my forgetfulness.

There were days when the information which I received happened to coincide most fortuitously with a relatively full pocket. For instance, Morris Fishman started his horse, Canada's Teddy, at Narragansett Park on Rhode Island and Morris liked his chances on that particular afternoon. I was temporarily in funds; anyhow, I felt flush enough to bet $200 to win. Canada's Teddy romped home and he paid $22.60. I should have gone home, but I stayed another day to bet $400 on another of Fishman's runners, Kanlee. Despite the fact that Kanlee ran ingloriously in the can it was, all told, a successful journey. A newspaperman doesn't win $1,660 every week.

It is axiomatic that liquor and gambling don't mix well. In my own case, the mixture frequently impaired my judgment, with lamentable results. It wasn't that I was prone to over-bet when I became foxed with the grape – it was much more usual for me to forget carelessly some unimpeachable information which had been whispered to me by a trainer or owner.

There was one hilariously memorable autumn afternoon at Woodbine. I had spent the previous evening with Doug Ness in his downtown Toronto hotel room, arguing over our copies of the *Daily Racing Form* and a couple of bottles of rye. Actually, there wasn't much argument – for once there was complete unanimity of opinion concerning the next afternoon's program.

Along about midnight, Ness and I put aside our Racing Forms and we agreed, with owlish solemnity, that we had four horses which on the morrow couldn't possibly lose. Ness was saddling Quick Bubble and Mountaloon in the first two races and thus he was monumentally confident that we could win the daily-double. Then my old horse Broom Time, which had been claimed from me a couple of weeks earlier, was running in the Breeders' Stakes. "That horse is going to win – off the training I gave him," Ness said sagaciously. "The old man who claimed him can't possibly mess him up in two short weeks. I'll go around and have a little chat with him in the morning." But it was in the seventh race of that day that we detected the opportunity for a really long-priced killing. Ness was starting his good mare, Play Flash, in the seventh race and she was razor sharp. Ness had been saving her for this very spot.

All would have been well, if at that juncture I had gone directly to my downy couch. Regrettably, I detoured via the Dancing Pig and spent a few hours philosophizing with Deacon Allen, who seldom went to sleep before dawn.

Accordingly, I was feeling no pain when I arrived at Woodbine the following afternoon. After purchasing a fistful of two-dollar daily-double tickets on the combination of Quick Bubble and Mountaloon, I repaired to the bar where Joe Perlove and the Caviar Kid were already working on an opened jug. I was becoming overly expansive even before the horses went to the post for the first race, and when Quick Bubble won on schedule, I felt impelled to share my blessings. Fully confident that Mountaloon would win the second race, I noticed two priests who were old friends of mine on the Club House lawn, and to each of them I gave one of my daily-double tickets.

The two priests were enchanted by this charitable contribution from a lapsed Protestant. However, a man who spends his life around the race track needs all the spiritual aid which is available.

When Mountaloon won the second race, the daily-double paid $33.25. I don't recall that I even momentarily regretted my donation to the Church of Rome. The sun was shining, the distiller's products were bubbling cheerfully in my bloodstream, and I wished the entire world to share my feeling of well-being.

After a few more visits to the bar, my mood was still exultant but my thinking-processes had become fuzzy. When the field was in the paddock for the Breeders' Stakes, I focused my gaze very carefully on the odds-board and perceived that Broom Time was being quoted at 25-to-1. I had intended to bet $100 on him, but the price shook my confidence. I was beginning to second-guess myself – and in gambling this is a fatal weakness.

Just before the pari-mutuel machines closed, I bet $50 to

win on Broom Time and I said: "Oh to hell with it" – thinking I had thrown the money out the window. The public couldn't be crazy, I reasoned; Broom Time was 25-to-1 in a small, six-horse field. Ness and I must be the only persons in the crowd who were daft enough to believe he could win.

Broom Time won. He paid $56.00 for every two-dollar wager. I swaggered into the Club House betting area to cash my tickets for a total of $1,402.50.

Instantly, I was overcome by an abounding affection for Broom Time. I arranged with the club house wine steward to liberate a couple of bottles of champagne, and with those protruding from my topcoat pockets I trudged towards the barns to visit Old Man Frost, who had claimed Broom Time from me. In this moment of affluence, I had only the friendliest feelings for the man who had taken my horse.

Mr. Frost was slightly surprised to see me arriving at his barn, agleam in goodwill and merriment. With little difficulty, I persuaded him to sit on a camp stool, testing the champagne while I grabbed Broom Time's shank and led the horse around the walking-ring. Broom Time and I had made ten or twelve circuits of the dusty little ring before a vagrant thought brought me to a halt. I remembered that Play Flash was on her way to the starting gate for the seventh race.

Fortunately, Frost's barn was close to the paddock, and at that moment a friend, nicknamed Winey, was scurrying past us on his way to make a bet on the seventh race. Holding Broom Time's shank in my right hand, I reached into my pocket awkwardly with my left hand and pulled out a few banknotes. I hailed Winey and asked him to bet the money for me on Play Flash, to win.

As luck would have it, I had pulled four twenty-dollar bills out of my pocket. My pocket was stuffed with fifty-dollar bills, but fate decreed that they should elude my groping fingers. Winey was in a hurry; he grabbed the money and sped away just in time to make his bets before the ticket-sellers slammed shut their windows.

Broom Time was just about cooled out and my feet were beginning to hurt when the distant cheering signified the finish of the seventh race. Mr. Frost and I were enjoying ourselves immensely, and in my fuzzy state I almost forgot my investment in Play Flash. Broom Time was regarding his owner and his amateur groom with some curiosity when Winey returned from the gambling pits. Play Flash had won the seventh race and she paid $19.30. Winey handed me $772, which I pushed into my overcrowded pockets without counting the money.

Naturally, I didn't go home directly. It was necessary to visit Doug Ness in his hotel room to congratulate him on his brilliant horsemanship. The celebration was protracted and noisy.

The next morning I awoke groggily and discovered that I was lying on a nest of money. I must have dumped the loot on my pillow when I arrived home and then after donning my pyjamas I had collapsed atop the heap of cash. I counted the banknotes dully and realized that, despite my merry debauchery of the previous day, I had come home with close to $2,200.

Ah – but I had blown the opportunity to win enough to make the down-payment on the Little Dream House. A man should keep his wits about him when he has advance information on four good-priced winners.

It is the nature of the bettor to remember only the good days at the track; he forgets about the bad days as quickly as possible. I remember a few very good days, but I never permitted my betting losses to get out of hand badly. I was a craven piker compared with many of my newspaper colleagues. I went to a Detroit track with a French sports-writer from Montreal and he won $3,600 in two days. Less than a week later, he had dissipated all his winnings and owed his bookmaker $4,000.

Even when I lost only what I was carrying in my pocket, I have been afflicted by profound depression. I was broke after the running of the fifth race one wet, gloomy afternoon at Woodbine. Feeling very lonely and neglected, I was walking through the rain towards the exit when I saw an equally forlorn figure leaning over the rail staring at the muddy track. It was Irwin Taylor, the Caviar Kid, and he had tapped out on the fifth race. I stopped to exchange commiserations.

"We are broke – but all is not lost," Irwin said sententiously. With which he reached into the extraordinarily capacious pockets of his custom-tailored rain coat. From one pocket he withdrew a jar of Romanov caviar. From the other pocket he plucked a large package of unsweetened English biscuits and a table knife.

For the next twenty minutes, oblivious to the rain which was dripping from the brims of our hats, we leaned over the rail, daintily eating biscuits which were slathered with Romanov caviar. Our spirits repaired rapidly. We strode out to the parking lot and grandly hailed a cab – which I charged to the *Globe and Mail*'s account. We drove to the Royal York Hotel and we signed ourselves into a small suite. After freshening up, we strode into the Imperial Dining Room and summoned the chef to discuss a suitable dinner. Although neither of us had more than carfare in our pockets, the Caviar Kid nonchalantly scrawled his name on the dinner check, adding a fifteen per cent tip and, patting his stomach happily, he said: "Tomorrow, we'll kill 'em. I have a tip on a fifteen-to-one shot in the first race. He'll win by as far as you can throw a rock."

Do I feel a twinge of conscience or regret over the money which I dissipated in racetrack wagering over the past forty years? I kept a fairly accurate record of my betting from day to day. To put it in the very worst light, there was seldom a year in which I showed a net loss of more than $1,000. If I wished to stretch a point, I could say that my lifetime losses have been $40,000 – although I know that the total sum was considerably less than that.

The figure is purely relative. In the same forty years, it is quite likely that I have spent a total of $15,000 on my daily purchases of cigars. I have never belonged to a golf club – the average golfer certainly spends $1,000 per year on his hobby.

What could I have done with $40,000 if I had spent the past forty years storing it carefully in the bank, in the manner of a squirrel?

Well, I might have bought a very, very small yacht!

The mere mention of the word "yacht" nauseates me. I am one of those landlubbers who can be overcome by mal de mer in my own bathtub if, incautiously, I permit the water to run to a depth of more than six inches.

The money lost is inconsequential when compared with the mental stimulation provided by my daily visits to the racetracks. As Jim Speers said, "every man needs a hobby and a worry." He might have added that the observation of human behaviour on racetracks is a divertissement without parallel.

There were, for instance, the "stoopers."

A "stooper" is a man who scurries around the grandstand area of a racetrack with his keen eyes focussed on the ground. He picks up discarded pari-mutuel tickets. Racetrack patrons carelessly throw away an extraordinarily large number of good tickets. This happens particularly in a race where the official result has been delayed by a claim-of-foul. Many a bettor, watching his horse being beaten, angrily throws away his tickets before the official result is posted on the board. A claim-of-foul provides a field day for the "stoopers."

A professional "stooper" can make a reasonably good living. They abhor the amateurs who impede their path, grubbing around on the ground after a horse has been disqualified.

Watching a professional stooper in action is quite intriguing. They have photographic memories and they can spot a "good" ticket instantly, even when it is lying on the ground three or four yards in front of them. The stoopers don't bend down unless they're reaching for a cashable ticket – they have developed a trick of kicking tickets which are lying on the ground, face-down. With the toe of their right shoe, they flip the ticket into the air and they can read the numbers as the ticket is in flight.

There is one stooper who, as long as I can remember, has seldom missed a day of racing on an Ontario track. He is a loner, a big, clean-shaven man, dressed habitually in immaculately pressed trousers and an expensive leather jacket. He never stops moving, even while a race is being run; the cashiers testify that he earns a good living.

Joe Perlove, who was given to periodic bursts of whimsy, had a theory about this man. Perlove insisted that this stooper wore shoes from which the soles had been removed. Thus-equipped, the stooper could stand on a discarded ticket and he could "read" the numbers through the sensitive soles of his feet. This was one of Perlove's theories which I never bothered to verify: Joe gave me enough trouble with his tips on slow horses.

Stoopers are tolerated on most North American racetracks, but touts are the pariahs of the racing world, detested and pursued relentlessly by the security officers who police the grandstands, club houses and stable areas. The touts are despised because they prey on the most gullible among the spectators, seducing those suckers into betting on sure-things which seldom – if ever – win. If the horse happens to win, the tout clings to the sucker, demanding his share of the profits. If the horse loses, the tout disappears until the heat is off. A really busy tout will frequently have five or six persons betting on five or six different horses for him in the same race.

Since 1950, policing methods have improved so dramatically on North American tracks that it has become almost impossible for touts to operate for any length of time within an individual track. The touts have been forced to become "telephone-men," calling their alleged information to betting-clients in neighboring cities.

The truth of the matter is that many businessmen who maintain otherwise respectable fronts are full of cupidity. These businessmen are often eager to bet on a "fixed race." A tout who is a good telephone-man can still hustle plenty of "marks" who are more than ready to listen to even the most spurious information.

"Show me a man who boasts about how honestly he runs his own business," Doc Burns used to say cynically, "and I'll show you a sucker who's ripe for the picking."

In a profession with a high mortality rate, Doc Burns was uniquely durable. He was touting on Canadian tracks when I was a small boy, and he was touting until the day before he died in an Edmonton hospital in 1967. He had travelled a million miles after leaving the little town of Tredegar, in Wales.

Doc Burns was born Will Bernstein, a member of an eminently respectable family in Tredegar. His two maiden sisters were apothecaries in the Welsh town, and during the Canadian winters when the race track suckers were hibernating, Doc frequently flew home to visit them in their musty dispensary. The two old dears were under the impression that their brother was a prominent businessman in the Canadian West.

Tredegar was also the birthplace of the Rt. Hon. Aneurin Bevan, the perpetually dissident labour minister in Prime Minister Clement Attlee's British cabinet. In fact, Bevan and Will Bernstein had been schoolboy playmates.

When the Rt. Hon. Mr. Bevan visited Canada and, he made an important speech in Winnipeg, Doc Burns was sitting front and centre. After his speech, Mr. Bevan was delighted to embrace his long-lost schoolmate, little knowing or caring that Doc was persona non grata with law-enforcement agencies on Canadian race tracks. After all, Wales is greyhound country – the Welsh don't give a damn for thoroughbred horses.

Doc's family had outfitted him splendidly when they despatched him to North America shortly after World War I. His ultimate destination was Chicago, but he detoured via Winnipeg to see another old Tredegar schoolmate, Max Isaacs, a Winnipeg lawyer. Doc took residence in one of the city's most opulent hostelries, the Fort Garry Hotel, and he fell in love with a blonde. Coincidentally, he discovered the bright lights of the neighboring French community of St. Boniface. If you visited sleepy little St. Boniface now, you would have difficulty in accepting the legend that the town once was known as "the Tia Juana of Western Canada."

The blonde soon reduced Doc's bankroll to the size of a black-eyed pea and Burns abandoned his original itinerary, which led to Chicago. Through force of circumstances, he became a tout, with a transcontinental list of clients. He had an exceptional fondness for girls who, regrettably, usually proved to be avaricious, and he was forced to work very hard in his new profession.

Although I knew Burns for forty years, he never attempted to induce me to bet on a horse. Possibly, he was reluctant to put the zip on me because he remembered me as an innocent child who used to go to the races in Winnipeg with W. A. Dutton. Mr. Dutton never permitted himself to be touted by Burns, but he found him amusing and, daily, he would give Doc a handout of ten or twenty dollars.

Doc placed me in a special category on his list of clients. He had numerous acquaintances from coast to coast whom he "fined" regularly. The "fine" was a penalty which you paid for the dubious privilege of Doc's company. Burns would approach one of these clients and he would say curtly: "I'm a little short – let me have ten dollars." Because of my youth, he didn't bother me until I was earning my own living in the newspaper business. I knew that I had made my mark in the business world when Doc imposed my first "fine" of five dollars. In later years, when I was working for the Ontario racetracks as the director of public relations, he raised me to the ten-dollar category.

I paid my fines willingly. It was less expensive than betting on one of Doc's tips. Doc's tips were the kiss of death – he could have "stopped" Man O War. Sam Green, a man in Edmonton, had a special arrangement with Burns. During the Edmonton race meetings, Sam paid Doc twenty dollars per day "NOT to call me". Green estimated that he saved himself thousands of dollars by short-circuiting Doc's telephone calls.

I had no illusions where Doc Burns was concerned. He was a rough, tough hustler and he was merciless when he had a sucker on the hook. Racetrackers are inclined to ignore a tout's depredations of the general public, but they become wrathful when a tout victimizes a member of the racing family. Burns, who worked all the angles, destroyed many of his hard-won friendships on the backstretch when he became party to an elaborate con-game which seriously mulcted a prominent prairie physician. The physician had performed many acts of medical charity for Canadian horsemen and Burn's stock hit an all-time low when it became public knowledge that he had been involved in the rip-off.

In his latter years, the old tout cut a singularly unprepossessing figure. In fact, he usually resembled an unmade bed. Even the most expensive suit appeared to be second-hand after Doc had worn it for a couple of weeks. His hat would be crumpled; he seldom wore his false teeth and the butt of a dead cigar dangled from one corner of his flabby mouth as he stood outside the main gate of a racetrack. The detectives wouldn't permit him to enter the grounds of many tracks – usually, he watched the races peering drably through the railings of the steel fences which bordered the grounds.

Mind you, he bought expensive clothes but they lost their rich patina as soon as he donned them. One night he was walking down Jasper Avenue, in Edmonton, with another hustler named Fishy. They paused before the floodlit window of an exclusive men's shop. A beautiful $250 tan cashmere polo-coat was displayed in the window.

"Do you see that coat?" demanded Doc. "Well, if Percy

Yates wins the Canadian Derby tomorrow afternoon, I'll be wearing that coat tomorrow night."

Fishy's mind boggled at the mere thought of Doc buying such a lovely coat. Relating the incident later to associates in the cafeteria of the Macdonald Hotel, Fishy blurted: "Can you imagine Burns wearing that coat? He'd look like a hog all dressed up in a tuxedo."

Everyone in the racing business regards a bookmaker as fair game in any devious plot. A bookmaker siphons off racing's lifeblood – the money – without making any significant contribution to the sport. Accordingly, any gambler who manages to past-post a bookmaker is hailed as an emancipator. Past-posting is an act of larceny which depends upon elaborate split-second timing; the object is to bet on a horse *after the horse has won.*

During one summer race meeting, when he was denied the privileges of the Edmonton race course, Doc Burns was listening on radio to the "live" broadcasts of the Edmonton races as he sat in his Edmonton hotel room. Doc cooked up a deal with Stanley Zedd, in Winnipeg. Stanley, the proprietor of the world's oldest permanent floating crap game, had been put out of business by a new reformist civic administration, and, additionally, his betting-luck had turned sour.

So each afternoon, Stanley would go into a small Winnipeg club which was operated by a bookmaker. Stanley would pass the time, studying the racing form for the Edmonton races and, he would make a few modest build-up bets.

The conspirators had devised a ludicrously simple code. The letter "A" represented the Number One horse, the letter "B" represented the Number Two horse, etc., etc. They agreed that they would confine their betting to the fifth race on the Edmonton program.

A couple of minutes before the broadcast of the fifth race in Edmonton, Doc would put in a telephone call to Max Isaac's Winnipeg office where – unknown to the senior partner of the firm – a struggling law student had been impressed into participating in the scheme. As the horses crossed the finish-line in Edmonton, Doc would shout into the phone: "Number One wins it!"

Hanging up the phone, the law clerk quickly would dial

the number of the Winnipeg bookmaker's club. When the bookmaker answered, the law clerk would ask: "Is Mr. Allen in the club?"

The bookmaker would turn to his clients and demand: "Is there a Mr. Allen in the room?" No answer! The bookmaker would hang up the phone after telling the caller that Mr. Allen wasn't present.

Meanwhile, Stanley Zedd had tabbed the name of the Number One horse in the fifth race. Nonchalantly, he would say to the bookmaker: "I'm going home, but before I go I might as well bet $100 on this bum in the fifth race at Edmonton."

Winnipeg is a small city and news travels swiftly there. Stanley Zedd won only three bets, spaced carefully over an entire week, before the indignant bookmakers refused to handle his action.

In my years around the tracks, I have heard many variations of his hoary past-posting wheezes, but most of them were one-shot deals. Many of them deserve only to be listed in racing's apocrypha.

Irish Davy Ambersley used to delight in telling the story of how he and Tom Hayes accompanied a Hamilton gambler named Harney to New York, where they sat in an afternoon table-stakes poker game operated by a certain Mr. Dwyer (no relation to Big Bill Dwyer). Harney had played at Dwyer's table before and he was acutely aware of the fact that he had little chance of winning – two of the daily participants in the poker game were on Dwyer's payroll.

Dwyer's office was in a second-floor loft in the New York garment district. Dwyer also "booked" horses on a big scale and a bettery of manned telephones lined the wall beside the poker-table. Just to be certain that there were no intrusions, Dwyer locked the door of his office at noon each day and it wasn't opened again until the afternoon's last race had been run.

Harney had made elaborate preparations for this particular session of Dwyer's table-stakes poker game. He had a mendicant accordion player stationed across the street from Dwyer's office. In a corner tobacco shop, a confederate was receiving the results of the Belmont Park races by telephone. They had worked out a complete musical program to cover the afternoon of racing at Belmont.

When Cup Cake won the second race at Belmont, the accordion player lustily squeezed out the strains of "The Sidewalks of New York."

Harney, who was losing steadily in the poker game, turned to Dwyer and snarled: "I'm hooked for $500 in this damn game. You'd better book me for $200 on Cup Cake in the second at Belmont. There's no point in going back to Hamilton without any money."

The accordion player continued his concert throughout the afternoon. Harney was no fool – deliberately, he blew a few bets on the Belmont horses. However, when the day's gambling was completed, the Hamilton trio had dropped more than $3,000 at the poker table and Harney had won more than $8,500 betting on horses.

Needless to say, that was the last occasion on which Harney, Hayes or Ambersley ever visited Mr. Dwyer's poker game. "To tell the truth," Irish Davy used to say. "I've never gone back to New York City since that day, although more than twenty years have passed. Mr. Dwyer didn't smile much; he struck me as a man who wouldn't be happy about being cheated."

The Doc Burns story of past-posting is true. I know it's true, because the law clerk, who grew up to be an eminently respected solicitor, told me the story himself. As for Irish Davy – well, the good man has been dead these many years, God rest his immortal soul.

Occasionally, bookmakers are the victims of their own cupidity. When Harry Lahman and Lou Chesler owned horses on Ontario tracks, they bet with such unrestrained enthusiasm that bookmakers were anxious to handle their business. Two Toronto bookmakers – Slow and Palooka – courted Lahman and Chesler assiduously, with the result that Lahman and Chesler invited them to Long Branch on a summer afternoon. The delighted bookmakers didn't realize that they were walking into a set-up; Morris Fishman was starting Indian Giver, one of Lahman's horses, and the canny little trainer was virtually certain that the horse would win at a long price.

Much liquor was consumed in Lahman's car after Harry

parked in the stable area at a spot which provided a good view of the racing strip. The build-up was planned carefully. After their tongues had been loosened by whiskey, Slow and Palooka boasted about the size of bets which they could handle.

"Could you handle $2,000 on a horse?" Lahman asked silkily.

The two bookies, their egos and their ambitions enlarged by the liberal intake of good whiskey, replied scornfully that a $2,000 bet was a mere bagatelle.

"Well," said Lahman, keeping one eye on the starting-gate, where Indian Giver just had been led into his stall, "you have a $2,000 bet on Indian Giver in this race."

The two bookmakers looked around, panic-stricken. They were trapped. They couldn't run to the pari-mutuel machines in time to lay off a portion of the $2,000 bet. With rueful sighs, they sat back in Lahman's car to watch the race.

Indian Giver won handily and he paid $13.65.

Personally, bookmakers provided me with headaches, but touts provided me with entertainment. Occasionally, when I was visiting foreign lands on an expense account, I permitted myself to be touted just for the hell of it. At Leopardstown, outside Dublin, I ran into a delightfully garrulous Irish tout named Casey, who stiffed me on five consecutive losers. Then he conned me into taking him back to the Gresham Hotel in Dublin for dinner. To top the evening, the Gresham charged me three quid for the silver fish-knives which Casey secreted in his raincoat pocket when he was leaving.

At Happy Valley, in Hong Kong, I permitted myself to be touted again by two sampan coolies who couldn't have handicapped a race between the Star Ferry and RMS *Queen Mary;* and, at a track outside Tokyo, I was touted by an old lady who had so many gold teeth in her head that her open mouth resembled an overloaded charm-bracelet.

Yes, but when it came to touts there was only one Doc Burns, thank God! The world wasn't large enough to accommodate more than one.

Doc Burns has gone now. His bones lie in an Alberta graveyard, far from his native Welsh village. I knew him for forty years and in that time he was never guilty of doing an honest day's labour. He proved conclusively that touting can be a financially rewarding profession.

Of course, those "fines" which he imposed on his acquaintances helped to sustain him.

A year or so before he died, I checked into the Hotel Vancouver. I had left the race tracks, and once again I was writing a newspaper column; this one was syndicated to twelve or thirteen Canadian papers. I had told no one that I was coming to Vancouver, and as the bellboy hung my topcoat in the cupboard I was astonished to hear the ringing of my room telephone.

I picked up the phone and I heard his hoarse, commanding voice: "This is Doc. I want to see you. Come down to the lobby."

Before going to the lobby, I put my bankroll in my left trouser pocket. I peeled off one ten-dollar bill and I put it in my right trouser pocket.

After Burns and I had exchanged a little chit-chat, I pulled the ten-dollar bill out of my pocket, handed it to him surreptitiously, and began to walk away.

"Hey," he called after me, loudly. "I need twenty dollars from you!"

I whirled on him indignantly. "What the hell's come over you?" I snapped. "You've never fined me more than ten dollars. After all, I'm only a newspaper columnist."

"Yeah," he said with a crooked smile. "But I've just learned that your column is being syndicated. I've decided to give you a promotion."

I paid my fine of twenty dollars. It was a small price to pay for belated public recognition of my new elevated status in life. I miss the crafty old rascal.

18

The Other Side of the Fence

The important decisions in men's lives customarily are made after intelligent consideration of all the alternatives. I decided to leave the newspaper business while I was sitting, one evening, in Morris Fishman's licensed tavern, the Paddock.

The Paddock had become my second-office. The switchboard operators at the *Globe and Mail* knew where to reach me if I didn't answer the telephone in my cubby-hole at the newspaper. For many years I had longed to be turned loose behind the well-stocked bar of a licensed tavern to mix my own drinks. On this particular evening, Morris had given me permission to be my own bartender. Making full use of my temporary visa, which permitted me to join the regular bartenders in their oak-bordered island, I was mixing champagne cocktails for myself and stingers for Deacon Allen.

The details of that evening still are remarkably clear in my mind. The Deacon and I were sitting at a table with Miss Aletha Granger, a beautiful songstress who had poured herself into a sheer white gown. Miss Granger was magnificently constructed and her bodice was overflowing.

I remember distinctly that when Miss Granger arrived at our table Mr. Allen, Mr. Fishman and I arose from our chairs. And when the Deacon attempted to sit down again, some clod had removed his chair. The Deacon sat down heavily on the carpeted floor, but with the elastic reflexes of a veteran and accomplished drinker, he didn't spill a single drop of his stinger, which he was holding in his right hand.

I remember distinctly, too, that when the time came for Miss Granger to rejoin the instrumental trio on the bandstand, she said in her lovely contralto voice: "Excuse me, gentlemen; I'm due back on the stand."

The Deacon arose gravely: instead of looking into Miss Granger's beautiful face, his gaze was directed into her cleavage. "When you go, Madam," he said to her softly, "will you be kind enough to leave one of those for me?"

Miss Granger laughed warmly. She regarded the Deacon as a kindly old soul.

While Miss Granger was singing, I walked into the tiny office of the Paddock. Deliberately, I telephoned the *Globe and Mail* and told Tommy Munns, the managing editor, that I was quitting. I returned to the table and I didn't tell anyone what I had done.

The next morning, the gravity of my act struck me. I told my shocked family what I had done, but I was too stupidly pig-headed to acknowledge that I might have made a mistake. When my column didn't appear in its customary place on the sports pages of the *Globe and Mail,* the paper informed a few curious callers that I was on vacation. Two days later, I bought a small display advertisement on the same sports pages, soliciting job-offers.

The response to the advertisement temporarily allayed my family's fears for my sanity. I had managed to acquire a normal quota of friends who, while they may have deplored my stupidity, didn't wish to see my family starving. There were some interesting offers; there were calls from genuine friends who were ready to advance financial aid, if it was needed; and there was one call from an elderly gentleman, whom I respected greatly, who asked if I might be interested in joining the newly-formed Toronto group of Alcoholics Anonymous. Far from resenting his suggestion, I thanked him for his concern. I should have listened to him.

One offer I snapped up immediately. Three Toronto businessmen had decided to introduce standardbred-racing, with pari-mutuel wagering, to Ontario's largest city. They hired me as assistant general-manager with supervision of the new harness-racing track's advertising and public relations.

Those three men, Herbert E. Hatch, Harry W. Knight and Jules Mendelsohn, launched me on a twelve-year excursion into the business offices of the racing industry. They provided me with immensely pleasurable employment for three years and, when they sold out their interests to E. P. Taylor's expanding empire, I was one of the chattels which were included in the sale.

Having spent so many years around the thoroughbreds, I shared the running-horsemen's lofty contempt for the "jugheads." Toronto was traditionally running-horse territory and Torontonians regarded the trotters and pacers as interlopers and country bumpkins. I confess that I took my new job with my tongue wedged firmly in my cheek. I suspected that the project was doomed to long, hard impoverishment, but the challenge offered very interesting possibilities.

In the first place, the new venture had been planned as a night-racing operation. My former employer, George McCullagh, was the implacable foe of one member of the syndicate – Jules Mendelsohn – and George exerted very strong influence in provincial political circles. McCullagh persuaded the provincial government that they would be unwise to permit the introduction of night racing to Ontario. George, of course, was a thoroughbred man, and quite apart from his dislike of Mendelsohn he did not desire to see standardbred racing obtain a foothold in Toronto, where the thoroughbreds had held undisputed sway for ninety years.

George McCullagh reasoned that if the standardbred promoters weren't permitted to have night racing they would go broke within three years. He was close to the mark. He erred in underestimating Messrs. Hatch and Knight. Julie Mendelsohn was essentially a promoter, who put up little of his own cash. However, Hatch and Knight were both wealthy and stubborn and they were prepared to lose a fortune in their campaign to establish the standardbreds in Toronto.

Despite the fact that they absorbed three years of unrelieved financial reverses, I never heard a word of complaint or reproach from Messrs. Hatch and Knight. Well, there was *one* beef: only hours before the opening of our inaugural 42-afternoon meeting, I was escorting Mr. Hatch through the catering area, beneath the grandstand.

He pointed at one concession stand, which was being stocked with Coca Cola. Mr. Hatch surprised me by giving me one of the few direct orders I ever received from him. "Get that Coca Cola out of here," he demanded.

"But, Mr. Hatch," I protested, "you can't run a race track without Coca Cola."

"You can run MY racetrack without it!" he roared. "Those are the sons-of-bitches who brought Prohibition to America."

Probably no other racing venture ever opened under less auspicious circumstances. We had purchased a mobile starting gate, mounted on a Cadillac car. The contraption was painted bright gold with "Thorncliffe Raceway" lettered in black on its sides. A few weeks before our opening, we decided to obtain some publicity by taking our mobile gate to New Hamburg, Ontario, where the Canadian Pacing Derby was being contested. New Hamburg normally has a population of only 2,500. However, the population is doubled on Derby Day when the harness-racing afficionados from all over the province descend on the little town.

Our collective hearts were bursting with pride as Thorncliffe's expensive Cadillac gate drove onto the track to start the field for the first race on New Hamburg's afternoon program. The car roared down the backstretch as the harness-horses paced behind it in perfect alignment.

Regrettably, the official starter wasn't accustomed to operating such a large gate.

On the outside of the turn, leaving the backstretch, stood a gigantic oak tree. The starter was just a bit slow in retracting the two extended arms of the starting gate. One of those extended arms struck the oak tree at a speed of fifty miles per hour. The oak tree withstood the impact – the arm of our precious starting gate was ripped right out of its housing.

I didn't dare to look at my three employers, who were sitting beside me in the grandstand. The crowd, who had been applauding our new starting gate when it appeared on the track, dissolved in derisive laughter. There is, I suppose, something hilarious about the sight of a lordly Cadillac disemboweling itself on an oak tree.

Further calamities awaited us. Our Cadillac was repaired

in time for Thorncliffe's opening day, but two simultaneous incidents almost provoked me into cutting my throat:

As the field came onto the Thorncliffe track to be paraded before our inaugural race, Torey Gregg, our public-address announcer, pressed the electric switch to open his microphones. It had rained heavily the previous night and there was water on the floor of the announcer's booth. As Torey opened his mike, he stepped on a naked wire on the wet floor of the booth; the shock almost paralyzed him.

The first words ever heard over the public-address system by a Thorncliffe harness-racing crowd were Torey Gregg's frightened scream:: "JESUS H. CHRIST!" The apocalyptic shout was heard clearly by almost everyone who lived within a two-mile radius of the track.

You are quite correct if you imagine that the crowd was rolling in the aisles after Gregg's welcoming words. Then, Torey urged the customers to turn their attention to the head of the stretch, where the field for the first race was preparing for the post-parade. The horses were ready, but the Cadillac wasn't ready. The Cadillac simply wouldn't start. To our acute embarrassment, our shiny new Cadillac eventually led the horses on parade – the Cadillac was being hauled by an incredibly dust-stained tow truck. The spectators were emitting snarky catcalls.

The mystery of the non-starting gate soon was solved, later. The previous night, one of my assistants had asked the general manager if he could borrow the Cadillac to call on his girl-friend. The general manager, assuming that the girl lived in Toronto, had given his assent. It transpired that the girl-friend lived in the town of Barrie, sixty-five miles away. It wasn't mechanical failure which had caused the Cadillac's ignominious official debut – simply, the return trip to Barrie had emptied the gasoline tank. The official starter had filled the tank before he left the track the previous afternoon and it never occurred to him to check the gas gauge before the first race.

Things were rapidly going from bad to worse. We had invited a throng of newspapermen and radio announcers to our opening and I had commandeered a large room above the racing-secretary's office as a press entertainment room. The room had been stocked liberally with whiskey, beer and assorted cold cuts. As the starting gate was being towed down the track past the jeering crowd, I rushed towards the press room, nourishing the faint hope that all the media reporters would be so engrossed by the free liquor that they wouldn't have observed our public discomfiture.

The door of the press room was locked. Cursing, I opened the door with my own key and barged in. There wasn't a single newspaperman or radio commentator in sight – the only occupants of the room were Fisher First and Benny, both of whom were sitting dully in chairs, stoned out of their minds. Fisher First was the Thorncliffe porter, an aged gentleman who habitually moved so slowly that, by comparison, he would have made Stepin Fetchit resemble an Olympic Games sprint-winner. Benny was a Thorncliffe hanger-on who, on Fisher First's earnest supplications, I had hired as steward of the press room.

I fired Benny on the spot although, later that evening, I relented after Fisher First bent my ear with an interminable story about Benny's urgent need of employment. I didn't fire Benny, but I banished him to the menial job of attendant in the men's washroom of the grandstand.

Benny was utterly incorrigible. Within two days at his new post, I discovered that he had invented another racket – he was selling ice water, at ten cents a glass, to patrons who found it necessary to visit the washroom.

My world was crumbling around me on Thorncliffe's opening afternoon. Leaving the press to pour their own drinks, I took a turn around the grounds and, along about the fourth race, I decided to inspect the little tea room in the club house. This room was packed with dear ladies who, parking their handbags on tables, were being served with afternoon pick-me-ups of tea, coffee and petit fours.

As I stood in the doorway, overseeing this charming scene, my heart jumped into my throat.

Smack-dab in the middle of the room, completely surrounded by these unsuspecting ladies, sat Toronto's two most notorious pickpockets. I knew them well – we had spent many off-duty hours together in bootlegging joints in the past, although I had never been rude enough to question them about the ethics and techniques of their profession.

The sight of the two light-fingered gentlemen was too much for me, on top of everything else which had occurred during the afternoon. I rushed towards them, red-faced with anger.

The older and smaller of the pair instantly recognized my intention. Standing up, he said politely: "Don't get excited, old pal. We are not here on business – this is strictly a social occasion. Won't you sit down and join us for a cup of tea?" True to their word, they departed after the last race, without even lifting a finger-bowl.

Things moved more smoothly after that horrific opening, although George McCullagh had assessed the situation shrewdly when he prophesied that Thorncliffe would suffer from slow economic strangulation if we were forced to race in the afternoons, in the hours traditionally reserved for thoroughbred racing. It was painstaking work, breaking down the customer-resistance of Torontonians who regarded the trotters and pacers as "country" horses. Grudgingly and very slowly, they came through our gates in increasing numbers; albeit in the first three years we never came close to attaining the break-even point. Almost against my will, I found myself being enchanted by the harness-horses and by the men and women who owned them. The first time I realized that they "had" me was when I was standing by the rail one evening, watching Earl Rowe driving two trotting mares in tandem. As I watched those two mares swinging through the homestretch with their hooves flying over the hard dirt surface in perfectly matched rhythm, I couldn't choke down an involuntary cry of delight. God, they were pretty!

Harness racing at Thorncliffe had a family-atmosphere, sharply reminiscent of the prairie thoroughbred days of my childhood. The three promoters had constructed a half-mile training track in a meadow, southeast of the main racing strip and, beside this, in the shelter of a copse of elms, they had staked out a trailer-village, complete with outlets for electric power. The horsemen moved their trailers into this pleasant spot and they brought along their wives, children and pets. It was the first time that I had seen children living on a race track.

I found the atmosphere so enjoyable that, frequently, I stayed on the grounds overnight, sleeping in the trailer owned by Harvey Fleet, a carefree ex-pugilist who raced a small stable of pacers. The idyllic serenity of the summer nights was destroyed occasionally after a flighty Irish lady, who owned horses, married her trainer, who was a genuinely wild Irishman. He moved into his bride's trailer and, more than once, he felt impelled to advertise his connubial enthusiasm by smashing all the windows in the bridal caravan. The newlyweds kept several glaziers busy that summer, until their marital ardour cooled down.

Three years passed swiftly, although I confess that I accepted with alacrity when E. P. Taylor offered me the job of publicizing all the thoroughbred tracks. Messrs. Hatch, Knight and Mendelsohn, who recouped most of their losses when they sold out to the Taylor interests, gave me their blessings. I was grateful to them for subsidizing my apprenticeship in the field of sports public relations. They had permitted me to make my mistakes without uttering a word of censure. Any success which I enjoyed in later years was due to the lessons which I had learned while spending the largesse of my uncomplaining employers at Thorncliffe. And the fact that harness-racing ultimately became the more profitable division of Taylor's turf enterprises could also be attributed – at least, in part – to the missionary sacrifices of Hatch, Knight and Mendelsohn.

There was one lingering regret as I left Thorncliffe. That little harness track had provided me with the highest priced winner of my life, although I take no credit for perspicacity; it was simply a case of dumb luck.

Morris Fishman, sneering gently at my association with the jugheads, had accepted my invitation to spend an afternoon at Thorncliffe, where the press bar had been operating with moderate efficiency ever since the ineffable Benny had been banished to custodianship of the men's washroom. Morris made a few polite remarks about our training facilities, our barns and our trailer-village, and just about the time that he was ready to bow a tendon, I led him into the control-room of our tiny pari-mutuel department. A field of eight undistinguished trotters was going to the post, and because we were playing rueful hosts to one of our smallest weekday crowds the betting was progressing very slowly.

I glanced at the calculating-machines and I noticed that,

although only six minutes remained before post-time, very little money had been wagered on a mare named Exeter Lady. She was being quoted at 100-to-1. With nonchalant bravado, which I hoped would impress my reluctant guest, I asked the mutuel-clerk to give me a couple of tickets on Exeter Lady. I knew no more about the mare than I know of nuclear fission.

Tucking the tickets in the breast pocket of my shirt, we went out onto the spacious lawn in front of the grandstand. As the field for that particular race was turning into the home-stretch for the final brush to the wire, the odds-on favorite broke stride and came to pieces like the innards of a three-dollar watch.

In the tangled confusion, Exeter Lady found racing-room along the inner rail. To the surprise of everyone – including me – Exeter Lady won handily.

She paid $254 for every two-dollar ticket. As far as I know, Exeter Lady was the longest-priced winner in the history of Thorncliffe.

When Mr. Taylor brought me back to the world of the runners, I was as ecstatic as a six-year-old boy who is turned loose in a candy factory. The preliminary negotiations were spasmodic and protracted, because Mr. Taylor had more important matters on his mind. Eventually, when he summoned me to his brewery headquarters to give me my terms of reference and strike a salary bargain, I had difficulty in restraining a smile of wild exultation from spreading ear to ear. As I walked away from his office, I was so happy that I was completely oblivious to a cloudburst which soaked my new cheap camelhair topcoat, causing it to stretch until it resembled a spaniel's drooping ear.

The mere idea of anyone *paying* me to spend my life on the thoroughbred racetracks struck me as hilariously amusing. It was a job which – if I had been fortunate enough to have an independent income – I would have been happy to perform without receiving any salary. I plunged into my duties with enthusiasm and I discovered that, although I had assumed that the horsemen contributed most of the gaiety to the racing world, there were some interesting personalities working on the other side of the fence.

Taylor had decided to concentrate Ontario's thoroughbred racing on three tracks. Ultimately, he closed Thorncliffe, Long Branch, Dufferin, Niagara Falls and the Hamilton Jockey Club. Coincidentally, he built a vast new Woodbine and, the name of the Old Woodbine was changed to Greenwood. Fortunately, he decided to retain and rebuild the Fort Erie track which, with its magnificent infield gardens, its lakes and its pastoral surroundings, became one of the most beautiful race courses in North America. The long summer meetings at Fort Erie were glorious. Audax Minor, the celebrated turf columnist of the *New Yorker* magazine, visited Fort Erie frequently and, for unspoiled beauty, he preferred it to immortal Saratoga.

Many of Fort Erie's patrons travelled daily from Toronto, ninety miles distant. The Canadian National Railways operated a race-train which was nicknamed "The Agony-Stricken Limited." Few trains in the history of Canadian transportation achieved comparable fame. It was reputed that the locomotive engineer was Charon, the boatman who, in Greek legend, ferried the dead across the River Styx. The "Agony-Stricken Limited" pulled out of Toronto's Union Station each morning with a full load of hopeful investors and the passenger-list included sundry touts and hustlers who operated poker-games and, surreptitiously, victimized the innocents in the nefarious pastime of Three-Card Monte while the train rumbled slowly through the Niagara Peninsula.

If the train was late – which it was, occasionally – the start of Fort Erie's first race was delayed by the management. The other track patrons, who already had purchased their daily-double tickets and were impatiently awaiting the beginning of the afternoon's action, would cheer sardonically when the locomotive, pulling its string of olive green day-coaches, appeared through the trees, rumbling towards the race track siding.

Neither flood nor fire nor hurricane can discourage a race-track patron who is anxious to bet on the daily-double. When the "Agony-Stricken Limited" was running late, the passengers would be leaping from the open doors of the coaches while the train was still a hundred yards from its destination. They would fall sprawling on the cindered right-of-way, and without bothering to brush themselves free of grime they would sprint heroically towards the Jockey Club gates. The wounded lay where they fell – no one ever bothered to stop and assist a maimed passenger who was lying, face-down in the cinders. Fortunately no one was ever killed in those crash-landings, although the casualty rate was quite high on wet afternoons when the footing was even more precarious than usual.

One afternoon, when the carnage among the disembarking train passengers was exceptionally high, my sense of duty impelled me to visit the track hospital, to offer words of comfort to the injured. Dr. Thoreau O'Mulvenny, the distinguished race-track surgeon, was ministering to one of the train-passengers, whose face was decorated with blood and railway cinders.

Dr. O'Mulvenny, who was dabbing the victim's lacerations with iodine while he instructed a nurse to apply bandages to the more ghastly contusions, gave me his Irish leprechaun grin as I hovered over the operating-table.

"He's going to miss the daily-double," said Dr. O'Mulvenny, employing a pair of tweezers to extract a particularly large cinder chunk, "but I'll have him back in action before post-time for the second race."

By an odd coincidence, that was the same afternoon on which one of our race horses decided that he was a swimmer. Puss N Boots, a two-year-old trained by Frank Merrill, was leading by five lengths as he sped towards the finish line, on the grass course. Without breaking stride, Puss N Boots jumped the inner hedge of the grass course and he headed for the largest and deepest of the lakes in the infield. With rare presence of mind, Jockey Ronnie Behrens bailed out, just before the horse dove into the deep water.

Trainer Merrill doffed his expensive jacket and, otherwise fully clothed, dove in to rescue his floundering horse. Merrill's stable foreman, an enthusiastic character named Reggie "Muscles-of-Steel" Anderson, dove in to rescue Merrill.

Anderson threshed the deep water for a few convulsive seconds and then screamed: "Migawd – I don't know how to swim." With which, he sank beneath the surface.

Saner heads took charge of the rescue operations and all participants in the impromptu bathing-sequence, human and equine, were rescued. Puss N Boots went on to establish a reputation for even greater eccentricity during his racing career: Muscles-of-Steel Anderson died of a heart attack a few years later, although there was no medical evidence that his maritime misadventures contributed to his untimely demise.

The box-office side of any race track is rich in salty characters, and two in particular who endeared themselves to me during my years as a racing publicist were Revolving Ossie Gelber and Thomas J. Bird.

Gelber like myself was a racing-nut, although we took different routes to the Lotus Land. I gave Gelber his nickname, because he has a peculiar habit of circling you continually while he is talking to you. I knew him first when he turned up at Thorncliffe Park with his one-horse stable – a selling-plater which he had purchased from Col. Fred Scott of Calgary. Coincidentally, Revolving Gelber had wormed his way into the editorial sanctum as the unpaid racing handicapper for the *Tribune*, a short-lived Toronto morning newspaper. Gelber was delighted to act as the paper's handicapper, without pay – his job provided him with press passes to all the tracks in Ontario.

Almost simultaneously, the *Tribune* went broke and Gelber's one-horse stable broke down. Undismayed, Revolving Gelber became Canada's first race-track pest-exterminator. He arrived at Woodbine one morning driving a battered old truck with a huge cylindrical drum mounted on it. Attached to the drum were hoses with spray nozzles. The contraption looked as if it had been assembled by a mad inventor.

Then, Revolving Gelber arrayed himself in a gas mask, white coveralls and thick gauntlets, and he proceeded to spray an empty barn. Woodbine officials watched apprehensively as Ossie, resembling a spaceman in his outlandish gear, ventured into the barn. He emerged with an impressive collection of rats, mice and luckless horse-flies which had been gassed into extinction.

Gelber was hired as the Jockey Club's official exterminator although officials eyed his jerry-built machine with some misgivings. One of the Woodbine officials asked Gelber if his equipment could exterminate household pests. "Sure," said Revolving Ossie, adding that it would be wise for the man to move his family into a hotel for the night and he would fumigate the house the following morning. He jotted down the address of the Woodbine man's home and promised to be Johnny-At-The-Rathole at 6 a.m. the next day.

So, the following morning, Gelber donned his protective

equipment; backed his old truck to the front of the house and opened the nozzles on his spray-hoses.

As the clouds of gas engulfed the little house, the doors burst open and a terrified man, his wife and their three children fled for their very lives.

Revolving Ossie Gelber was spraying the wrong house!

A man with Gelber's dedication couldn't be downed by such minor setbacks. The last I heard of him, he had been appointed Consulting Exterminator to all the harness-racing tracks in North America.

I inherited Thomas J. Bird when I joined Mr. Taylor's racing enterprise and the inheritance was one of the most rewarding experiences of my life. Tom Bird had been the official clocker at Woodbine since the days of walk-up starts but, at the age of seventy-five, he couldn't qualify for the pension plans and social security programs which Mr. Taylor's collection of eager-beaver cost accountants were attempting to install as they consolidated the financial statements of all the tracks which Mr. Taylor had purchased. Accordingly, I asked for Mr. Bird to be assigned to my department, where my generous budget permitted a few extravagances. It proved to be a most felicitous arrangement; Tom's security problems were solved and I had the daily delight of his company until he died, seven years later.

Tom Bird carried his age lightly. He stood as straight as a ramrod and, even in his late seventies, he was a formidable physical antagonist. He came into the office one morning with his right hand in a plaster cast. Under questioning he admitted, with embarrassed satisfaction, that he had flattened "some young whippersnapper" who had dared to question his veracity.

Tom was touchy on the subject of his veracity. I'll put it this way: Tom occasionally enlarged on the truth, if slight embellishment could improve a story. He vowed that, personally, he had clocked every horse which took a workout on the Woodbine track, and when Tom reported on a workout to an impressionable owner the owner usually came away from the conversation with the strong impression that his horse was a legitimate rival to Man O War. "What the hell," Mr. Bird would snort when anyone suggested that he was overstating the case. "The man paid a lot of money for that colt. I just want him to feel good."

Tom may have missed a few workouts, but seriously, I doubt it. Harry Giddings told me once about working a horse in total darkness at 3 a.m. because he didn't wish Bird to report the workout to his wealthy betting-clients.

While Woodbine slept, Giddings boosted his exercise boy onto the horses' back. He told the boy to gallop the horse slowly for a half-mile and then to set him down for the final half-mile. Giddings walked over to the finish-line and he pulled out his stopwatch. He had stationed a stableboy with a lantern at the half-mile pole. It was pitch dark, and the stableboy was instructed to drop the lantern to the ground as the colt began the four-furlong sprint.

The secret workout was conducted flawlessly. The boy dropped the lantern as the horse sped past the half-mile marker. Giddings clocked the horse, snapping the "stop" button on his watch as the horse's nose hit the wire.

Chuckling to himself, Giddings turned to walk across the infield to his barn. He was startled as a tall figure emerged from the tiny judges' stand on the finish line. Tom Bird was walking towards him gleefully.

"I caught him in $47\frac{2}{5}$, Harry," cackled Old Tom. "How fast did you make him?"

Tom Bird was not only my friend and associate, but he appointed himself my protector. One afternoon, I was sitting at my desk when a visiting drunk from Kitchener barged into my office to protest noisily because the stewards had disqualified a horse on which he had wagered. He was shouting and yelling; a display which didn't bother me particularly since I knew him as a loudmouth who was really quite harmless.

I was unaware that Tom Bird had come into my ante-room, where he could hear the uproar. He stuck his head around the corner of my door and said to me:

"Son, if this son-of-a-bitch is bothering you, just let me know – and I'll shift his chin six or seven inches."

At eighty-two Mr. Bird still was more than capable of handling any situation. The intruder snapped his mouth shut and left without another word.

There were times when our departmental secretary, Mary Guadagno, didn't share my unqualified enthusiasm for our veteran clocker. She loved him, but when he sat down at her desk each morning to dictate the times of the day's workouts to her, he had a truly distressing habit of taking his false teeth out of his mouth and placing them conspicuously on her desk. Mary had difficulty in concentrating while Tom's teeth were glaring at her from the polished desktop.

He used to boss her around scandalously, but she never objected. It was only those false teeth which upset her – particularly when she had come to the office without having had her breakfast.

One morning, Tom came into the office with something on his mind. A veteran racetracker and a very good friend of all of us – Joe "The Belgian" Kane – had been taken to hospital a few days earlier after suffering a heart attack.

"Mary," Tom roared at the young lady, as he strode up to her and deposited his false teeth on her desk, "Phone St. Joseph's Hospital and ask how Joe Kane is doing. I hear he had a bad night."

"Oh, Mr. Bird," cried Mary, her big eyes filling up suddenly. "I thought you'd heard . . . Mr. Kane died at five o'clock this morning."

"Jesus Christ!" barked Tom, picking his teeth off the desk and jamming them back into his mouth. "Joe had a REALLY BAD NIGHT!"

19

A Headstone for the Good Ones

The entire lure of horse racing is built upon a dream. Show me a man who goes to the races regularly and I'll show you a man who builds castles in the air. In the secret recesses of his mind, he cherishes the dream of winning that astronomically-priced daily-double. He chuckles to himself as he contemplates escape to that South Sea Paradise, or the previously-unattainable blonde mistress brought to bed in the Florida hotel suite; he eases his conscience with the imagined purchase of a sable coat for his wife, the summer holidays for his children in luxury-camps; but, essentially, the dream always represents escape from the treadmill of his dull daily existence.

The horse-owner is a dreamer, too. As he sits down at the end of the month to write the cheques for his trainer, his veterinary and his farrier, the horse-owner comforts himself with his dream of winning the Kentucky Derby, the Grand National Steeplechase or L'Arc de Triomphe. I can laugh, now, when I recall my own harmless fantasy of winning the Queen's Plate, the gracious speech which I was going to make in the winner's enclosure, the lordly distribution of largesse to the trainer, the jockey, the grooms and the members of my family who silently had suffered my madness.

Hope is the key. Without Hope, there is no point in living. Hope is woven through the entire fabric of horse racing, from the backstretch to the totalisator machines. You can bet on eight consecutive losers today, but tomorrow will bring riches. Hope is the drug, the eternal placebo.

God forgive me if all I carried to my grave from horse racing was the recollection of a few winning bets. Could I forget my debt to Lester Knifong and Doc Ronald and Stub Barnes? Could I forget the summer mornings on the back-stretch? The long, wonderful, untroubled afternoons in the little club house at Whittier Park? The touch of my father's hand on my cheek, awakening me at Saratoga?

The best part of it is that, as I lie here now, I find myself remembering the good ones, the men and horses who through force of character etched themselves forever on my memory-pads. They were not great men or great horses in the generally accepted use of that overworked adjective; they were little men and little horses, undistinguished in terms of public recognition, but they were deep through the heart. Could I tell you that Duchess of York and skinny Joey were the equal of Man O War or Nijinsky? Could I expect you to share my sorrow and strange pride as Ada Whittier – her suspensory ligament cut clear through by another horse's pointed steel shoe – ran across the finish line on three legs, won the race, and then stood there with her severed leg dangling, waiting quietly for the track veterinarian to end her life? You must take my word for it: they had character.

I remember one afternoon, sitting in the office of the Vancouver *Daily Province,* when inspiration struck me. There was approximately one hour remaining before post-time for the running of the British Columbia Futurity at Lansdowne Park. I had smoked out an eagle bird among the two-year-old entries, a little chestnut gelding named Simosee, who hadn't done much racing. Simosee's mother was Tennessee, a mud-running phenomenon. Rain had been falling during the early part of that summer afternoon and the Lansdowne track would be muddy, ideal conditions for Simosee.

My pockets contained a total of two dollars and fifty cents. Quickly, I dialed the telephone number of the Cannibal Cab Company and I asked for George Naylor, a driver who would permit me to put my fares on a charge account in these moments of crisis. Actually, the taxi company was the Blue Line, but it was known in newspaper circles as the Cannibal

Cab Company because one of its drivers had bitten off another driver's ear when they had a slight disagreement.

George Naylor drove me to Lansdowne Park on Lulu Island and we arrived at the gate just as the field was leaving the paddock to parade for the running of the British Columbia Futurity. Grandly, I gave Naylor a fifty-cent tip, and with my remaining two dollars clutched in my hot little hand I raced for the nearest wicket to bet the two dollars on Simosee's nose. It never occurred to me to figure out how I would get home if I lost my bet.

Simosee won and, he paid $23.65.

I remember distinctly, standing on the Club House lawn after I had cashed my ticket. The rain had stopped about thirty minutes before the race; the sun was shining hotly. Not for an instant did I think of going home and tucking away my $23.65, which would go a long way towards paying my monthly rent of $40. I thought of going home with the money, alright, but I had other plans for the $23.65.

I remember standing there, thinking to myself: "This is going to be my lucky week . . . I'm going to come out here tomorrow and I'm going to bet $10 on the daily-double . . . Suppose I win the daily-double? . . . If it's an $80 payoff, I'll have a total of $418. . . . Then, I'll bet $200 on a 10-to-1 shot . . . ." I was brought back from the clouds abruptly by the realization that there was a small hole in the sole of my right shoe and the grass on the club house lawn was quite wet.

I have so many graves on which I must place flowers. This is the penalty which I must pay for getting into this racing game too young and outliving the men and horses who enthralled me. One by one they went and they left me here alone, idiotically babbling names which have no more present-day relevance than the Bobbsey Twins or Tom Swift and His Wonderful Flying Machine.

Still, there is a debt to be paid. Too many people are still beckoning to me, signalling for recognition: Banjo Jack, wheezing asthmatically and whining in the quaint argot of Ireland-cum-Liverpool; Chicken Pie wandering through the stable yard, hawking his wares which invariably seemed to have a few wisps from his soup-strainer moustache mixed with the chicken; Jimmy Lardus swimming in the infield lake at Oaklawn with his fully-grown pet bear. There is too widespread a public misconception that horse racing is only a gambling device, in which the principal motivation is avarice. Too often, the Good Men have been ignored, the men who left a tiny but important legacy of kindness.

I could name you a hundred men who ignored the cynical backstretch adage: "Never fall in love with a horse." There was old Andy Robinson and Sunny Marcus, who was a genuine rogue. Sunny Marcus had the disposition of an enraged rattlesnake; he smashed starting gates; he bucked frightened jockeys to such heights that they came down with snow in their hair; he had a lifelong feud with most members of the human race, but Andy Robinson understood him and gave him the patient care and affection which a father would give to a prodigal son.

Sunny Marcus raced for Andy Robinson until the gelding was ten years old. Then one afternoon Andy entered Sunny in a claiming race at Edmonton. An American horseman, a newcomer who was unaware of the unusually close attachment, claimed Sunny Marcus.

Andy simply refused to honour the claim. He took Sunny Marcus back to his barn and he stood outside the stall door, daring the American horseman to invade his domain. The horsemen held an emergency meeting that night as they knew that, under the laws of racing, Andy was certain to be suspended if he refused to yield a horse. Eventually, a compromise was reached: Andy was persuaded to let Sunny Marcus go to the American's barn for a few days – on the strict condition that Sunny Marcus's regular groom went along, too. A week later, the American sold Sunny Marcus to Andy at a modest profit. The old gelding died in Robinson's barn and Andy buried him under the poplar trees on the banks of the Red River, behind Whittier Park in St. Boniface, Manitoba.

Andy Robinson was the last human being to leave Whittier Park when the floodwaters of the Red River engulfed the track in 1950. After the last horses had been removed, a rescue-squad led the protesting old man from the little apartment in the yearling-barn, which had been his permanent off-season home for many years. As they led him atop the high railway right-of-way on the southern perimeter of Whittier Park, Andy took one last long look down at his flooded home. He never went back – he died in a nursing home.

But even the best nursing home – what a hell of a place for Andy Robinson to die! He would have been happier beside old Sunny Marcus, down under the poplars on the banks of the Red River.

The afternoon that Spud Murphy won the Canadian Derby with Brother Leo, I found myself thinking about Spud and another horse, named Joe Geary. This is "Calgary Spud" Murphy I'm talking about and he isn't to be confused with "Milk River Spud" Murphy, who is reputed to have given Johnny Longden his start as a jockey, riding in Indian pony-races at the little one-day fairs in Montana and Southern Alberta. The similarity of names around race tracks often is confusing: there was a time when I couldn't walk a quarter-mile without bumping into "Calgary Red," "Montreal Red," or "Society Red."

Well, Spud was standing there in the sun-splashed infield enclosure, receiving the Canadian Derby trophy from His Honour, the Lieutenant-Governor of Alberta. The official representative of Her Majesty, The Queen, was dressed formally in grey topper, swallowtail coat and striped trousers. Spud was wearing his best tan suit and his round red face glistened with pleasure and embarrassment. The crowd was applauding loudly because Spud was a very popular little man, a racetrack gypsy who, after years of earnest hustling, had hit the jackpot.

As Spud shifted his weight from foot to foot, while waiting for His Honour and the other members of the viceregal party to depart the scene in their horse-drawn landau, I was aware that I was watching the climax of the movie-type racetrack Success Story.

Exactly forty-nine weeks earlier, I had been beside Spud on a platform in front of the grandstand in the Calgary Stampede grounds. As a visitor with racing connections, I had been pressed into making the official presentation to the winner of the second division of the Stampede Futurity for two-year-olds. Brother Leo was a front-running winner of the race, and a few minutes later Spud and I stood on that platform while the photographers snapped pictures of us holding a sterling silver tray. As the photographers reloaded, Spud jocularly whispered into my left ear: "This purse is going to come in mighty handy – the telephone company just notified me that they're going to disconnect my line."

Murphy may have been exaggerating slightly, but we had been friends for so many years that he could be certain that I was aware of the ring of truth in his limp jest. Spud, a middle-aged bachelor, had his permanent home in the winter-barn on the Stampede grounds. He had converted a tackroom into a comfortable little apartment, complete with telephone, stove and electric refrigerator.

During the long, cold Alberta winters, Spud cooked gargantuan stews in his racetrack apartment and shared his food with many indigent swipes and ginnies who couldn't find employment until the snow disappeared and the horses came out of winter quarters to prepare for the summer racing.

Brother Leo changed Spud's life. After that Canadian Derby victory, Murphy received several offers for his colt and, weighing all the probabilities, he eventually accepted one of those offers. When the financial transactions had been completed, the accumulated purses and Brother Leo's sale-price left Spud with a sum in the neighbourhood of $50,000. It wasn't a fortune; nevertheless, for a middle-aged gypsy-trainer, it represented security. Spud bought himself a nice little house in Calgary – and he moved out of the racetrack tackroom which had been his home for so many years.

Spud died less than two years after he bought that house. It is my considered opinion that the soft living – the electric heating in that house, plus all the new-fangled contraptions such as air-conditioning and a constant supply of hot water for his showerbath – undermined his health. It is probable that Spud never really felt comfortable in that house, removed from the salubrious aroma of horseshit.

All this is beside the point. On the day that Brother Leo won the Canadian Derby, a great wave of sentimental pleasure swept down from the grandstand and rolled over the modest roly-poly man who was accepting the winner's trophy from the frock-coated Lieutenant Governor. Every knowledgeable racing patron who witnessed that afternoon's triumph shared Spud's delight. Because a large percentage of the crowd knew the story of Spud Murphy and his affection for an old horse, Joe Geary.

Thirty years earlier, when Spud was hustling with Kinky King on Western Canada tracks, he got his first horse. They pooled two dollars to buy a Quinella ticket at Winnipeg one afternoon and Spud was so confident that their combination would win that he stuck the ticket in his pocket and went downtown without waiting for the result of the seventh race. He took a young lady to dinner at The Cave, a supper club which enjoyed considerable popularity at the time.

A couple of hours later, Kinky King sauntered into The Cave and said to Spud: "How much do you want for your half of the Quinella ticket?" Without removing his gaze from the face of the young lady, who was sitting opposite him, Spud replied: "No Sale." The Quinella ticket was worth $550 and, with the proceeds, the partners bought two horses – Matilda Jane and Time Ball – for $300 down and $300 on-the-cuff. Before the season ended, they won six races and they sold the two horses for $600.

It was about then that Murphy began to live in tackrooms. He wasn't extraordinarily successful as a trainer; he managed to keep his nose above water. He got his hands on a nice old crippled horse, Joe Geary, and they campaigned back and forth across the Western prairies for several seasons. As Spud used to say: "Joe has two bad wheels and he has a heart as large as a watermelon." The itinerant pair didn't win much money, but always won just enough to keep Joe Geary in oats and Spud Murphy in stew-ingredients. Spud and Joe became quite famous among the regular patrons of the western tracks. When a bettor approached Murphy to ask if his horse was ready to win, Spud would reply: "I'm not sure – you'd better ask Joe how he feels about it."

As Joe Geary became older and increasingly infirm, the purses came in very slowly and they had one particularly bad summer. On the final day of the racing season at Winnipeg, Joe Geary broke down completely and Spud was broke, too.

The morning after the Winnipeg meeting ended, Spud Murphy was into the office of Lou Davies. "Joe has reached the end of the line," he said, "and I've tapped out; I can't even ship myself home to Calgary. There's a guy over in Barn Five who's offered me $100 for Joe."

Davies remembers that a strangely stubborn look came over little Spud's face and, then, Spud added: "I'm not going to take the $100. That man would patch up Joe and he'd try to bring him back to the races next year. Joe has been too damn good a friend to be treated that way. So, I want you to lend me twenty dollars. You won't get it back until next season."

Davies peeled off two ten-dollar bills and gave them to the little horseman. Spud went out to get the track veterinary surgeon, who gently led old Joe Geary into the infield at Whittier Park. While Spud turned his back, the veterinarian ended Joe's life quickly and painlessly. Little Spud borrowed a shovel and he buried Joe Geary under a tree on the club house turn at Whittier Park, where the old horse always would lie within listening distance of the thudding hooves.

Then, Spud went down to the Canadian Pacific marshalling yards and – without a dollar to his name – he climbed into an empty boxcar for the long ride home to his tackroom in Calgary. The stews had little meat in them, that winter.

He was an uncomplicated little man; unusual only in that he would put himself into hock for twenty dollars to spare an old friend the possibility of continued suffering.

I am remembering the Good Men. There are other trainers who brutalized their horses, treating them as mute, insensitive machines. The latter type of human is distinctly in a scorned minority around the race tracks. It is normal for the agony of a four-legged animal to arouse only compassion in the man who owns him.

I watched Mess Hall die, one moonlit night at Fort Erie. Mess Hall wasn't a great horse, but he was a courageous horse and the manner in which he met death demonstrated that the will to live is as strong in horses as it is in human beings.

Mess Hall's deathbed was a manure pile. The death scene was set between two barns; the horse framed in the headlights of automobiles which ringed him. Mess Hall had contracted pneumonia while he was being vanned from Florida and his demise was speeded by that strange equine malady which, for want of a better name, is known as shipping-fever. The simple mathematics of such diseases decreed that he should have been dead a week earlier. He displayed incredible stamina, fighting off the terminal diseases for seven days, scarcely able to move, his every breath a stentorian sob.

Then, about nine o'clock on this particular night, he pitched forward on his head. After lying inert for five minutes, Mess Hall stuck his nose through the open door of his stall and he appeared to wish to get into the open air. Five men attempted to help him, but even five men can't lift 1,000 pounds of inert horse.

Mess Hall wasn't finished. Gathering strength from some mysterious inner source, he lurched to his feet; he took a few stumbling steps and pitched forward, again, into a shallow ditch. This time, you would have bet 1-to-100 he was gone.

As Mess Hall lay there, a groom rushed away to put in telephone-calls to the owner and the veterinary who had been treating the dying horse. Two cars purred into the stable area; their lights were left on to provide illumination for the doctor.

When a horse is dying, the racetrack's Old Men appear, unsummoned. The mysterious adventure of death fascinates old men. Mess Hall's death watch was conducted by Percy Pearson, who, at the age of eighty-six, was still riding his pony on the track every morning, and Mose Dunn, a lean, moose-nosed man, who had been around horses for more than sixty years.

Then, Mess Hall did something which raised the hairs on the backs of men's necks. Mess Hall arose from the shallow ditch; stiffly and slowly he walked through the headlights, heading for the manure pile, as if drawn by a magnet.

Little Tak Inouye, a Japanese hot-walker who later was to ride a Queen's Plate winner, stood shivering and he displayed emotion for the first time in his three years around the track. "I won't watch him die," Tak whimpered and he ran away, to hide behind the barn.

Mose Dunn watched Mess Hall lurching towards the manure pile and he said fervently: "Gamest son-of-a-buck I ever saw."

Mess Hall's owner was acting as if one of his own children was dying. A big rough man, who was no stranger to human mayhem, he growled: "You're damn right this is a game horse. He ran a mile and a half for me and he ran the first six furlongs in 1.11. This is just too much horse to accept the fact that he's licked. Where the hell is that goddam vet?" And, furiously, he cursed the entire profession of veterinary surgeons.

It's funny what horses will do, when they're going to die," Mose Dunn whispered, as he stood in the darkness, just out of the ring of headlights. "I had that old mare, Double-L, and she was meaner than cat-piss. The only human who could get near her was my old lady, who trained her to come to the back door and rub her nose against the screen. Whenever she rubbed the screen, my old lady would give her a lump of sugar.

"Well, we had to leave that place and we gave the old mare to the people who took over. They never could get near her – they just used to pitch her feed into the backyard. Well, one day she came up to their back door and she rubbed her nose against the screen. Then, she dropped dead – just like that!"

At that instant, the veterinarian, a young, prematurely grey-haired man arrived and he leaped from his car. The vet had been dining in the nearby American city of Buffalo. He took one look at Mess Hall and, quickly and efficiently, he filled a syringe with a massive dose of strychnine.

Standing there in the headlights, Mess Hall must have known what was going to happen. His sobs stopped abruptly and he appeared to hold his breath as the syringe jabbed him and death rushed into his heart.

As the vet stepped back, someone thoughtfully extinguished the car headlights. Mess Hall was not to be denied the dignity of privacy in his last seconds.

As the lights went out, Mess Hall gave one wild snort of despair – or was it defiance? – and, in the darkness, we could hear him crash to the ground.

This time, he didn't get up.

In the darkness, the owner, his voice breaking unexpectedly, was commanding: "No one take the shoes off that horse. He ran in those shoes."

Then the man turned his face to the barn wall and he wept, like a broken-hearted child.

20

The Second Time Around

I have been lying here all night, remembering – just the two of me.

There is a breeze blowing quite briskly; the bedroom curtains are billowing in the dawn light like mist drifting above the Woodbine shedrows in the hour before work begins. The old house is creaking in the morning breeze. Probably, the old house is creaking under the weight of the mortgage. That damn mortgage wraps itself around the old house's rickety chimney, clinging like an albatross.

I must write down my night-dream while it's fresh in my mind. I'll hide it away in a trunk because my wife might find it some day and she'll blow her stack when she reads that part about how much money I spent on the horses. My wife has a hell of a good sense of humour about everything, with the sole exception of money. She becomes very narrow-minded when I complain about the manner in which, occasionally, she overspends her household budget. One of her hang-ups is basic insecurity. I can't understand this slight flaw in her character because, always, I have sublimated my whims to her demands. It's my own fault that she becomes testy; I have been too good to her. She is a very fortunate woman; she might have married a man of wealth and then she would have developed gout or cirrhosis of the liver. This life which we have led has compelled her to stay healthy. Someday, she'll be grateful to me when she realizes that I saved her from gout or cirrhosis.

This long night of lying awake, watching it all pass before my eyes on the room-wide screen, has left me curiously refreshed. I wish that they'd outfit my brain with a cathode tube, so that I could dream in Living Colour. My dreams are always viewed in black-and-white. Funny, though, there are colour-shots in some of my rememberings – that bit about the morning in Saratoga, for instance: I could see the dull red of the old grandstand; my father's tie was deep blue with small white dots; that chestnut colt, racing along the track, was the colour of a robin's breast.

The two of me lie here in this bed and I must decide which one will get up this morning.

Will it be the drab me which my family has learned to accept in these latter years? The testy old man who grumbles about taxes, as he sticks his grapefruit spoon carelessly in his eye while he reads the front page of the morning paper? The anonymous, inconspicuous man who rides the subway to work, frowning back at the hordes who frown their way through the doors of the train?

Or will it be Walter Mitty who gets out of bed this morning? The secret bon vivant; the little man with a tiger in his soul; the unsuspected plotter who, in his battered brief case, carries the bomb which will blow the whole bloody world to kingdom come? Some mornings, I am Trock Estrella, the sinister hood in "Winterset," doomed to die of consumption in six months, and bitterly intent upon straightening out a few of his underworld associates as he rasps: "I'm rotten inside . . . it'll kill me . . . but before that happens to me, a lot of these healthy boys'll know what it's like!" I rather like that role for myself – always charming!

Every dawn, each man is offered, again, the freedom of choice. He can continue his slow but inexorable downhill slide or he can grab the brass ring. While life remains, there is always the opportunity to remake the world.

This is one of those mornings when I have decided to stay around a bit longer.

I hope that she isn't running the dishwasher or the washing machine. With the old-fashioned plumbing in this house, I can't get any hot water for my showerbath when she's running the hot taps in the kitchen. Oh, to hell with a hot shower! A cold shower will do me good; it'll get my blood circulating again. It may give me a heart attack, but I'll take the chance.

Jee-sus! This water must have come straight from the Arctic Ocean. I'll turn on the hot tap, just a little bit. There's no point in killing myself. There, that's better, I can breathe again, I was beginning to believe that my lungs had been frost-bitten. Anyhow, you can't get a decent lather with cold water. There's no point in taking a shower if you don't wash yourself, too. Standing under a stream of ice cold water is simply a refined form of Chinese torture.

Hmmm! I'm beginning to feel like a human being. If I straighten my shoulders and pull in my stomach, maybe I can see my toes again. Hello, toes! No, I'd just as soon not look at them. The male human's pedal extremities never were intended for admiration. Men's feet resemble something that should be kept on the lower layer of the household freezer. There's something obscene about men's feet. God must have decided to play a practical joke when he got around to designing feet. He ran out of material.

Really, I'm not in bad shape, considering the life I've led. I'm only seven pounds heavier than I was fifteen years ago. My biceps wouldn't frighten Charles Atlas, but you can't keep all your muscles in shape when you spend most of your time pounding a typewriter. It's funny that I've never developed stenographer's spread. My buttocks still are no wider than a couple of soda-crackers. There's one good thing about having a few financial problems; they keep you thin and nervous.

That shower really made me feel good. I'm going to give them a surprise this morning. I'll bet they faint dead away when I come down to breakfast wearing my new sport-jacket, the maroon shirt and the white tie with the big sunflower.

Let's see what the mirror tells me this morning. Still enough hair to keep my head reasonably warm. It's funny that I've never become very grey-haired. Probably, it's because I have no conscience. Teeth in pretty good shape; they're all still there although the lower ones, in front, are beginning to be worn down slightly. They ought to last me for another fifteen or twenty years.

How old would I be in another fifteen or twenty years? Oh, hell – I don't want to last that *long. I'd just like to get through today, another week, another year.*

I've just decided that it's about time that I bought another race horse. Looking at the lather forming on my face reminds me of all the mornings when I stood in front of the mirror like this, plotting what I'd do if Leonforte won the Queen's Plate. I used to laugh to myself and everyone in the house thought that I was crazy. Well, maybe I was *crazy.*

Johnny Wayne wants me to pick out a horse and go into partnership with him. Now, there would be a hell of a fine partnership of horse-owners: a professional comedian and a sports-scribbler. I wonder how long Wayne's sense of humour would survive the trials of horse-ownership. He'd wind up playing Hamlet and Othello.

Why not, though? We could get a decent yearling for $5,000 and we could throw another $5,000 into the pot to pay the expenses for the first year. I could fly out to Vancouver and persuade Bobby Hall to sell me one of his George Royal yearlings. I know damn well that those George Royals are under-rated; one of these seasons, pretty soon, a George Royal colt is going to come along and he'll beat the whey out of those expensive Northern Dancer and Nearctic two-year-olds. It's just a matter of being lucky – as long as a colt is sound, there's no telling how much dynamite is hidden in his heart.

As soon as I have breakfast and get out of the house, I'll phone Wayne from the office. I've been good for a long time, now. I've kept my nose clean; I've paid my bills regularly; I've got enough insurance to keep the family in modest comfort if I happen to croak without warning. It's about time that I had a little fling.

Johnny and I could have a lot of fun, fooling around with a horse. This time, I'll let Johnny take all the bows. I'll just stay in the background and do the planning. Two of my old trainers are still in the business: we could turn over the colt to Duke Campbell or Morris Fishman. Either of them will give us a square shake: I'll tell them we want to go slowly with this colt. We won't run him until he's really ready – and then we'll just drop him into soft spots, where he isn't going to be overmatched before he grows into his full strength.

It would be a joke if I happened to pick out a decent horse. If we were very careful with him, we might nurse him along and we might get lucky in one of those big two-year-old stakes, late in the autumn. If he won the Coronation Stakes or the Cup and Saucer, we'd pretty well be forced to give him his chance to run in the Queen's Plate, the following year.

Johnny would get a tremendous belt out of a horse carrying his colours in the Queen's Plate. It would be strictly a moon-shot, but stranger things have happened in horse racing: I mean, things stranger than a comedian and a newspaperman winning the richest horse race in the country. I wonder if Johnny would want our jockey to wear the sock and buskin? or a fool's cap and bells? Maybe we should call this colt Will Somers; that was the name of the jester in the court of King Henry VIII.

This is crazy, of course, but what if Will Somers happened to win the Queen's Plate? Well, I'd let Wayne lead the colt into the Winner's Enclosure to accept Her Majesty's gift of Fifty Guineas from the Governor General. I'd just stand in the background, waiting to get my hands on the cheque for $55,000 which goes to the winning owners. If Johnny forced me into the presentation ceremonies, I'd make that little speech which I rehearsed for Leonforte, so many years ago: You know, the one about paying tribute modestly to the horse, the trainer and the jockey. I rehearsed it so often that it's still engraved on my brain. (Where did I put that tie with the big sunflower?)

That colt would be worth a lot of money, if he happened to win the Queen's Plate. Someone might offer us $100,000 for him after the race. Johnny might not want to sell, but he'd get one hell of an argument from me. $100,000 is a heap of money. A man never should fall in love with a horse – not when someone is willing to pay $100,000 for that horse.

Let's see, now! We'd split $100,000 from the sale of the colt and we'd split another $40,000 or so, after we divided up the purse for the Queen's Plate. We'd have to give a ten per cent stake to the trainer; we'd give another ten per cent to the jockey; and we'd give another $1,000 to the boys around the barn. That means that Johnny and I would take down about $70,000, each, after the smoke cleared. Maybe we'd give *another $10,000 to the trainer when we sold the horse, so each of us would have $65,000.*

A few years back, I could have done a lot of damage with $65,000. None of that nonsense this time. I'll just buy myself a tiny place in the country, just a couple of acres beside a stream, a three-room house where I can sit on the verandah in a rocking-chair, sitting there, thinking and listening to my hair growing. Possibly, there'd be room for a little barn where I could keep one old horse. The horse wouldn't have to do anything except eat – I'd just go out to the barn and stand there, leaning against his stall door for a few minutes every morning, just looking at him.

God dammit – here I go again!